Prescription for a Miracle

Prescription for a Miracle

A DAILY DEVOTIONAL FOR DIVINE HEALTH

by

Mark Brazee

Harrison House
Tulsa, Oklahoma

Second Printing

Prescription for a Miracle—
A Daily Devotional for Divine Health
ISBN 1-57794-208-6
Copyright © 1999 by Mark Brazee
Mark Brazee Ministries
P. O. Box 1870
Broken Arrow, Oklahoma 74013-1870

Published by Harrison House, Inc.
P. O. Box 35035
Tulsa, Oklahoma 74153

FOREWORD

I was saved in 1972 while attending Michigan State University. I grew up in a good, Christian home, and as far back as I can remember, I had a love for God.

As a child I knew I had a call of God on my life; however, I ran from God as long and as hard as I could for years. Being a Christian seemed to me to be a boring life with no apparent benefits—except that at the end one would go to heaven instead of hell. I wanted in on the heaven part! But I could not understand a God who would pay the price to purchase me and to cleanse me from my sins and make me new inside yet leave me to fend for myself down here on earth.

When I finally surrendered my life to God and asked Jesus into my heart, I found a life of excitement and adventure beyond my wildest dreams. I also found that God doesn't leave us helpless down here; in fact, I found just the opposite.

After being saved, I returned to my hometown and started working in the real estate business. Suddenly I began encountering great financial difficulty. After trying everything else, I opened my Bible to see what God had to say about my finances—if anything.

To my amazement, I found that God had already taken care of my financial needs, and through the truths I found in His Word, He would give me faith to walk in His blessings of an abundant life.

I also discovered Philippians 4:19, which says, **But my God shall supply all your need according to his riches in glory by Christ Jesus.**

Over a period of time the truth of that Scripture settled down into my heart, and my financial situation began to change. God had become my source of supply, and He has been faithful to me in the area of finances for more than twenty-five years.

Through that experience, I discovered that God would not only save me but He would also bless and take care of me. But at times I had needs in my physical body as well. Would God make provision for them?

I decided to search the Scriptures and see if healing was a part of what Jesus had provided for me through His death, burial and resurrection. And as I studied God's Word in the area of divine healing, I found truths that have changed my life.

Consistently "feeding" on God's Word on the subject of healing produces faith in anyone's heart. Jesus said that all things are possible to those who believe (Mark 9:23), and that includes healing for the body.

I believe that the daily nuggets of truth in this book on God's healing plan will both produce healing to all of your flesh and keep you in divine health all the days of your life.

PREFACE

Suppose you went to the doctor to receive relief from pain or sickness and he told you, "I have a new wonder drug I'm going to prescribe for you. There are no side effects, and it's guaranteed to heal you of your condition. Not only that, but it will actually bring health to every part of your body, no matter what the problem or ailment! However, you have to faithfully take it exactly according to instructions."

After hearing that, I bet you'd listen very carefully as the doctor explained how to use this wonderful medicine. You'd want to take your prescription just as instructed so you could receive its full benefits!

You may say, "Well, that's a nice thought, but it's all hypothetical. There is no such wonder drug that can do all that."

I have some good news for you—that imaginary prescription isn't imaginary! The medicine that the Great Physician has provided for you does all that and more!

You see, God says that when you attend to His Word, it's actually life to you and health, or *medicine,* to your flesh. (Prov. 4:20-22.) When you take God's medicine according to His instructions, it goes to work in your body to drive out pain, sickness and disease. And it doesn't stop until it's made you whole from the top of your head to the soles of your feet!

But in order to walk in divine health, you have to take your medicine every day according to the Great Physician's prescription. That's where this daily devotional comes in.

Prescription for a Miracle provides a daily dose of God's medicine for you to take as you're on your way to health and wholeness. Make sure you take your divine prescription as instructed. In other words, don't just read your daily dose and then forget about it as you go on your way. Read it over and over. Meditate on its truth until it's planted down in your spirit. Throughout the day, release your faith by saying the confession at the end of each devotion out loud.

As you do so, faithfully acting on the Word you are learning, your health will improve. In fact, I believe it won't be the same at this time next year, but you'll see the effects of God's medicine at work in your body for 365 days—making you healed, strong and whole!

JANUARY 1

Plant God's Word in Your Spirit

If ye abide in me, and my words abide in you, ye shall ask what ye will, and it shall be done unto you.
—*John 15:7*

Many people in the body of Christ today are not walking in health. They may believe in their *heads* that healing belongs to them, but they haven't received the revelation of it in their *spirits*.

But if Christians want to walk in health, they need to get the basic truths in God's Word on healing lodged deep down inside them so they can become an effective, working part of their lives. Only then will they begin to see healing manifested in their bodies.

When I was just beginning to learn how to live by faith, I walked around confessing, "I know I'm healed. I believe I'm healed. I know I'm healed. I believe I'm healed." The problem was, my body still felt sick! But I kept reading, studying and meditating on the Word, and God's truth about healing finally dropped down into my spirit. The stronger the Word of God grew on the inside of me, the more I was able to walk in health. Of course, I still have "opportunities" to be sick, but now I choose not to accept them.

This is how I see it: How in the world can we get sick when God's Word regarding what Jesus Christ purchased for our physical bodies is lodged in our spirits? What more do we need to know than, "Surely he hath borne our griefs [sicknesses], and carried our sorrows [pains]...and with his stripes we are healed" (Isa. 53:4,5)?

So when the devil tries to offer you some "lying vanity" symptom, just say, "No, I'm not taking that. That isn't mine. Jesus took my sickness 2000 years ago!"

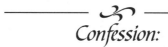

Confession:

Father, I abide in You, and Your words abide in me. I choose to believe Your Word, which says healing and health belong to me. I walk in divine health because Jesus took my sicknesses and carried my pains.

For therein is the righteousness of God revealed from faith to faith: as it is written, The just shall live by faith.   —Romans 1:17

JANUARY 2

Don't Wait on God for Your Miracle

The Word of God tells us we are to live by faith. Now, what if you need a miracle, but God doesn't move sovereignly through the gifts of the Spirit to give it to you? Don't be surprised if He doesn't; He never promised He would. In fact, God didn't design the gifts of the Spirit to be used on behalf of the Church. He intended them to be divine "advertisements" to an unsaved world operating as signs following as believers preach the Gospel.

Of course, God loves us so much that He does manifest spiritual gifts within the body of Christ for our blessing. But God doesn't expect us to sit and wait for a sovereign move of His Spirit in order to be blessed with miracles.

How do I know that? Well, look at 2 Corinthians 5:7: "For we walk by faith, not by sight." Notice this verse does *not* say, "For we walk by the sovereignty of God, and we hope He operates quickly." Nor does it say, "For we sit back and wait for God to move on our behalf, even if it takes forty years." No, it says, "For we walk by *faith,* not by *sight.*"

What happens when a person walks by faith? The same thing that happened to the woman of Canaan in Matthew 15:22-28. Jesus said to her, "O woman, great is thy faith: *be it unto thee even as thou wilt*" (v. 28).

God doesn't expect us to sit back and wait for miracles to happen. He expects us as believers to use our faith to initiate a miracle. We can receive a miracle at our own will—according to our faith.

So don't sit back and wait for God by His sovereign will to do something. Go to His Word and *find out* His will; then just reach out by faith and take hold of what already belongs to you!

Confession:

I walk by faith and not by sight. Jesus' body was broken for me so I could live free from sickness and pain. Therefore, I receive my healing now by faith.

JANUARY 3

Take God's Medicine

My son, attend to my words; incline thine ear unto my sayings. Let them not depart from thine eyes; keep them in the midst of thine heart. For they are life unto those that find them, and health to all their flesh. —Proverbs 4:20-22

In the original Hebrew, this Scripture literally says that God's Word is *medicine* to our flesh. (A marginal note in my *King James Version* Bible substitutes the word *medicine* for the word *health.*) Now, think about this: What if someone invented a medication that could cure anything wrong with the human body? He'd be rich overnight! People would take that medicine diligently to make sure it worked. Well, if we'd just give God's promises on healing the same credibility we give the medicines developed by medical science, we would have 100 times the results!

(Now, I'm not against medical doctors. In fact, I have several doctors in my close family. Thank God for doctors! They keep people alive until those people discover there is a better way.)

God's words may be medicine to all our flesh, but just like other medicine, we have to take it. If we just put it on the shelf and look at it, it won't do us any good.

How do we take God's medicine? We hear it and hear it and hear it. Romans 10:17 says, "So then faith cometh by hearing, and hearing by the word of God." When we take the time to continually hear God's Word, our faith hooks up and releases God's power—and we rise up healed!

Confession:

God's Word has the power to effect healing in my body. I hear the Word and faith rises in me, releasing God's power and producing what I need.

And Jesus went forth, and saw a great multitude, and was moved with compassion toward them, and he healed their sick. –Matthew 14:14

JANUARY 4

Keep Your Faith Hooked Up

My wife, Janet, and I were in Capetown, South Africa, some time ago to hold four nights of meetings. The first night, a lady in her fifties came forward for prayer. We noticed that someone had to lead her to the front and then lead her back to her seat after we prayed for her.

This woman attended each night of the meetings. At the end of the last meeting, she walked up to the front to talk with us. She said, "I've been blind for thirteen years, and I've suffered with migraine headaches for a long time. When you prayed for me on the first night, I was instantly healed of the headaches. But as I walked back to my seat, I still couldn't see a thing.

"But I kept coming back each night to feed my faith," the woman continued. "When I came here the first night, all I could see was a mass of gray. But tonight, I can tell what color your suit is. And by the time you come here again, I'll be seeing *you!*"

This woman kept her faith hooked up once she realized God wanted her healed. Knowing it is God's will to heal us is the foundation we all must have.

Once we know the Word of God on the subject, we must *act* on the Word we know. First we make a "point of contact" with our faith—that is, establishing a moment in time when we've taken our stance on God's promises. Then we hold fast to our confession of faith until our healing manifests in our bodies.

You can make your point of contact right now. Just say from your heart, "Father, I ask You for my healing. I believe I receive it and I thank You for it in Jesus' name. I believe it is mine!"

You may not look or feel any different, but just believe that you *are* different. Keep your faith hooked up. Continue to confess, "Thank God, I believe I receive my healing. I believe I'm healed." Your healing may come instantly, or it may come over a period of minutes, hours, days, weeks or months. *But it will come!*

Confession:

I believe God is able to heal me. I believe God is willing to heal me. Therefore, I believe I receive my healing!

JANUARY 5

Put Your Faith in God

My son, attend to my words; incline thine ear unto my sayings. Let them not depart from thine eyes; keep them in the midst of thine heart. For they are life unto those that find them, and health [medicine] to all their flesh.

—Proverbs 4:20-22

Someone may ask, "If I believe I am healed, does that mean I need to throw my medicine away?"

If you have to ask, you'd better not. You are *not* healed because you throw your medicine away; you are healed because you believe God.

Some people hear a message on how to live by faith and then go out and smash their glasses to pieces. They say, "I believe I'm healed," and then they walk into walls for six months until they get a new pair of glasses!

No, the glasses don't heal your eyes; they just enable you to see while *God* heals them. So every time you put your glasses on, make a practice of saying, "Thank God, I believe I'm healed."

Or if you're taking medicine, every time you swallow a dose, say, "Thank God, I believe I'm healed by the stripes of Jesus." The medicine doesn't heal you, but it helps keep your body working right while *God* does the healing.

Now, if God tells you to throw your medicine away, you should obey Him. In that case, however, you will know it is God and you won't have to ask anyone else what you should do.

So until God tells you to throw the medicine away, keep taking it. But always remember—don't put your faith in the medicine; put your faith in *God*.

Confession:

Medicine may be helpful, but God's medicine—His Word—is much more effective! The Word says healing is mine. Therefore, I believe that God's healing power is working in me now, making my body completely whole.

Wherefore take unto you the whole armour of God, that ye may be able to withstand in the evil day, and having done all, to stand.

–Ephesians 6:13

Having Done All–Stand!

I know a lady who, when she became pregnant, found out that a childhood case of rheumatic fever had permanently damaged her heart. Her doctor put her on heart medication indefinitely.

Later the woman discovered Mark 11:24—"What things soever ye desire, when ye pray, believe that ye receive them, and ye shall have them"—and began to feed her spirit on it. Then she prayed and believed she received healing for her damaged heart. For two years, every time she took her medicine, she'd say, "Thank God, I'm healed by Jesus' stripes. Medicine doesn't heal me; it just keeps my heart beating right while *God* does the healing." She kept standing on the Word.

One day, the lady went to get her medication out of the medicine cabinet. Suddenly the Holy Ghost spoke to her spirit, saying, *You don't need the medicine now. Throw it away.* (Notice that she didn't stop taking her medicine until she knew that God had told her to do it.) Some time later, she went to another heart specialist, who conducted more tests. After examining the test results, he said, "There must have been a mix-up in the original diagnosis, because your heart is fine." Now, heart damage doesn't just disappear. No, this woman supernaturally received her healing!

Someone may say, "Well, the woman must not have had faith for the two years she took her medicine." Yes, she did. Her faith may have just been a seed, but it was growing.

You see, we all want quick results to our prayer of faith—and at times we may receive them. If our faith is developed, sometimes we can grab our answers by faith and see them instantly manifested. But if our answers don't come quickly, we must keep standing. That's why Ephesians 6:13 says you may be able, "having done all, to stand."

So put yourself in a position to hear the Word. Feed continually on God's promises. Then take hold of your healing by faith, believing that you receive your answer when you pray. Once you've done all you know to do, get ready to *stand!*

Confession:

Although medicine may help me, Jesus is my healer.
Therefore, I say with confidence, "God's Word works,
and it is working in me now!"

JANUARY 7

Be Free From Condemnation!

Beloved, if our heart condemn us not, then have we confidence toward God. And whatsoever we ask, we receive of him, because we keep his commandments, and do those things that are pleasing in his sight. —1 John 3:21,22

Condemnation and disease go hand in hand. The devil puts condemnation on you not just to make you feel bad—although he succeeds in doing that—but also to destroy your confidence in God so you can't receive from Him.

God is never the One who shuts you off from receiving. But if you allow condemnation to operate in your life, it will stop your faith from working every time. Condemnation dogs your trail, making you say things like, "Well, God wouldn't heal me. God wouldn't do anything for me. I'm unworthy. I've made mistakes. Something's wrong with me."

The enemy likes to put you under condemnation for past sins, failures and mistakes until you lose all your confidence in receiving from God. The devil knows that if he can just put you under condemnation, he can keep you wrapped around his finger with sickness and disease.

But always remember that the devil is the one who condemns, not God. The Holy Ghost and your own spirit will only *convict* you of sin in order to draw you to repentance. Condemnation always comes from the kingdom of darkness.

So get yourself in a position to receive from God—absolutely refuse to allow condemnation in your life!

Confession:

*I am a child of God. My Father never condemns me,
so I do not allow condemnation in my life.
I hold fast to the truth that my Father loves me!*

There is therefore now no condemnation to them which are in Christ Jesus, who walk not after the flesh, but after the Spirit. —Romans 8:1

Freedom From Condemnation Changes Your Life!

One time during a service, the Spirit of God suddenly spoke to my spirit: *There's someone here who fell several years ago and injured the bottom part of her spine. Call her up here; I want to heal her.*

I spoke out what I'd heard, and immediately a lady came forward and said, "That's me."

I told the woman, "God just wants you to know He loves you." Then I laid hands on her and prayed.

The next day this woman related her testimony: "Some bad things happened to me as a young child that didn't happen to my friends. Because I had no teaching, I assumed that God caused everything that happened to people.

"So I formulated the opinion that there was something 'evil' about me, although I didn't know what it was. I always thought, *God loves my friends, and good things happen to them. But He doesn't love me, because there's something evil about me. That must be why bad things happen to me.*"

I asked her, "You've always been sickly, haven't you?"

"Yes, I have," she replied. "But today while I was at work, I thought, *Oh, it feels so good to feel good. The pain is gone!* Then suddenly it just registered on me: *God called me out. I was the only one in a whole crowd who had those symptoms. Not only did He call me out, He healed me from the top of my head to the soles of my feet!*

"Now I know that I was wrong all my life. God does love me. From now on, my life will be different. I know God loves me, and that has changed me forever."

God is in the "signs and wonders" business. When He moved on this woman's behalf, He instantly healed her from pain and sickness and freed her from a lifetime of condemnation. And, as she testified, that new freedom changed her life forever!

Confession:

My Father loves me. He doesn't condemn me; therefore I am not condemned. His best for me is that I walk in healing and health, and I walk in His best!

JANUARY 9

Hold Fast to Your Healing With the Hand of Faith

Behold, I come quickly: hold that fast which thou hast, that no man take thy crown.

–Revelation 3:11

So many times people go to large meetings and get healed. But six weeks or six months later, the same symptoms return to their bodies, and some, in fact, end up worse off than before they were healed.

You may say, "Well, I thought God healed them." Sure, He did. But the Bible says, "Prove all things; *hold fast* that which is good" (1 Thess. 5:21). Healing is good, so we have to hold fast to it. And the only way to hold fast is with the hand of faith.

So if you're in a big meeting and God reaches out and miraculously heals your body, don't turn it down. But once you're healed, run back home to your Bible and feed on God's Word. Get full of the Word on the subject of healing. Then if the enemy tries to steal your miracle, you'll be able to say with authority, "No, devil, you're not taking away my healing! God gave it to me. It's mine, and you're not stealing it!"

Rise up and take a stance of faith. Refuse to be moved. Hold fast to your healing with the hand of faith!

Confession:

Healing belongs to me! I meditate on the Word, which is greater than any sickness or disease. The devil can't make symptoms stick, because the power of God's Word in me drives them out!

For unto us was the gospel preached, as well as unto them: but the word preached did not profit them, not being mixed with faith in them that heard it. —Hebrews 4:2

Healing Is God's Will

Some people say, "Well, I know lots of people who prayed for healing, and they didn't get healed." But faith begins where the will of God is known. Did those people know that healing is God's will? Did they know it is God's will that they prosper and be in health, even as their souls prosper? (3 John 2.)

Your faith will never operate beyond your knowledge of God's will. Therefore, faith is simply taking God at His Word, which *is* His will.

So feed on the Word, and establish the truth in your heart that healing is God's will. Then you'll be able to say with confidence, "Father, You said it, I believe it, so that settles it."

Now just go act like God's Word is true—and receive your healing by faith!

Confession:

I know my Father wants me healthy. His Son, Jesus, bore my sickness and pain so I wouldn't have to bear them. Therefore, I receive the healing Jesus purchased for me.

JANUARY 11

Don't Waver!

If any of you lack wisdom, let him ask of God, that giveth to all men liberally, and upbraideth not; and it shall be given him. But let him ask in faith, nothing wavering. For he that wavereth is like a wave of the sea driven with the wind and tossed. For let not that man think that he shall receive any thing of the Lord.

—James 1:5-7

When we ask God for something, we must ask in faith, believing we receive our answer and not wavering in doubt. James 1:7 says, "For let not that man [the person who doubts] think that he shall receive any thing of the Lord."

Well, wouldn't healing be included in "any thing"? We could say, "Let not the man who doubts think that he shall receive *healing* of the Lord." What man? The one who doesn't ask in faith. And where does faith begin? *Where the will of God is known.*

Sometimes I think we ministers pray for people in healing lines too quickly— before we know if they are ready to stand in faith for their answer. For instance, many folks say, "Well, I sure would like to be healed."

I ask them, "Do you believe it's God's will to heal you?"

"Well, I hope so," they respond.

These people's words show they are only *hoping* they will be healed, but they are not in *faith*. And the more they are prayed for without results, the less they expect to receive the next time someone prays for them. They ask for prayer, but in their minds they think, *I know I won't get anything, but I'll give it a good try anyway.*

Don't let that happen to you. Spend time in God's Word. Find out what His will is regarding your need. Then pray the prayer of faith without wavering in doubt. *Expect* to receive from the Lord, and your answer will surely come to pass!

Confession:

I confidently pray for healing in faith.
I believe I receive my answer, because the Word
says that by Jesus' stripes, I am healed!

JANUARY 12

> *For whatsoever is born of God overcometh the world: and this is the victory that overcometh the world, even our faith.* —1 John 5:4

Real Faith vs. "That Faith Business"

Sometimes people say, "Well, I tried that faith business, but it didn't work." But these people never could have been in faith to begin with. If they'd really been in faith, they'd still be in faith. If they really believed they received their answer when they prayed, they'd still be believing. But if they were just hoping and praying that "that faith business" works, then it won't.

Why is that? Because real faith involves:

- Stepping out and believing God for what you know to be His will for your life.
- Finding out God's will regarding your need and then trusting Him to bring it to pass.
- Believing that God said what He meant and meant what He said and then trusting Him to do what He said.
- Acting like His Word is true and expecting Him to do the same.

So forget about "trying" faith. Either you believe the Bible, or you don't. Hope will give up, but faith has tenacity. Real faith digs its heels in and says, "I know what belongs to me, and I'm not going to live without it!"

Confession:

I believe that what God says will come to pass. I don't just hope to receive what I pray for; I know that when I pray according to God's will, I receive what I have asked for.

JANUARY 13

Discern the Lord's Body

For he that eateth and drinketh [communion] unworthily, eateth and drinketh damnation to himself, not discerning the Lord's body. For this cause many are weak and sickly among you, and many sleep. —1 Corinthians 11:29,30

Many times, the major reason many sick people stay sick is that they don't know whether or not God wants them healed. They don't understand why Jesus' body was broken. They are "...not discerning [not fully understanding or duly appreciating] the Lord's body."

Many people don't realize Jesus' body was broken for their physical health as much as His blood was shed for the forgiveness of their sins. Therefore, they don't know it is God's will to heal them.

I've heard people say, "Oh, yes, I believe that God heals today. But sometimes He does, and sometimes He doesn't. We can never know who will receive their healing and who won't."

But that isn't faith! Faith begins where the will of God is known.

Discern the Lord's body rightly; understand that it was broken for you. Feed your spirit with the truth that by Jesus' stripes, you were healed. (1 Peter 2:24.) Keep meditating on that truth until you know that you know God wants you healed. Then you can be sure when you ask God for your healing that you are truly praying the prayer of *faith*.

Confession:

Jesus' body was broken for my physical health as surely as His blood was shed for my sins. I believe I receive healing in my body now.

As the bird by wandering, as the swallow by flying, so the curse causeless shall not come.

–Proverbs 26:2

Don't Leave the Door Open!

If you were to leave the front door of your home wide open, any kind of animal—even a skunk—could walk right in. Spiritually speaking, Christians sometimes leave a "door" open to their lives for the enemy's "skunk" to enter.

Perhaps you're having trouble with obstacles the devil keeps throwing your way and you've done everything you know to do. Well, check to see if you've left a door open. By that I mean, for instance, are you walking in love? Are you harboring unforgiveness in your heart toward anyone?

You see, unforgiveness stops faith from working, because faith works by love, and love always forgives. (Gal. 5:6.) We may be trying to believe God for healing. But if we harbor unforgiveness in our hearts, our faith will not work.

Sometimes people think they just can't forgive. They claim that the devil just won't let them. No, it isn't the devil who won't let people forgive; it's their own flesh—and the flesh can always be put under.

Forgiveness is not a *feeling;* it's a *decision.* We may have to reinforce that commitment to forgive again and again, but it's well worth the effort. When we keep all our doors shut, no skunks can get in to steal our blessings!

Confession:

I refuse to walk in unforgiveness and open the door to the devil. I won't allow the enemy's curse to come back on me. I choose to forgive, no matter what anyone does. I walk in love!

JANUARY 15

Forgiveness and Healing–Both Are Yours in Christ

Bless the Lord, O my soul, and forget not all his benefits: who forgiveth all thine iniquities; who healeth all thy diseases. —Psalm 103:2,3

Scriptures from Genesis to Revelation show that both forgiveness and healing were provided on the Cross. These Scriptures show that when you are forgiven, you can be healed as well, and when you are healed, you can also be forgiven.

Forgiveness and healing go hand in hand and cannot be separated. We are made righteous through the shed blood of Jesus Christ, and we are healed through the stripes He bore.

You may ask, "But what if I'm sick today as a result of living in sin in the past?" Even if sin opened the door to sickness, you can be forgiven and healed at the same time because of God's love and mercy.

So don't take one part of Jesus' redemptive work and leave the other. If one part of God's plan of redemption is for today, then all of it is for today. Jesus' body was broken for you as surely as His blood was shed for you. You have as much right to be healed as you do to be saved and forgiven from sin. It's a package deal, and it all belongs to you!

Confession:

When I received Jesus as my Savior, I also received Him as my healer. I meditate on all of His benefits. His blood was shed for my sins, and His body was broken for my healing.

And when he had given thanks, he brake it, and said, Take, eat: this is my body, which is broken for you: this do in remembrance of me.

−1 Corinthians 11:24

JANUARY 16

Healing Belongs to You

When you found out Jesus' blood was shed for your sins and you believed in your heart and confessed Him as Lord, at that moment, *nothing* could stop your salvation.

Well, the same should be true when you make a declaration of healing by faith. You find out the truth in God's Word that Jesus' body was broken for your healing; you believe and confess Him as your healer. Then nothing can stop your healing!

For too long, Church tradition has taught people only half of redemption. All over the world, ministers have preached that "whosoever will" shall receive salvation. But at the same time, those same people have also told Christians, "Healing isn't for today. God *can* heal, but that doesn't mean He always *does* heal. Sometimes our prayers for healing work, and sometimes they don't." As a result, Christians often have to get rid of a lot of doubt and unbelief before they can take hold of the healing Jesus purchased for them.

It's different out on the mission field. Every time Janet and I visit a place where the Gospel has never been preached, we tell the people that Jesus Christ paid the same price for their sins and their sicknesses. The people eagerly receive what God reveals to them—and they get saved and healed at the same time!

Sickness is the price we pay for not understanding the Atonement. But bless God, we are as healed as we are saved! So freely come and receive, for healing belongs to whosoever will believe. Healing belongs to *you!*

Confession:

Healing belongs to me just as much as salvation does.
Jesus is as much my healer as He is my Savior.
I walk in the full benefits of my redemption!

JANUARY 17

Use Your Authority

And I will give unto thee the keys of the kingdom of heaven: and whatsoever thou shalt bind on earth shall be bound in heaven: and whatsoever thou shalt loose on earth shall be loosed in heaven. —Matthew 16:19

Many times wrong thinking opens the door to the devil in Christians' lives. They may assume God allows sickness to come. But in reality, it's not God who does it—it's *they themselves.* They don't use the authority Jesus gave them in His name.

In Matthew 16:19, Jesus was talking to Peter just after Peter had received the revelation that Jesus is the Christ, the Son of the living God. In another translation, Jesus says to Peter, "And I will give unto thee the keys of the kingdom of heaven: whatever you forbid on earth, Heaven shall forbid, and whatever you allow on earth, Heaven shall allow" (v. 19 RIEU).

You see, Jesus has all authority. But as the Head of the Church, He has given us the same authority He has.

Think about it this way: I have a pocketknife, but you can't use it. Why? Simply because I have it. As long as I have it, I can use it, and you can't. But if I give it to you, you can use it.

It's the same way with authority. God says His authority has been given to you. Therefore, *you* resist the devil, and he'll flee from you. *You* use the name of Jesus. *You* stand steadfast in the faith. *You* neither give place to the devil. Jesus said, "Whatever you forbid on earth, heaven will forbid. Whatever you allow on earth, heaven will allow. You make the decision, and We'll back you up."

Authority is like a traffic policeman. He doesn't have the physical power to stop a car. But when he holds up his hand, the authority of the city that hired him stands behind him and says, "When you hold up your hand to stop traffic, we'll back you up."

So use your authority in Christ to shut the door to the devil. As you do, all of heaven will stand behind you to make sure God's promise of healing comes to pass in your life!

Confession:

Jesus said that what I allow, He will allow and what I forbid, He will forbid. I refuse to allow sickness, and I forbid it to stay in my body. My body must come in line with the Word of God in Jesus' name!

And I will give unto thee the keys of the kingdom of heaven: and whatsoever thou shalt bind on earth shall be bound in heaven: and whatsoever thou shalt loose on earth shall be loosed in heaven. —Matthew 16:19

JANUARY 18

God Will Back You Up

Sometimes we ask, "Why did God allow this illness to come into my life?" But the truth is, *we* allowed it.

It's like driving down a highway at breakneck speed and then telling the policeman who pulls you over, "But, Officer, I didn't realize the speed limit wasn't 110 miles an hour. I'm sorry."

The policeman would *not* say, "Oh, bless your heart. Forgive me, I shouldn't have pulled you over. I didn't know you were ignorant of the law." No, he'd give you a ticket anyway. Ignorance of the law is no excuse.

The same thing is true in the spiritual realm. You may say, "I didn't know I allowed the devil to keep me from receiving my healing." Yes, but you have the Bible, which gives you all the answers. Ignorance of the Word gives you no excuse.

Sometimes we don't receive our healing because we allow a door to stay open to the devil. Often the open door is the result of wrong thinking, which is usually the result of wrong teaching. Wrong thinking produces wrong believing, and wrong believing produces wrong results.

The bottom line is this: If you close the door to the enemy and forbid his strategies against you, God stands behind you. If you sit and do nothing, allowing sickness or wrong thoughts to remain in your life, God stands behind you. Whatever you do, God backs you up. He leaves the decision to you—so choose wisely!

Confession:

My Father has given me authority to choose what to allow or forbid in my life. So I choose to allow only God's thoughts in my mind and His divine health in my body!

JANUARY 19

God Gives Abundant Life— Not Sickness

The thief cometh not, but for to steal, and to kill, and to destroy: I am come that they might have life, and that they might have it more abundantly. —John 10:10

Are you in need of healing? Make sure your thinking is in line with God's Word. Wrong thinking is one of the major things that can hinder you from receiving your miracle.

For example, some people think God causes sickness—by sending, commissioning, planning or allowing it. Therefore, they automatically conclude, "Sickness must be God's will for me. After all, He allowed this sickness to come on me."

But when people say that, they are saying, in essence, "Yes, I know the devil is the author of sickness, but somehow *this* sickness is God's will for me. God saw that I needed this to teach me something, so He and the devil joined hands and are somehow working together in this situation."

No, the devil hasn't worked with God for a long time. Long ago he was an archangel named Lucifer, created by God and living in heaven. But sin and iniquity were found in Lucifer, and he was thrown out of God's presence. (Isa. 14:12,14.)

Ever since then, God and the devil have never worked together. They are *not* a team. And they do not work together to perfect or mature you. How in the world could they work as a team? Amos 3:3 says, "Can two walk together, except they be agreed?"

No! God and the devil are not in agreement. Satan tries to destroy you, while God sacrificed His only Son, who offers you abundant life! Make sure your thinking is in line with God's Word in order to receive that abundant life!

Confession:

*My heavenly Father doesn't put sickness on me.
He only gives me life, and He wants me well. I walk in
the health and abundant life my Father God has given me.*

Then Peter said, Silver and gold have I none; but such as I have give I thee: In the name of Jesus Christ of Nazareth rise up and walk. —Acts 3:6

Refuse To Allow Sickness in Your Life

Sometimes people say, "God allowed the devil to put this sickness on me." No, *they* allowed it, and God didn't have any choice in the matter because He will not override people's wills.

Most of us have been guilty of the same thing at one time or another. We allow the devil to put sickness on us because we don't use our God-given authority. God doesn't allow sickness in our lives as a part of His divine plan and purpose for us. He only allows sickness when He doesn't have a choice.

You see, God has bound Himself to His Word. He said, "Whatever you forbid, I'll forbid. All of heaven stands at attention ready to back you up. But if you allow it, I have to allow it. Whatever decision you make, I'll back you up on it." (Matt. 18:19 RIEU.)

Just think about it. God doesn't have sickness to give. Remember, He lives in heaven. Do you think you'll see a lot of sick people lying around when you get to heaven? No! There is no sickness and disease up there.

You can't give something you don't have. If you don't have sickness, you can't give it. Well, that applies to God as well. If God doesn't have something, He can't give it.

So how would God give us sickness? Would He take a trip down to hell and borrow it from the devil? *No!* God is the One who sent sickness down to hell to begin with through the death, burial and resurrection of Jesus. If He didn't want it up in heaven, He sure doesn't want it on His children.

So follow God's example, and refuse to allow sickness in your life!

Confession:

I refuse to allow sickness or disease in my life! I want nothing from the devil. I give him no place in me. Therefore, I won't allow sickness in my body, and all of heaven backs me up.

JANUARY 21

My people are destroyed for lack of knowledge.

–Hosea 4:6

Set Free by Divine Knowledge

Sometimes we try to discover how we can receive our healing when what we really need to do is find out why we got sick to begin with. If we can find the answer to that question, we can correct the problem and be healed.

Why do Christians get sick? There are many different reasons, but a primary one is a lack of knowledge of God's Word. Isaiah 5:13 says, "Therefore my people are gone into captivity, because they have no knowledge." In *The Amplified Bible,* it says, "Therefore my people go into captivity [to their enemies] without knowing it and because they have no knowledge [of God]."

Many people are bound up and taken captive by the enemy through sickness and disease. Yet they think their physical condition is God's will because they don't have knowledge of His Word. These people say, "I'm sick for the glory of God!" because they don't know that Jesus paid the price for their healing. They don't have knowledge of the Word, so they are taken captive—and they don't even know it!

But when you get hold of the Word in your heart, it transforms your life. You're set free from the notion that God wants you sick for some purpose of His own, and you can receive the healing that rightfully belongs to you as a covenant child of God!

Confession:

My God is the God who heals me.
He gets glory from my being healthy.
Therefore, I walk in healing and divine health.

The Spirit itself beareth witness with our spirit,
that we are the children of God: and if children,
then heirs; heirs of God, and joint-heirs with
Christ; if so be that we suffer with him, that we
may be also glorified together. –Romans 8:16,17

Look in God's "Will" To Find His Will

In order to be healed, we need to be sure of the answers to certain questions: Is it God's will for us to be healed? Does He want us sick for a purpose or to teach us something? Does God have *anything* to do with sickness or disease?

The only way we can find out God's will on any subject is to read the "will" He left for us.

You see, suppose I had a wealthy relative who died and left not only an inheritance to me, but also a will explaining what was in the inheritance. I could sit back for years and say, "I wonder what the will says. I wonder what's mine in the will. I wonder what's included in the will." *Or* I could go read the will and find out what belongs to me!

It's the same with God. Jesus provided an inheritance for us because God first appointed Jesus heir of all things. Hebrews 1:2 says that God "hath in these last days spoken unto us by his Son, whom he hath appointed heir of all things, by whom also he made the worlds."

God made Jesus the heir of all things, and we're joint-heirs with Him. But we need to read the will to find out what God's will is. The New Testament is God's last will and testament. It tells us what belongs to us as children of God.

So is it God's will to heal you? Do you want to know for sure? Then take the time to read His will and find out!

Confession:

My Father wrote a will to tell me what is mine, and He sealed it with
the blood of Jesus. It tells me that healing is a part of my inheritance.
Because the will is now in effect, healing belongs to me now!

JANUARY 23

God Is a Rewarder

But without faith it is impossible to please him: for he that cometh to God must believe that he is, and that he is a rewarder of them that diligently seek him. —*Hebrews 11:6*

Do you want to receive God's covenant promise of healing? Then you have to believe that God *is,* and you have to believe He is a *rewarder.* If you don't believe you will receive a reward from Him, you won't.

Most of the time people don't go to God in faith. They may believe that God *is,* but they aren't sure He is a rewarder. So they say, "Oh, dear God, if it is Your will, please do this for me."

But you can go to God in faith, knowing exactly what His will is because you have His will to read. For example, you never have to say, "I wonder if it's God's will to heal me." You can just read the Bible and find out. It's His last will and testament to you.

When someone makes out a will, no one else has the right to take away from it or add to it. In the same way, we don't have a right to change God's will to us. All we can do is read what belongs to us and live by it.

So study God's last will and testament until you get these two truths lodged deep in your heart: God is, and God is a rewarder. Then diligently seek Him for your healing, and receive your reward!

Confession:

I believe my God is. He is alive, He is powerful and He is a rewarder. I live in line with His Word, and I receive all the benefits He has provided for me!

And he said unto them, When ye pray, say,
Our Father which art in heaven, Hallowed be
thy name. Thy kingdom come. Thy will be done,
as in heaven, so in earth. —*Luke 11:2*

JANUARY 24

God's Will Be Done in Your Life

Notice what Jesus said: "Thy will be done, as in heaven, so in earth." In other words, God's will on earth is no different than God's will in heaven.

I don't plan to see any sickness when I get to heaven, do you? There is no sickness in heaven. Sickness can't exist in the presence of God.

How do you know what God's will is here on earth? Well, find out what His will is in heaven, and you'll have a pretty good idea. Jesus said, "Thy kingdom come. Thy will be done in earth *as it is in heaven.*"

So if health is God's will in heaven, health is His will down here on earth too. If He's against sickness there, He's against sickness here.

God wants you healthy once you're in heaven, and He wants you healthy while you're still here on earth. So let God's kingdom come and His will be done in *your* life. Receive your healing and walk in divine health!

Confession:

Divine health is God's will for me even while I'm here on the earth. I walk in health because Jesus bore all my sicknesses and pains. Therefore, in Jesus' name I am healed!

JANUARY 25

God Wants To Heal All

Is any sick among you? let him call for the elders of the church; and let them pray over him, anointing him with oil in the name of the Lord: and the prayer of faith shall save the sick, and the Lord shall raise him up; and if he have committed sins, they shall be forgiven him.

—James 5:14,15

James was writing to believers here—to the Church of the living God. He asked, "Is there any sick among you?" Notice that He didn't say, "If there is any sick among you, let him pray and see if, by any chance, God might want him healed." Nor did James say, "Let him fast and pray for three weeks to see if it's God's will to heal him."

Nothing is said in this Scripture about whether it is God's will or not. And it doesn't say, "The Lord shall raise him up—if he is one of the few destined to get healed because the Lord is in a good mood."

James just tells us, "If there is any sick in the church, let him come up to the front and have the church elders pray over him, anointing him with oil in the name of the Lord."

Then James says, "And the prayer of faith *shall* [not *might*] save the sick, and the Lord shall raise him up" (v. 15).

Who is the "him" this verse refers to? "Him" is *any sick in the church.*

Now, God isn't confused or mixed up. If it weren't His will for all to be healed, why would He tell sick people how to get healed? God reveals His will right here in this Scripture. It is His perfect will to heal His children—*any* who are sick.

Confession:

God has given me several ways to receive my healing. According to His Word, when I ask the church elders to anoint me with oil and pray, the prayer of faith will heal me, and God will raise me up!

And he said unto them, Go ye into all the world, and preach the gospel to every creature. He that believeth and is baptized shall be saved; but he that believeth not shall be damned. And these signs shall follow them that believe; In my name...they shall lay hands on the sick, and they shall recover. —Mark 16:15-18

JANUARY 26

Healing and the Gospel Are for All

At times I've prayed, "Lord, I laid hands on Brother so-and-so over there, and he didn't get any better." But notice in this passage of Scripture that God didn't say, "Just go lay hands on the sick, and they will recover." No, He starts out by saying, "Go into all the world and preach the Gospel to every creature." *Then* He says, "And these signs shall follow them that believe...."

We aren't supposed to just go around looking for sick people to lay hands on. They will run away from us if we do that. First, we have to tell them what God's Word says. We have to tell them the good news of the Gospel—that it's God's will for them to be healed and that if we lay hands on them, they will recover.

We make a mistake when we rush out and try to lay hands on everybody without teaching them to cooperate with the Word. I remember a case like that. People laid hands on someone to pray for him. But the moment they were done praying, the person receiving the prayer said, "Well, that didn't work." He didn't expect it to work, because no one had taught him how it was supposed to work.

But if that same person hears the Gospel, he can get in agreement with the person praying for him. He'll know for himself that God's will is *healing for all.*

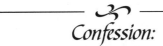

Confession:

God's Word lives richly in me, so I'm always ready to give God's Word to someone with a need. I speak the Word, knowing that the power in the Word produces faith in me and everyone who hears.

JANUARY 27

Jesus: The Image of the Father

[The Father] hath delivered us from the power of darkness, and hath translated us into the kingdom of his dear Son: in whom we have redemption through his blood, even the forgiveness of sins: who is the image of the invisible God, the firstborn of every creature.

–Colossians 1:13-15

The world has always had such a warped idea of what God is like. People often think God is causing all their problems. They have a mental picture of God sitting up in heaven with a big club. They think He's waiting for them to make a mistake so He can hit them on the head—in other words, make them sick, steal their money or kill their family.

But if you want to know what God is really like, look at Jesus. Seeing Jesus gives us a picture of God. In Colossians 1:15, Jesus is called "the image of the invisible God." Jesus Himself said, "If you've seen Me, you've seen the Father." (John 14:9.)

Follow Jesus' earthly ministry to see God's will in action. You see, everything Jesus did (or didn't do) represented God's will.

Jesus led a perfect life. He never committed a sin. He never made anyone sick. He never stole, never killed and never destroyed. He never left anyone sick who wanted and believed Him to be healed. He never said, "This sickness is here to teach you something, to perfect you, to correct you or to make you more pious." He never said, "This sickness is good for you." He just healed anyone and everyone who desired to be healed.

Jesus acted out God's will for mankind. He never refused healing to anyone, and He won't refuse healing to *you.*

Confession:

*Jesus healed everyone who came to Him in faith.
Hebrews 13:8 says He is the same yesterday, today and forever,
so I come to Him in faith, knowing He will heal me too!*

And ye shall know the truth, and the truth
shall make you free.   *—John 8:32*

JANUARY 28

God Wants To Heal All

People who say, "God doesn't heal anymore," evidently never read the Bible. Hebrews 13:8 says Jesus is the same now as He has ever been. If He healed while He walked on this earth, He still heals today.

Most people believe it is God's will to heal *some*. But the big question remains, "Is it God's will to heal *all?*" Some say, "Well, that can't be true because I knew Brother so-and-so, and he wasn't healed."

If we go by the experiences of people we know, we may conclude it isn't God's will to heal everyone. But we must gather together all the experience, tradition, doctrine, theory and denominationalism we've ever heard and just push it aside. We must look at nothing but God's Word and find out what *He* has to say.

Let me illustrate. If you wanted to know my will about something, for example, I hope you wouldn't go ask some guy out on the street corner who doesn't know me. There's no telling what that person would say!

But most of us have done that with God. When we've wanted to know God's will, we've sometimes gone to people who don't even know Him and asked what they thought. They may have given us all kinds of wild opinions, not having the faintest idea what the Bible says.

So if we want to find God's will on a subject, we have to go to Jesus. He is the express image of God. Jesus said, "He that hath seen me hath seen the Father" (John 14:9). He also said, "And ye shall know the truth, and the truth shall make you free" (John 8:32). He didn't say theories or doctrines will make you free; He said *knowing the truth*—His Word—will make you free.

Thank God, the Bible is truth! And in the Bible, we find it is God's will to heal *all*.

Confession:

I know the truth that God wants to heal me, and the truth sets
me free from any sickness or disease. I've found it in the Word;
I know it's God's will. So I believe I receive my healing now!

JANUARY 29

Look to Jesus To Know the Father

Philip saith unto him, Lord, shew us the Father, and it sufficeth us. Jesus saith unto him, Have I been so long time with you, and yet hast thou not known me, Philip? he that hath seen me hath seen the Father; and how sayest thou then, Shew us the Father? Believest thou not that I am in the Father, and the Father in me? the words that I speak unto you I speak not of myself: but the Father that dwelleth in me, he doeth the works.
—John 14:8-10

Philip had one burning desire in his heart—for Jesus to show them the Father. You see, before Jesus walked on this earth, the world didn't understand God. They didn't know what God looked like. Then Jesus came along as love manifested in the flesh, and He said, "If you want to know what the Father looks like, look at Me. I'll show you what the Father looks like, sounds like and acts like, because I only do that which I see my Father do." (John 5:19.)

That's a strong statement! Jesus also said in that verse, "The Father in Me is doing the work. I'm not healing people; *God* is healing them through Me." Therefore, everything Jesus did had to be the will of God, because if it wasn't God's will, Jesus couldn't do it. If God didn't supply the power, Jesus couldn't give it out.

Jesus acted out God's will for the human race. And what did Jesus do? He healed all those who would receive their healing in faith. What *didn't* He do? He didn't *make* people sick, and He didn't *leave* them sick if they believed Him to be healed.

So study the ministry of Jesus, and you'll know for a fact—sickness isn't God's will, but healing is!

Confession:

While Jesus walked on this earth, He revealed the Father's desire to heal His people. Just like Jesus, my Father heals me when I come to Him in faith to be healed. My God is a good and merciful God!

And when Jesus was come into Peter's house, he saw his wife's mother laid, and sick of a fever. And he touched her hand, and the fever left her: and she arose, and ministered unto them.

—Matthew 8:14,15

JANUARY 30

Jesus—The Will of God in Action

When Jesus came to Peter's house, Jesus didn't fast and pray to see what the Father wanted Him to do. He just knew that God's will is healing for *all*. Therefore, it had to be God's will for Peter's mother-in-law to be healed and whole.

You can come to that same conclusion yourself just by studying the Gospels. For example, think about this: How many people did Jesus walk up to and make sick? *None.* How many people did He tell, "This sickness is for the glory of God, so keep it awhile"? *None.* How many times did He say, "No, I can't heal you"? *Never.* How many people who wanted healing did He turn down? *None.* How many times did He say, "No, wait until later; I'll do it in My own good time"? *Never.*

Remember, Jesus' every move in His earthly ministry was the will of God in action. He said, "If you've seen Me, you've seen the Father." So when we see that Jesus never turned anyone down, that tells us that God never turns anyone down. Jesus never said, "Wait," so God never says, "Wait." Jesus never said, "This sickness is good for you," so God never says, "This sickness is good for you." Jesus did nothing but set people free; therefore, God does nothing but set people free.

Jesus is all the proof we need that it's God's will to heal *everyone!*

Confession:

I see my Father when I look at Jesus. Just as Jesus is the same, yesterday, today and forever, so also my Father never changes. His will was healing then, and His will is healing for me now. So I say, "Let Your will be done, Lord!"

JANUARY 31

Hear and Be Healed

And [Jesus] came to Nazareth, where he had been brought up: and, as his custom was, he went into the synagogue on the sabbath day, and stood up for to read. And there was delivered unto him the book of the prophet Esaias. And when he had opened the book, he found the place where it was written, The Spirit of the Lord is upon me, because he hath anointed me to preach the gospel to the poor; he hath sent me to heal the brokenhearted, to preach deliverance to the captives, and recovering of sight to the blind, to set at liberty them that are bruised, to preach the acceptable year of the Lord.

–Luke 4:16-19

There is a definite connection between *hearing* and *being healed*. You can find several instances in the New Testament where people refused to hear the Word and therefore were not healed.

In this passage from Luke 4 Jesus quoted from the book of Isaiah, but the people wouldn't hear it. Verse 28 tells of their response to Jesus: "And all they in the synagogue, when they heard these things, were filled with wrath."

If the people had been willing to hear, they would have been filled with faith to receive their healing—not to mention all the other benefits of believing in Jesus. But they missed out on God's blessings because they refused to hear.

During Jesus' three years of ministry on this earth, we never find Him leaving anyone sick—except the people who wouldn't receive from Him. For instance, in His own hometown, the people didn't receive healing because of their unbelief. Mark 6:5-6 says, "And he could there do no mighty work, save that he laid his hands upon a few sick folk, and healed them. And he marvelled because of their unbelief."

God won't force anything on anyone. He's a gentleman. But when you come to Him in faith, it's His delight to heal you and set you free.

Confession:

I choose to hear God's Word and accept His will, which is my healing. I will not allow doubt and unbelief to keep me from receiving from God.

*If ye abide in me, and my words abide in you,
ye shall ask what ye will, and it shall be done
unto you.* —John 15:7

Ask What You Will

From this Scripture we understand that it is God's will to heal everyone, because it is God's will to answer prayers. God promises to answer any prayer that lines up with His Word.

We know that healing lines up with God's Word because Psalm 107:20 tells us God sent His Word to heal us. We know healing lines up with His Word because Matthew 9:35 tells us Jesus went through all the cities and villages, teaching, preaching and healing every sickness and disease among the people. We know healing lines up with His Word because Hebrews 13:8 says Jesus is the same yesterday, today and forever.

Jesus said, "If you abide in Me, and My words abide in you, you shall ask whatever *you* will, and it shall be done."

"Well, Lord, what if I will to be healed?" God's will is to heal you. And if healing is what *you* will, too, then you can be sure it shall be done unto you!

Confession:

*I abide in the Lord Jesus Christ, and His words abide in me.
So I ask my Father in prayer, believing I receive my healing today.
By faith, it is done—I am healed!*

FEBRUARY 2

Ask, and You Shall Receive

And in that day ye shall ask me nothing. Verily, verily, I say unto you, Whatsoever ye shall ask the Father in my name, he will give it you. Hitherto have ye asked nothing in my name: ask, and ye shall receive, that your joy may be full.

–John 16:23,24

One way we know our heavenly Father wants to heal us is by this verse, which tells us that He wants to answer our prayers. Out of all the things He said we could ask for in prayer, Jesus never excluded healing. In fact, He said, "Verily, verily, I say unto you, *whatsoever* ye shall ask the Father in my name, he will give it you." He didn't say, "He will give you whatsoever you ask—unless it's healing"!

Jesus said, "Ask, and ye shall receive, that your joy may be full."

"What if I ask for healing?" you may say.

"Ask, and ye shall receive, that your joy may be full."

"What if it's a physical need?"

"Ask, and ye shall receive, that your joy may be full."

Does God want us healed? He must, because He promised to answer our prayers—including our prayers for healing—when we pray to Him in Jesus' name.

Confession:

God's ears are open to my prayers for healing.
I receive what I pray for in Jesus' name,
and I am filled with joy!

For I am the Lord that healeth thee.

–Exodus 15:26

FEBRUARY 3

Our Creator and Our Healer

For years as a young man, I had problems with my throat. It kept closing up on me. At times I'd almost go into a panic because it would become so tight that I could hardly swallow. I went to a doctor, who gave me various pills, but none of the medication helped.

Finally, I saw an allergist. He informed me that I was allergic to weeds, most foods, dust and other allergens that are hard to avoid. He began giving me regular serum injections, and for the first time in five or six years, my throat started to loosen up. I was supposed to take those injections for the rest of my life.

Shortly after that I was born again. When I was home from college for the summer, I held youth meetings five to seven nights a week. We sang and prayed a lot at the meetings, but we didn't have any real teaching from the Word. You see, I was the leader, and I didn't know anything! I certainly couldn't teach the Word—I didn't even know God could heal!

Then my throat began to tighten again, and I realized I hadn't brought the serum home with me from college. As my throat got tighter and tighter, I kept thinking, *I'll have to go get that serum!*

One day we were all praying together when I felt my throat tighten again. Suddenly panic and fear hit me. (I didn't know I'd been delivered from fear when I'd gotten saved.) But then gradually, a deep realization that God is God began to rise up from my spirit.

I said quietly, "Lord, I've had this problem a long time. But I figure that if You're smart and powerful enough to put this body together to begin with, You sure ought to be able to fix one defect like this. Would You do that for me?"

Within five minutes my throat had returned to normal, and it has never tightened up like that again. My healing came the moment I realized God could heal. It was a revelation that has changed my life. God *created* me—surely He could fix me!

Confession:

My God is the Creator of the universe, and He upholds all things by the Word of His power. He is the God who heals His people, and He is the God who is able and willing to heal me!

FEBRUARY 4

Getting Past the Invisible Wall

The heart of the prudent getteth knowledge; and the ear of the wise seeketh knowledge.

—Proverbs 18:15

After God healed me of allergies, I went through a real struggle the next time I needed healing. The thought came into my mind, *Yeah, God is able to heal me, but is He willing?* (I bet you know what that voice in your mind sounds like!)

So when I prayed for healing the next time, I said, "Lord, I sure would like You to heal me—if You really want to." But I wasn't healed, and I couldn't figure out why. I prayed again, "Lord, here I am! You did it last time; why don't You do it this time?"

I didn't understand that I'd hit an invisible wall because, although I knew God was *able* to heal, I still didn't know He was *willing*.

Then came the thought, *Maybe God wants me sick for a purpose.* I didn't get that thought from a church or from a book; it came straight from the source of doubt and unbelief. That thought came to my mind, and then it took root. For years, I had trouble getting rid of that wrong way of thinking.

That's the point most Christians have come to in their spiritual walk. They know God is *able,* but they aren't sure God is *willing.*

Your faith will never operate beyond your knowledge of God's will. So root out wrong thinking that isn't in line with the Word. Seek knowledge in God's Word until you know it's His will to heal everyone. Then believe Him for *your* healing. Take God at His Word, and expect His promises to come to pass in your life.

Confession:

I'm so glad my Father wants me well. I root out every thought that would tell me otherwise! God sent His Word to heal me. And by Jesus' stripes, I am healed!

And the people, when they knew it, followed him: and he received them, and spake unto them of the kingdom of God, and healed them that had need of healing. —Luke 9:11

God Is Able and Willing

When I first started hearing the truth of God's Word about healing, I studied the subject with great interest. But whenever symptoms hit my body, my first thought was *I wonder why God allowed this to happen?* It took me years to get rid of that doubt and unbelief the enemy had planted in me.

When we know God's ability but doubt His willingness, it's like slapping Him in the face. Stop and think about it. Suppose you came to me and said, "Now, Mark, I have a real problem here, and I know you'd help me if you could. But I realize you don't have the capability or the equipment to help me." I'd feel good that you thought I cared enough to help if I could.

But suppose you said, "Now, Mark, I have a real problem here. I know you could help me if you wanted to, but I don't know if you want to." It would hurt my feelings that you found me so uncaring!

How much more, then, does it hurt our Father when we go to Him and say, "I know You're able, Lord, but I don't know if You're willing"? The worst part is that God's Word tells us He *is* willing, but many of us haven't bothered to take the time to search out the truth.

So don't insult your heavenly Father by doubting His willingness to heal you. He is able *and* willing to heal you. You have His Word on it!

Confession:

I will never insult my Father by doubting His willingness to heal me. God's will is health and healing. He is able and willing to heal me, so I honor Him by receiving His healing touch today!

FEBRUARY 6

"That It Might Be Fulfilled"

When the even was come, they brought unto him many that were possessed with devils: and he cast out the spirits with his word, and healed all that were sick. —Matthew 8:16

What if God didn't want to heal everyone who came to Jesus? What if a few people God didn't want to heal slipped into that crowd and received their healing from Jesus before God knew about it?

No, that couldn't happen. You see, for Jesus to heal anyone, it had to be God's will, because Jesus only did what He saw His Father do. (John 5:19.)

When Jesus walked into a multitude of people, He cast out *all* the devils and healed *all* the sick. He never refused one person; He never turned anyone down. He never said, "I'll heal you later; you need to learn a few things before you get healed." Instead, He always said things like, "I will—be thou clean," or "I will—come and be healed."

Jesus always healed all who were in faith. Here's why:

That it might be fulfilled which was spoken by Esaias the prophet, saying, Himself took our infirmities, and bare our sicknesses.

Matthew 8:17

The Bible says Jesus healed *in order to fulfill the Scriptures*. Every time He healed the multitudes, He proved once more that God's will is healing for *all*.

Confession:

*Jesus took my infirmities and bore my sicknesses.
I believe that He is able and willing to heal me;
therefore, right now I receive my healing by faith.*

And this is the confidence that we have in him, that, if we ask any thing according to his will, he heareth us: and if we know that he hear us, whatsoever we ask, we know that we have the petitions that we desired of him.

–1 John 5:14,15

FEBRUARY 7

God Is Willing To Heal

Physical healing is a great need in the body of Christ today. The greatest hindrance is not knowing that God is willing to heal. Hosea 4:6 says, "My people are destroyed for lack of knowledge."

The marginal note in my Bible says that the word *destroyed* literally means "cut off." So that Scripture could actually be rendered, "For a lack of knowledge people are cut off from the blessings of God."

If we don't know that God is willing to heal us, we are cut off from His blessings of healing and health. You see, faith must have a foundation. In order to confidently receive what Jesus purchased and provided for us, we must know it is our Father's desire to give it to us.

God wants us to come boldly to the throne of grace to receive the healing we need. (Heb. 4:16.) That kind of boldness comes only from strong faith—a faith born of knowing the Father's willingness to heal.

Confession:
I am confident that God is willing to heal me. Therefore, I'm confident He hears me and gives me the petition of healing I desire!

FEBRUARY 8

Healed in Order To Serve

And when Jesus was come into Peter's house, he saw his wife's mother laid, and sick of a fever. And he touched her hand, and the fever left her: and she arose, and ministered unto them.

—Matthew 8:14,15

God lets us know in this Scripture what our motive should be for wanting to be healed. We should want to get healed so God can use us in service to Him, not just so we can go play tennis or golf.

Now, there's nothing wrong with tennis or golf, but our primary motives for wanting to be healed ought to be first, because Jesus purchased our healing with His own precious blood, and second, because we want to be able to serve God with all our strength.

When Samuel was sent to anoint David to be king, God said something to Samuel that shows how important right heart motives are to Him: "The Lord seeth not as man seeth; for man looketh on the outward appearance, *but the Lord looketh on the heart"* (1 Sam. 16:7).

We need to keep our motives right. Wrong motives will keep us out of God's blessings. James 4:3 says, "Ye ask, and receive not, because ye ask amiss [or with wrong motives]."

So keep your motives pure and your heart right, and then believe God for your healing. Faith inspired by right motives for healing and health will quickly move the hand of God!

Confession:

The main purpose of my life is to minister to the Lord, putting my hand to the work He gives me to do. I thank God for healing me, that I might be effective and unhindered by pain, sickness and disease.

*I have been young, and now am old; yet have I
not seen the righteous forsaken, nor his seed
begging bread.* —Psalm 37:25

Healing–The Children's Bread

God doesn't want His children begging for what already belongs to them. To the woman of Canaan who begged Him to heal her daughter, Jesus said, "It is not meet to take the children's bread, and to cast it to dogs" (Matt. 15:26).

So according to Jesus, healing is the children's bread.

Healing belongs to us. It is part of our redemption, our covenant, our spiritual inheritance. It belongs to us as blood-bought, new creatures in Christ.

When a believer begs for healing, God doesn't have the slightest idea why. God says, "Child, healing belongs to you; it's yours! When you accepted Jesus, He became your healer. You don't have to beg."

So get the revelation in your heart that as God's child, healing is your "bread." That's 99 percent of the battle right there!

Confession:

*As a joint-heir with Jesus Christ, I have a covenant right
to receive healing and to walk in divine health. I receive
my inheritance of healing by faith. Healing belongs to me!*

FEBRUARY 10

No Longer Just a Promise

According as his divine power hath given unto us all things that pertain unto life and godliness, through the knowledge of him that hath called us to glory and virtue. —2 Peter 1:3

Under the old covenant, God kept telling Israel about the Redeemer, the Messiah, showing them pictures of redemption in types and shadows. Thousands of years passed, and people continued waiting for God's redemptive promises to be fulfilled.

Then Jesus came to this earth, fulfilling the will of God through His death, burial and resurrection. Under the new covenant, Peter could say, "His divine power *hath given* unto us all things that pertain unto life and godliness." What was a promise is now a fulfilled fact. Now God says, "I've done My part." The responsibility to act switched from Him to us.

You see, if someone says to you, "I want to give you a book" but then just sits there, doing nothing, you have to wait to receive the book you've been given. But if he says, "I want to give you this book" and then places the book beside you, then it's your responsibility to pick it up.

In the spiritual realm, we know that God "hath given unto us all things that pertain unto life and godliness." Well, healing pertains to life and godliness. So if we want the healing God has already given us, we have to "pick it up." We don't wait for God to heal us. We just reach out and take hold of what He's already done. That isn't forcing God's hand. That's saying, "Lord, You did it. I believe it. I take it!"

Thank God, we don't have to wait until God completes the plan of redemption. We aren't looking ahead to what God will do someday. We're looking back to what He did 2000 years ago! He has already redeemed us from the curse of the Law. He has already redeemed us from sickness and disease. It isn't just a promise anymore—it's a fact!

Confession:

I'm redeemed by the blood of Jesus, set free from all the effects of the curse. Sickness and disease are no longer a part of my job description. I'm free!

He sent his word, and healed them, and delivered them from their destructions.

–Psalm 107:20

Healing Is a Fact

Divine healing belongs to us. We aren't waiting for God to heal us; God is waiting for us to *take* the healing that's already ours. God wanted us healed so much that He didn't just *promise* to heal us; He sent His Son to purchase our healing with His broken body. Therefore, healing is not just a promise—it is a *fact!*

Years ago, I looked at healing as a promise. Then one day I read, "Who his own self bare our sins in his own body on the tree, that we, being dead to sins, should live unto righteousness: by whose stripes ye were healed" (1 Peter 2:24). He didn't say you *may* be healed or you *will* be healed. He said, "Ye *were* healed"—past tense. It isn't what God is going to do; it's what He already did. The day I found that Scripture in the Bible, it turned my life around.

Healing is a fact. As far as God is concerned, His part is done. Now He's waiting for us to do our part—to reach out and take what is already ours!

Confession:

I want what the Word says and nothing less! I want God's best, and that includes healing for my body. By faith, I reach out and take the healing that is already mine!

FEBRUARY 12

Healing Is God's Idea

But my God shall supply all your need according to his riches in glory by Christ Jesus.

—Philippians 4:19

God designed the plan of redemption long before we were ever born. Remember, He called Jesus "the Lamb slain from the foundation of the world" (Rev. 13:8). In His plan of redemption, God provided us with certain benefits—salvation, the infilling of the Holy Ghost, divine healing and so forth—through the death, burial and resurrection of the Lord Jesus Christ.

God gives us these benefits, not because of anything we've done, but because of what He's done through the blood of His Son. We're not pushing God to heal us; He *chose* to do it. It was His idea. We aren't forcing His hand; we're accepting His Word. Our part is to say, "Lord, You said You'd supply every need, so I believe it and receive it."

Make sure you fulfill your part. Don't be like some people, who look at God's promise of healing and say, "Well, I don't know if I can go along with that." That's like slapping Jesus in the face! In essence, those people are saying, "Jesus, the Word says You shed Your blood to purchase healing for me. But my religious doctrine says it isn't true, so I'll take my doctrine instead."

You can't receive healing for your body with that kind of attitude! You have to come to the place where it doesn't matter what you've heard or been taught. In order to receive God's benefits, you must agree with His Word.

Confession:

When I ask for healing, I'm not forcing God's hand. Healing me is His idea! He made healing available for me. God's way is blessed, right, healthy and joyous. I choose to believe God's Word!

And [Jesus] was teaching in one of the synagogues on the sabbath.

–Luke 13:10

FEBRUARY 13

The Importance of Hearing the Word

Jesus' teaching ministry was important. You see, His teaching of the Word is what caused His healing ministry to flow and operate.

Under Jesus' ministry, most people had to hear Him teach the Word to get healed. Luke 5:15 says, "Multitudes came together to hear, and to be healed." That means most of the people were healed as a result of hearing the Word and then receiving by their own faith.

For example, Jesus said to two blind men, "According to your faith be it unto you" (Matt. 9:29). To a centurion, He said, "As thou hast believed, so be it done unto thee" (Matt. 8:13). Jesus told a leper, "Thy faith hath made thee whole" (Luke 17:19). And to the woman with the issue of blood, Jesus said, "Daughter, thy faith hath made thee whole" (Mark 5:34).

Many Christians are not healed today because they don't take time to listen to the Word of God. They want someone to get them healed so they can get on with life. "Hurry up and lay hands on me so I can get back to what I was doing!" With that kind of attitude, it's no wonder these people don't receive their healing.

Take the time to hear the Word. Feed your spirit continually with God's promises of healing and health. As you are faithful to hear and hear and hear the Word, your faith will rise up to make you whole!

Confession:

I continually put myself in position to hear the Word, and faith rises up strong within me. As I act on God's Word, I receive all I need to make my life full and rich with God's blessings.

FEBRUARY 14

Hear With Your Spiritual Ears

Let these sayings sink down into your ears: for the Son of man shall be delivered into the hands of men.

–Luke 9:44

There is a direct connection between hearing the Word and being healed. Many people are not being healed because they are either not hearing at all or they are not hearing enough.

Someone may say, "Well, I heard the Word; I know what it says; but it didn't work for me." No, that's not possible. The Word always works. Sometimes *we* fail to receive the benefits of the Word, but the Word never fails. The failure is on our part.

When Jesus told His disciples, "Let these sayings sink down into your ears," He meant that you must hear the Word over and over and over with your spiritual ears—the ears of your inner man—until those truths finally get down on the inside of you. Only then will you be able to receive the benefits of healing that are rightfully yours.

Confession:

I'm hearing and hearing and hearing the Word. The Word is sinking down into the "ears" of my spirit so it can produce fruit in my life. The Word always works, and it's working in me, producing health in my body.

Wherefore let him that thinketh he standeth take heed lest he fall. —*1 Corinthians 10:12*

FEBRUARY 15

Faith Comes by Hearing

Several years ago, after I'd been walking in health for a number of years, allergy symptoms once again attacked my body. I started waking up in the middle of the night, sneezing off and on for hours.

So I began declaring, "Bless God, I stand on the Word. Thank God, I believe I'm healed!" Nothing happened. Then I said, "I rebuke these symptoms in Jesus' name. Leave my body *now!*" Nothing happened. I cursed the symptoms and commanded them to go. And yet they stayed. I asked someone to agree with me for healing; still nothing happened.

I tried everything I knew to do—I pulled every lever, flipped every switch, pushed every button, pulled every knob—but got no better fast. Finally, I went to the Lord and said, "Dear God, I know You don't miss it. It's not Your fault; it's mine. I'm missing it someplace. If You'll tell me where it is, I'll correct it."

About that time, I was asked to minister on healing for a week in a Bible school. I hadn't taught on healing for about a year and a half. And because I hadn't been teaching on healing, I hadn't been studying the subject either.

Well, faith cometh by hearing—and it goeth by *not* hearing! I had what you would call a faith deficit because I hadn't kept my faith built up in the area of healing. The enemy made use of that weakness and strapped some symptoms on me.

Because I was going to teach on healing, I spent a week studying the subject from one to eight hours a day. The entire week I kept hearing, confessing and meditating on healing Scriptures.

Toward the end of the week, I asked my wife, Janet, "When did I stop sneezing?" I had been healed so fast that I didn't even know I was healed! I was so busy enjoying my healing that I didn't even notice when all the symptoms lifted! I *heard* and was healed!

Confession:

Because I am His child, God gave me access to the power in His Word. As I hear, believe and confess His Word, it produces healing in my physical body.

FEBRUARY 16

Faith—
The Product
of Hearing
the Word

*And Jesus went about all Galilee, teaching in
their synagogues, and preaching the gospel of
the kingdom, and healing all manner of sickness
and all manner of disease among the people.*

–Matthew 4:23

Did you ever notice that in Jesus' ministry teaching and preaching came before healing? You see, there's a direct connection between hearing and being healed. The very best thing you can do if you need healing in your body is to keep hearing and hearing and hearing the Word of God. Hear it with your physical ears so many times that you finally hear it with your spiritual ears.

In Romans 10:10, Paul said, "For with the *heart* man believeth." Real faith is of the heart—the inner man. You don't believe with your head. The Holy Spirit didn't say through Paul, "With the *head* man believeth." It's when the Word of God goes down into your spirit—when the Word is mixed with your "believer"— that faith emerges. Faith is the product, or the fruit, of your knowledge of God's Word having moved from your mind to your spirit. When you put the Word in your spirit, faith is always the result.

Confession:

*With my heart, I believe whatever I hear the most–the Word.
I choose to hear the truth of God's Word. It's easy to believe
God's promises because I keep hearing and hearing the Word.*

How then shall they call on him in whom they have not believed? and how shall they believe in him of whom they have not heard? and how shall they hear without a preacher?

–Romans 10:14

FEBRUARY 17

The More You Hear, the More You Believe

Several years ago, I went with a group of five other ministers to India to conduct a ministers' seminar for about 130 native ministers. Each of the six of us taught on a different subject. I had it in my heart to teach on healing. I taught for three and a half weeks, one hour every day. God dealt with me to teach most of the time on the Atonement—what Jesus purchased for us on the Cross.

On the first day, different ministers asked me to pray for their healing, but the Spirit of God wouldn't allow me to do it. I told them, "Not yet; we'll do it later." Each day, another person would ask me to pray for him, and I'd say the same thing—"No, I can't do it yet." I knew that if I laid hands on these ministers and prayed for their healing, they wouldn't receive. They didn't know enough of the Word to have strong faith, because they'd just begun to hear the Word on the subject of healing.

The last day of the meeting came, and I taught on healing one more time. Then the Lord spoke to my spirit, *It's time to pray! But don't you pray or lay hands on them. They are ministers; let them pray for each other.*

I obeyed the Lord, and when the ministers finished praying for each other, I asked, "All right, how many needed healing?" Many hands went up. Then I asked, "How many received your healing?" A large number of hands went up again. "How many received manifestations of your healing?" Hands went up again.

After these ministers had heard the Word day after day after day, they were ready to receive. They could hardly wait for me to finish the message so they could pray! They had heard the Word, and their faith had grown strong. They were ready to receive!

Confession:

Faith rises up in me when I hear God's Word.
I take time to hear His Word on healing, and my faith
increases and grows stronger and produces healing in me!

FEBRUARY 18

Activate Jesus' Healing Power With Your Faith

And [Jesus] came down with them, and stood in the plain, and the company of his disciples, and a great multitude of people out of all Judaea and Jerusalem, and from the sea coast of Tyre and Sidon, which came to hear him, and to be healed of their diseases; and they that were vexed with unclean spirits: and they were healed. And the whole multitude sought to touch him: for there went virtue out of him, and healed them all.
—Luke 6:17-19

During Jesus' ministry, people who wanted their lives changed came to hear Him and be healed. Verse 19 reveals what happened when they came: "For there went virtue out of him, and healed them all." You see, the virtue, or power, of God flowed out of Jesus to heal the multitude when the people operated in faith. And when did they operate in faith? After they heard the Word.

Once the people heard, their faith rose up and released the healing power in Jesus. But the power didn't flow out of Him until after the people heard His teaching.

If you need healing or a miracle from God, you, too, can draw on Jesus' healing power with your faith. However, the first step is to hear what the Word of God says. You must hear it and hear it with your physical ears until you can hear it with your spiritual ears. As the healing virtue flowed out of Jesus then, it still flows out of Him today—activated by your faith.

Confession:

The same virtue that flowed out of Jesus to heal the multitude heals me now as I hear the Word and draw on His power. Jesus is the same now as He was then. He was the healer then, and He's still my healer today.

And [Jesus] could there do no mighty work, save that he laid his hands upon a few sick folk, and healed them. And he marvelled because of their unbelief. And he went round about the villages, teaching. —Mark 6:5,6

FEBRUARY 19

Keep Teaching Others How To Be Healed

Jesus had gone into His own hometown, and the power of God was present to heal. Jesus was anointed with the Holy Ghost and with power, but just a few in Nazareth received their healing. Most of them wouldn't receive because their unbelief was so strong. So what was Jesus' solution to that situation? (Remember, there is a connection between hearing and healing.) "And he went round about the villages, *teaching*" (v. 6).

When Jesus couldn't get anything else to happen, He taught. Jesus did that all through His ministry. When He encountered the hard places, He'd just lean back and teach. When people weren't receiving their healing, when He couldn't do any mighty works, when no gifts of the Spirit were operating and no one was receiving the anointing, Jesus would teach and teach and teach.

Jesus is our example. When people won't receive, just keep teaching. That was a major part of Jesus' ministry, because when He taught people, they were healed. The only way to cure unbelief is to keep teaching the Word. Someone will take hold of it because there's a connection between hearing and being healed.

Confession:

*As the Word becomes life and healing in me,
I can teach others. The healing power of
the Word works in all who hear.*

FEBRUARY 20

My soul, wait thou only upon God; for my expectation is from him. —*Psalm 62:5*

Keep Hearing the Word

Janet and I recently ministered in a Sunday morning church service, where we told the people, "Come back tonight expecting God to do something. Meditate on the Word. If you need something from God, find out what the Word says about it. If you need healing, find healing Scriptures and meditate on them. Dwell on them. Say them out loud to yourself all afternoon, and then come back tonight expecting."

Some people came up to us after the service and said, "Just give us a couple of Scriptures, and we'll go home and meditate on them." Others said, "We're going home to pray and listen to the Word all afternoon. We'll come back tonight expecting."

The people did what they said they were going to do. They went home that afternoon and did their spiritual homework. They schooled themselves in faith— and what a difference it made!

I'm telling you, that night we had *church!* People were filled with the Holy Spirit and many others healed—all because they took the time to hear the Word.

When you set yourself to continually hear the Word, you build up your faith to be healed, filled with the Holy Spirit and set free from fear. *Whatever* God promises in His Word will manifest in your life—as long as you keep hearing the Word and building your faith for it.

Confession:

The Word of God is stronger than any sickness or disease.
As I hear God's Word, I expect its power to work in
my body, bringing about the healing I desire.

Be not deceived; God is not mocked: for whatsoever a man soweth, that shall he also reap.

—Galatians 6:7

Sow the Word–Reap Healing

Whatever seed you plant, you will reap that kind of harvest. God's entire kingdom works on this principle. Whatever you sow in your heart is what you will reap in your life. So if you sow God's Word on healing, you will reap healing.

Many people are trying to reap a harvest of healing, yet they've never sown a seed. Hearing and healing go hand in hand. "Faith cometh by hearing." Whatever we plant on the inside, we will see on the outside. What we are, what we have and what we look like on the outside is a result of what we have—or haven't—put on the inside.

I've noticed that whenever symptoms try to come on my body, it's usually when I haven't been putting enough of the Word down on the inside for it to manifest on the outside. So I go back and study the Word.

Janet and I made a tape on healing several years ago. We received reports from people all over the country who, when they played that tape over and over, were healed. So Janet decided to try it. We were on a plane heading for the Philippines when various symptoms attacked her body. She put that tape in a recorder and listened to it over and over again for about four hours. By the time we got to Manila, every symptom was gone. As Janet planted seeds of the Word in her heart, the Word drove those symptoms out. That's the connection between hearing and healing!

Confession:

Whatever I sow in my life, I reap. I sow the Word of God and reap life, joy, love, healing, protection, guidance, peace and safety!

FEBRUARY 22

First Hearing, Then Believing

For whosoever shall call upon the name of the Lord shall be saved. How then shall they call on him in whom they have not believed? and how shall they believe in him of whom they have not heard? and how shall they hear without a preacher?
—Romans 10:13,14

Hearing the Word produces belief. You can't call on God unless you believe, and you can't believe unless you hear. That's why hearing and healing go hand in hand. Once you hear, you can believe; and once you believe, you can be healed.

Romans 10:17 says, "So then faith cometh by hearing, and hearing by the word of God." Hearing God's Word causes faith to rise up on the inside. When you release that faith, you get results. That's why Mark 9:23 says, "All things are possible to him that believeth."

God made it easy for you. He said simply to hear and be healed. So if you're having trouble believing God for your healing, don't try to work it up. Go back to the Word and "hear" what He said. Then just keep on hearing until faith rises up on the inside. Healing will be the result!

Confession:

Because I hear the Word of God, faith produces healing in my physical body. Whosoever shall call upon the name of the Lord shall be healed. I hear, I call, I believe—and I am healed!

For whosoever shall call upon the name of the
Lord shall be saved. —*Romans 10:13*

Call on the Lord in Faith

Biblically speaking, the word *saved* or *salva-tion* means the sum total of all the blessings bestowed on man by God in Christ through the Holy Spirit. Salvation also includes healing.

Knowing that, let's word this verse another way: "Whosoever shall call on the name of the Lord shall also be healed."

However, to receive the blessing of healing, we must *believe*. Romans 10:14 says, "How then shall they call on him in whom they have not believed?" If we don't believe the Word, either we won't call on God at all, or we won't call on Him in faith.

Many have endeavored to call on God without actually believing. There was a time when I was doing a lot of calling, but I wasn't doing much believing; therefore, I wasn't getting any answers. I prayed for two years without seeing any results. I almost threw away my sign that said, "Prayer Changes Things"!

Finally I read Matthew 21:22: "All things, whatsoever ye shall ask in prayer, *believing,* ye shall receive." I had missed that part about believing!

Also, notice that Jesus said, *"All things,* whatsoever ye shall ask in prayer." Well, healing is part of "all things." Therefore, healing is possible to him who believes.

You must believe to tap into the source of God's healing power. You can't call on Him unless you believe, and you can't believe unless you hear. That's why hearing and healing go hand in hand.

Confession:

All things are possible to me because I believe.
I believe God sent His Word to heal me. I call on
the name of the Lord in faith, and I am healed.

FEBRUARY 24

The Hearing of Faith

This only would I learn of you, Received ye the Spirit by the works of the law, or by the hearing of faith? —Galatians 3:2

I once heard a minister say that 99 percent of the problems we have living by faith or receiving from God result from a lack of knowledge. If we are having trouble receiving from God, we need to hear more Word and get more knowledge.

Paul asked, "Received ye the Spirit by the works of the law, or by the hearing of faith?" Well, we didn't receive the Spirit because of any works of the Law, so we know it is by the hearing of faith. When we hear the Word, it builds our faith to receive.

Now look at Galatians 3:5: "He therefore that ministereth to you the Spirit, and worketh miracles among you, doeth he it by the works of the law, or by the hearing of faith?" Again, the hearing of faith produces miracles. God works miracles after we hear His Word. We hear, and then God works the miracles.

Why do we have to hear first? We do because when we hear, faith rises up, and faith is the spiritual force that releases God's power.

Confession:

Receiving from God is easy. I hear and hear and hear the Word until I believe it in my heart. Then I speak the Word from my believing spirit and release power to accomplish healing in my body.

And [Jesus] went out from thence, and came into his own country; and his disciples follow him. And when the sabbath day was come, he began to teach in the synagogue: and many hearing him were astonished, saying, From whence hath this man these things? and what wisdom is this which is given unto him, that even such mighty works are wrought by his hands? ...And they were offended at him.

—Mark 6:1-3

FEBRUARY 25

Let Jesus Do a Mighty Work in You!

When Jesus was in His own country, the people in the synagogue listened to Him, but they really didn't *hear* Him. They said, "Where does Jesus get these things? What wisdom is this?" The people were offended, so we know they didn't really hear what Jesus said, nor did they allow the Word to produce faith. They were listening, but in reality they weren't hearing.

Verse 5 says, "And he could there do no mighty work, save that he laid his hands upon a few sick folk, and healed them." Think of it: Jesus of Nazareth—God manifested in the flesh, the One anointed with the Holy Ghost and power, the One infilled with the Holy Spirit without limits"—could there do no mighty work."

The Bible didn't say Jesus *wouldn't;* it said He *couldn't!* He couldn't do any mighty work "save that he laid his hands upon a few sick folk." I like the way Brother Hagin translates it; he says Jesus laid his hands "upon a few people *with minor ailments.*"

Jesus went in equipped with signs, wonders and miracles, but only a few people with a cold or the flu were healed. Thank God for the ones who *were* healed, but that isn't what Jesus went to His own hometown to do.

Make sure you allow Jesus to perform His will in *your* life. Don't just listen to the Word—*hear* it with your spiritual ears, and build up your faith to receive. Let Jesus do a *mighty* work of healing on your behalf!

Confession:

The power of the Lord Jesus Christ is present to heal me right now. That power is working in my body to effect healing as I hear and believe the Word.

FEBRUARY 26

Recognize When It's Time To Change

And he could there do no mighty work, save that he laid his hands upon a few sick folk, and healed them. And he marvelled because of their unbelief. And he went round about the villages, teaching. —Mark 6:5,6

Jesus had been teaching and preaching all over the region where He grew up. But when He came to the part of His message proclaiming God as healer, no one got it. So what did Jesus do? He went back to traveling around the region, teaching the Word.

That was always the progression of Jesus' ministry on this earth: teaching, preaching and healing. If the people weren't getting healed, Jesus knew their faith wasn't strong enough to take hold of the truths He taught. They hadn't sufficiently heard the Word. So He'd back up and start teaching again, feeding them more Word to build their faith.

Notice that Jesus didn't give up on the people in His own country. He didn't say, "I quit. I throw in the towel. I'm done with you folks. That's it—I'm out of here. I'm going someplace where people are hungry."

Jesus knew when the truths He taught hadn't sufficiently registered in people. He knew that the minute the truth did register, it would produce healing and wholeness.

Be smart enough to recognize when your faith doesn't seem to be working in your life. If you've endeavored to believe for your healing but nothing is happening, you probably need to change in some area. Ask the Lord, "What should I change? What should I be doing differently?" Then back up and start hearing more of His teaching from the Word. Keep hearing it until you get so full on the *inside* that it shows up as healing on the *outside!*

Confession:

*My Father isn't withholding anything from me.
I hear His voice and obey Him when it's time to change,
so by faith I am able to receive what I need from Him.*

For [God's words] are life unto those that find them, and health to all their flesh.

–Proverbs 4:22

Take a Daily Dose of God's Word

One day Janet and I were talking to a man who was badly in need of healing in his physical body. We advised him, "Feed on the Word daily. Take your daily dose of God's medicine. If you'd take God's Word as faithfully as you take other medicines, we guarantee you that there isn't a sickness or disease that can stay in your body. God's Word is medicine to *all* your flesh."

The man replied, "Oh, I've been studying the Bible every day. I've been doing a thorough study on the book of Revelation."

But the man needed to understand that every seed produces after its own kind. In other words, he needed healing in his body, so the best thing for him to study was healing.

Thank God for the book of Revelation. It will get you ready to go on to heaven. But if you're sick, right now you need to know how to live in victory over sickness on this earth. So if you need healing in your body, feed on healing Scriptures. Whatever you feed on is what you will have faith for.

And realize that even if you fed on healing Scriptures last week, last month or last year, that Word gave you faith for your answer then. However, that doesn't mean you will have strong faith for the answer you need *today.* Faith comes by hearing the Word on a daily basis.

"Well, Brother, I've heard that before," I hear people sometimes say. When people say that, you can tell that their faith isn't working.

You see, it isn't what you *have heard;* it's what you *are hearing* that counts. Even if you heard healing taught a week or a month ago, a lot of unbelief may have been pumped into your spirit through your ears since then. That's why what you are hearing *now* is what counts.

So what are you listening to these days? A good dose of God's Word or a lot of doubt and unbelief? The answer to that question makes all the difference to your receiving healing.

Confession:

When I need healing, I go to God's Word and build healing Scriptures into my spirit. My body is healed as the Word becomes life to me.

FEBRUARY 28

Apply Your Heart to the Word

Bow down thine ear, and hear the words of the wise, and apply thine heart unto my knowledge.

–Proverbs 22:17

Some years ago Janet and I taught for several days in a small campmeeting. While we were there, we noticed a young woman who came to every service. She used crutches and couldn't walk at all without them.

One afternoon we taught the congregation to feed on healing Scriptures when they needed healing. That evening another evangelist preached. When he called for the sick to come forward for prayer, this woman was the first one to the front.

The minister laid hands on her to pray, and the woman was instantly healed. Later she testified, "For a long time, I suffered with multiple sclerosis. I couldn't even walk without crutches. The doctors told me my condition would only get worse. But I've been coming regularly to this church, endeavoring to feed on the Word, keep a good confession and believe God for my healing.

"This afternoon I heard the message on the importance of feeding my faith with healing Scriptures. I'd been doing all I knew to do, but until then I hadn't *saturated* myself with God's Word on healing.

"So this afternoon, I opened my Bible and started studying healing Scriptures. I studied for hours. Suddenly, my heart got so full of the Scriptures I'd been meditating on that my faith rose up inside me. I came to church tonight and wrote inside my Bible with today's date, 'Healed by the power of God!' I just knew in my heart things were going to change tonight."

Now, taking hold of a miracle by faith doesn't necessarily work this quickly for everyone. But how did this woman know her healing would manifest that night? She got so full of the Word on the inside that it produced faith in her that was unstoppable.

You see, many times we wait for God to drop an extra measure of faith on us. But faith comes from the inside. We cannot produce faith on our own. Faith only comes by applying our hearts to the Word of God.

Confession:

Faith builds up in me when I hear and hear the Word. I hear the Word of God, and hearing produces faith in me.

And Jesus saith unto them, Believe ye that I am able to do this?

They said unto him, Yea, Lord.

Then touched he their eyes, saying, According to your faith be it unto you. And their eyes were opened. —*Matthew 9:28-30*

FEBRUARY 29

Set Your Faith Limits High!

Jesus said, "According to your faith be it unto you." I always thought He meant, "If you believe, you'll receive"—and that's true. But there's more to what Jesus is saying here than that. He is saying, "According to your faith—or according to *what* you believe—be it unto you."

For instance, in Matthew 8:5-10, when the centurion came to Jesus on behalf of his servant, Jesus said, "I'll come and heal him."

But the centurion replied, "I'm not worthy that You should come under my roof. Just speak the word only, and my servant will be healed." What happened? Jesus spoke, "and his servant was healed in the selfsame hour" (Matt. 8:13).

In Mark 5, a man named Jairus approached Jesus about his little girl, who was at home at the point of death. Jairus said to Jesus, "If You will just come and lay Your hand upon her, she'll be healed and live."

But when Jesus came to the home, she'd already died! Then Jesus said, "She's not dead; she's just sleeping." He threw out all the unbelief, took the child by the hand and raised her from the dead. (vv. 22-24,35-42.)

Two blind men believed Jesus was able to heal them, and He did. The centurion said, "Speak the Word, and my servant will be healed," and it happened. Jairus said, "Touch my daughter, and she'll be well," and it came to pass just as he believed.

Notice that in each of these cases, it wasn't just the fact that the people believed that brought their miracles—it was *what* they believed. They set their own limits, and Jesus ministered to them according to those limits.

Jesus says to His people, "You believe it, and I'll do it. I will meet you at the point where you set your faith."

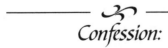

Confession:

I set my faith in line with God's Word to receive all Jesus purchased for me. Healing is one of the benefits provided for me, and I believe I receive it now!

MARCH 1

He Sent His Word To Heal You

He sent his word, and healed them, and delivered them from their destructions.

—Psalm 107:20

How did God send His Word to heal us? He gave us sixty-six books of His words—the Bible. As we hear the Word, it starts working inside us to make us completely healed and whole.

When you go all through the Gospels, in most cases you'll find that hearing came before healing. And if it worked that way under Jesus' ministry, it still works that way today.

When you need healing, the best thing you can do is to hear and hear and hear and hear. Keep that Word going into your ears every way possible. Keep hearing what God says about your healing.

Many people want to go to one particular meeting and miraculously receive their healing. They aren't interested in hearing. Sometimes God in His mercy does manifest Himself, and people receive their healing. But most of the time, they have to take time to hear before they are healed.

You see, walking by faith doesn't come from leaving your Bible on the shelf until it's time to dust it off and carry it to church. Your faith grows as you get into God's Word. It builds in your spirit as you hear it from the preacher, cassette tapes and out of your own mouth.

He sent His Word, and it heals you. When does it heal you? When you take the time to hear it.

Confession:

God sent His Word to heal me. His Word is life to me and medicine to all my flesh. I hear His Word and obey it, and I am delivered from sickness and disease.

But Christ being come an high priest of good things to come, by a greater and more perfect tabernacle, not made with hands, that is to say, not of this building; neither by the blood of goats and calves, but by his own blood he entered in once into the holy place, having obtained eternal redemption for us.

—Hebrews 9:11,12

MARCH 2

Jesus Took Our Place

After Adam's fall, man inherited a load he couldn't carry—a load of death, sin, iniquity, sickness and disease. The old covenant provided for man's sins to be covered for a year at a time through the shedding of the blood of bulls and goats. Man could also experience healing in his body through animal sacrifices. But those sacrifices had to be made every year because they were only temporary. They could only cover sins, not wash sins away.

Then Jesus Christ came and took the place for our punishment, dying on the Cross as our substitute. Most people have no problem believing that Jesus bore our iniquities on the Cross and set us free from sin—and He did. He paid the price for our sins so we could stand before Him forgiven. Through Jesus, we don't have to be bound to a sin nature anymore. We live in right standing with God, and sin cannot dominate us any longer.

But most Christians believe that Jesus left us with our sicknesses, intending to decide on an individual basis who should be healed. These people believe that salvation belongs to everyone but that you never know who's going to get healing.

That's what most Christians believe, but that is *not* what the Bible says. Isaiah 53:5 says that Jesus "was wounded for our transgressions, bruised for our iniquities: the chastisement of our peace was upon him; and with his stripes we are healed." He took our sin, pain and sickness and nailed it all to the Cross, setting us free.

Jesus already took sickness. Anyone can be saved, and anyone who is saved can be healed. Healing belongs to us!

Confession:

When I called on Jesus to be my Savior and made Him my Lord, He also became my healer. By faith I receive the healing that is mine. I walk in the divine health that Jesus bought and paid for!

MARCH 3

Two Sides of the Atonement

Bless the Lord, O my soul: and all that is within me, bless his holy name. Bless the Lord, O my soul, and forget not all his benefits: who forgiveth all thine iniquities; who healeth all thy diseases. —Psalm 103:1-3

This Scripture tells us, "Forget not all his benefits." What are God's benefits? He forgives all our iniquities and heals all our diseases. Now, verse 3 lists these two benefits in the same breath, so to speak, meaning that Jesus provided both when He died on the Cross and was raised from the dead.

Forgiveness of sins and healing go hand in hand: Jesus shed His blood for the remission of sins, and His body was broken for us so we could enjoy physical healing and health. He provided both benefits at once, and there's no place in the Bible that tells us to separate these two sides of the Atonement. Healing belongs to us as much as salvation does.

Confession:

When I received Jesus as Savior, healing came in my "benefits package" as well. I don't have to be sick. My healer bore my sicknesses and pains so I wouldn't have to bear them. By His stripes, I am healed.

For ye are bought with a price: therefore glorify God in your body, and in your spirit, which are God's.   *—1 Corinthians 6:20*

MARCH 4

Healing—Not Just a Divine Afterthought

Did you notice God talks about healing before He talks about salvation? He says, "Glorify God in your *body,* and in your spirit." Healing was not a divine afterthought. It was instituted before the new birth.

Look at what Isaiah 53:4-5 says:

> **Surely he hath borne our griefs** [or sicknesses]**, and carried our sorrows** [or pains]**: yet we did esteem him stricken, smitten of God, and afflicted. But he was wounded for our transgressions, he was bruised for our iniquities: the chastisement of our peace was upon him; and with his stripes we are healed.**

Healing is revealed in verse 4 and salvation in verse 5. Does that mean healing is more important? No, but God knew the body of Christ would have more trouble believing for healing; perhaps that's why He put it first.

Jesus bore stripes on His back before He hung on the Cross. He paid the price for our physical health before He paid the price for our new birth. Healing isn't more important, but God wants us to know it is equally as important to Him as salvation. God wants us to have both salvation and healing, and we receive both the same way—by faith.

So study what the Bible says about the Atonement and the death and resurrection of Jesus Christ. As you do, you'll come to a firm persuasion, an unshakable confidence, that you are as healed as you are saved.

Confession:

The work of the Savior is complete. Jesus paid the price so I could not only be saved, but healed as well. I live free of sickness and disease. I am healed, I am well, I am whole!

MARCH 5

How Many Sick People Does God Want To Heal?

Go ye into all the world, and preach the gospel to every creature.

And these signs shall follow them that believe; in my name shall they cast out devils; they shall speak with new tongues; they shall take up serpents; and if they drink any deadly thing, it shall not hurt them; they shall lay hands on the sick, and they shall recover. —Mark 16:15,17,18

How many sick people is Jesus talking about in verse 18? He's talking about *all* sick people. God wants all healed, and we know this from what Jesus said: "Go into *all* the world and preach the Gospel to *every* creature. And when you find any who are sick, lay your hands on them in Jesus' name so they can recover." If God didn't want every sick person healed, Jesus wouldn't have told us to lay hands on sick people so He could heal them!

And by virtue of the fact that this is the last thing Jesus shared with His disciples while on earth, we know how important it is. It's like this. Suppose you were going to leave for a long period of time, and you wanted your close friends to remember something important. Wouldn't you make sure the last thing you said to them before you left was the message you really wanted them to remember?

That's just what Jesus did in this passage of Scripture. It is called the Great Commission, and it still hasn't been totally fulfilled. Therefore, every part of it is still for today.

In the Great Commission, Jesus tells us God wants every person to be saved, healed, set free and delivered. God doesn't leave anyone out. But He doesn't force His blessings on anyone either. God won't force us to be saved, He won't force us to be filled with the Holy Spirit and He won't force us to be healed. God is a gentleman, and He only leads if we yield to Him.

God offers to mankind all that salvation encompasses and says, "Whosoever will, let him come." He wants every creature to hear the Gospel, and He wants every creature *healed!*

Confession:

My Father wants me healed. I believe God's Word and receive healing for myself in Jesus' name. And when I lay hands on the sick, they recover!

> *Go ye into all the world, and preach the gospel*
> *to every creature. He that believeth and is*
> *baptized shall be saved; but he that believeth*
> *not shall be damned. And these signs shall*
> *follow them that believe; in my name...they shall*
> *lay hands on the sick, and they shall recover.*
>
> *—Mark 16:15-18*

MARCH 6

Our Divine Commission

It's significant that in this passage of Scripture Jesus didn't say, "When you run across sick people, fast and pray to see if they are part of the chosen few God wants to heal." Nor did He say, "Lay hands on the sick, and if it's My will, they will recover." Jesus said, "Go find the sick and preach the Gospel to them; then lay hands on them, and they will recover." This is one of the signs He said would follow all believers.

We should be interested in learning how to operate in faith so we can take hold of our own healing. However, if we're going to be assets to the kingdom of God, we should be even more interested in learning how to minister healing to sick people ourselves. That's what God has been trying to get across to us for years.

Another thing I want to point out about this Scripture is that it doesn't say, "And these signs shall follow *apostles and prophets.*" No, it states, "These signs shall follow *them that believe.*" You see, we all have a divine commission to preach the Gospel, and the supernatural signs Jesus listed in these verses will follow us as we preach the Gospel to others.

So tell people the good news that it's God's will to heal them. Then lay hands on them, and watch God's promise of healing come to pass in their lives!

Confession:

I tell others the good news that Jesus died and was raised from the dead to deliver them from sin and sickness. I also help others receive healing: I lay hands on the sick, and they recover!

MARCH 7

Making Your Point of Contact

Now when the sun was setting, all they that had any sick with divers diseases brought them unto him; and [Jesus] laid his hands on every one of them, and healed them.

–Luke 4:40

Jesus was the will of God in action. He constantly showed people that God wanted them healed.

God wants *you* healed, and once that truth is lodged in your own heart, your next step is to make a point of contact. This "point of contact" refers to the moment you begin to release your faith for your healing. After finding out God's perfect will in the matter, you make your petition: "Thank God, I believe I receive my healing. Thank God, I'm healed by the stripes of Jesus."

A point of contact can be made in two basic ways. One way is through prayer, according to Mark 11:24: "What things soever ye desire, when ye pray, believe that ye receive them, and ye shall have them." Another way is through the laying on of hands: "In my name...they shall lay hands on the sick, and they shall recover" (Mark 16:17,18).

When a person makes his point of contact, at that moment he begins to believe he receives his healing. He may not feel it or see it, but he still believes he has received his answer. You may hear him say, "I believe I received three days ago when I prayed" or "I believe I received yesterday when hands were laid on me."

"Do you feel any different?" Someone might ask.

"No, but that doesn't make any difference, I believe I received!"

That's the confession of faith!

Confession:

I know God's will, so I pray, believing I receive what I desire through my own prayer of faith. Another way I receive from my Father is through the laying on of hands. When hands are laid on me or I pray, my healing begins at that point of contact.

Therefore I say unto you, What things soever ye desire, when ye pray, believe that ye receive them, and ye shall have them. —Mark 11:24

How To Receive From God

How do we receive all that Jesus bought and paid for through His death, burial and resurrection? Well, we know that faith operates on God's known will. So first we must look into the Word, where we find it's God's perfect will for every person to be born again and healed. Next, we make a point of contact, which occurs when we believe we receive—not necessarily when we see our petition come to pass.

Imagine a reservoir of water held back by a dam and a dry valley below. The two represent a "greater" and a "lesser"—a reservoir full of water and a valley that's dry. If you were to open the spillgate so that contact is made between the two, the greater would flood into the lesser.

In the same way, our point of contact can be likened to "opening the spill-gate." The moment we release our faith—the point of contact—the greater anointing and power that is in Jesus Christ begins to flow into the "lesser," our bodies, whether we feel it or not. God's healing power begins to effect a healing in our physical bodies the moment we believe we receive.

In John 11:40, Jesus said to Martha, "I told you if you'd believe, you'd see the glory of God." Notice He didn't say, "I told you that when you see God's glory, then you'll believe."

Anyone can believe when he sees or feels something. But as Christians, we're supposed to believe we receive our answer *before* we see or feel it, because we believe the Word.

What else are we supposed to do? We are to *say* what we believe: "Thank God, I believe I'm healed by the stripes of Jesus." Do we necessarily feel any different? Not always, but that's all right. Our feelings won't change God's Word, but God's Word will definitely change our feelings when we hook up with Him!

Confession:

*Today I make my point of contact with God. By faith
I open the spillgate of His goodness, and His
healing power flows into me as I believe I receive!*

MARCH 9

The Laying on of Hands

Therefore leaving the principles of the doctrine of Christ, let us go on unto perfection; not laying again the foundation of repentance from dead works, and of faith toward God, of the doctrine of baptisms, and of laying on of hands, and of resurrection of the dead, and of eternal judgment.
—Hebrews 6:1,2

This Scripture gives us the basic fundamental principles of the doctrines of Christ. Have they passed away? Let's look: "Let us go on to perfection; not laying again the foundation of repentance." Has repentance passed away? No, repentance is still a foundational principle of the doctrine of Christ.

What about what that verse says next—faith toward God? Is that finished? It can't be, because we are saved by grace through faith. (Eph. 2:8.) If faith has passed away, we are all in trouble.

What about the doctrine of baptisms or the doctrine of the resurrection of the dead? Are baptisms going to continue? Are the dead going to be resurrected? Yes! What about eternal judgment? Has that passed away? No, it is still in the works.

Only one foundational principle remains, and if all the others haven't passed away, then this one hasn't either. Right in the middle of those verses, it says, "...not laying again the foundation...of laying on of hands." This is one of the fundamental principles of the doctrines of Christ, and it hasn't passed away. It's still in effect.

What happens when you lay hands on people, especially sick people? Mark 16:18 says, "They shall lay hands on the sick, and they shall recover." If laying on of hands is one of the fundamental principles of the doctrine of Christ, then apparently healing is too, because when believers lay hands on the sick, they are healed. If laying on of hands is for today, then healing is still for today as well. It's just that simple!

Confession:

God's foundational principles haven't changed. Believers still lay hands on the sick, and the sick still recover. God's compassion and healing mercies haven't changed either. He is still the God who heals me!

[Jesus] was delivered for our offences, and was raised again for our justification.

–Romans 4:25

What Was Accomplished on the Cross?

Millions of people around the world believe that Jesus died on the Cross. But not everyone believes He was raised from the dead. And very few people, even Christians, know what He actually accomplished when He went to the Cross.

Why did Jesus shed His blood? Was it just for forgiveness of sins alone, or was it for more than that? First, Jesus was delivered unto death for the payment of our sins. Then He was raised again for our justification so we could be placed in right standing with God.

When Jesus shed His blood, it was for the forgiveness of our sins. His resurrection from the dead made the new birth available to us. We can now receive Jesus as our Savior and become brand-new creatures on the inside. (2 Cor. 5:17.) And our newly re-created spirits are infused with the nature of God.

Our sins are not just forgiven but *remitted*—totally removed as though they'd never happened. God takes out the old, hardened heart of stone and puts in a heart of flesh. (Ezek. 36:26.) He not only delivers us from our sins but He delivers us from the power sin once had over us.

You see, it wouldn't have been enough just to have our sins forgiven, because our nature would still be the same; we'd still continue to sin. God wanted to deliver us from the power of sin and all its effects, including the curse of sickness. Jesus died to pay for our sins, and He was raised from the dead to deliver us from sin, sickness and disease.

Confession:

I'm a new creature in Christ. The old sin nature has been removed and holds no more power over me. God has placed His nature in me. Now I live a clean, holy life, free from sickness and disease.

MARCH 11

Portraits of Our Redemption

And all things are of God, who hath reconciled us to himself by Jesus Christ, and hath given to us the ministry of reconciliation; to wit, that God was in Christ, reconciling the world unto himself, not imputing their trespasses unto them; and hath committed unto us the word of reconciliation. —2 Corinthians 5:18,19

God redeemed the world to Himself through Jesus' work on the Cross. That's why John the Baptist referred to Jesus as "the Lamb of God, which taketh away the sin of the world" (John 1:29).

Jesus' work on the Cross is available to anyone and everyone who believes. Therefore, it behooves us to learn what Jesus accomplished on that Cross. When we find that out, we'll know what belongs to us in Him. If physical healing was a part of what Jesus accomplished, then we'll know that healing is God's will and that we can expect divine healing to be a part of our spiritual inheritance.

When we look in the Gospels, we discover what literally happened to Jesus on His way to the Cross: He was beaten. His back was laid open with a whip. He was spat upon, and a crown of thorns was placed on His head. Finally, He was nailed to the Cross, where He hung until He died.

But the Gospels don't really tell us what Jesus *purchased* for us on the Cross. We can go to the Old Testament to discover more about that. All through the Old Testament, God gives us portraits of our redemption—"word pictures" of what Jesus did for us when He went to the Cross. These portraits are so clear and vivid that everyone should have recognized Jesus when He came to the earth.

For the next several days, let's study more closely these pictures of the Cross. Let's get a greater revelation of our redemption in Christ!

Confession:

To walk in the fullness of God's blessings, I must know what Jesus did for me on the Cross. My faith grows stronger as I receive a greater revelation of the finished work of redemption.

> *Speak ye unto all the congregation of Israel, saying, In the tenth day of this month they shall take to them every man a lamb, according to the house of their fathers, a lamb for an house: and if the household be too little for the lamb, let him and his neighbour next unto his house take it according to the number of the souls; every man according to his eating shall make your count for the lamb.* —Exodus 12:3,4

MARCH 12

Jesus, Our Passover Lamb

Exodus 12 gives us one of God's portraits of redemption, a picture of what Jesus did for us in His death, burial and resurrection. At this time, the children of Israel were in bondage in Egypt.

In the Old Testament, Egypt is a type of sin, bondage or Satan's kingdom—the kingdom we lived in before we were born again. As the ruler of Egypt, Pharaoh is a type of Satan.

Israel, on the other hand, is a type of the Church. Moses, God's man, is a picture of Jesus Christ coming on the scene with signs, wonders and miracles to deliver God's people. Israel's deliverance out of Egyptian bondage into freedom is a type of the new birth. Just as the Israelites were allowed to leave Egypt, so is a new believer translated out of the kingdom of darkness into the kingdom of God's dear Son.

Finally, the miracle that produced Israel's freedom centered around a lamb—what the Bible called a Passover lamb. What the Passover lamb in the Old Testament accomplished for the children of Israel through its death is a clear picture of what Jesus accomplished for us through His death, burial and resurrection.

That's why John the Baptist called Jesus the Lamb of God. (John 1:29.) And in Revelation 13:8, Jesus was called "the Lamb slain from the foundation of the world." Jesus is our Passover Lamb, whose death provided a way for those who believe in Him to be saved, delivered, healed and made whole.

Confession:

The Old Testament Passover lamb opened the way for the Israelites to be delivered from Egypt's bondage. Jesus is my Passover Lamb. His blood opened the way for me to come into the family of God and enjoy my inheritance!

MARCH 13

Christ, Our Passover

In the tenth day of this month they shall take to them every man a lamb, according to the house of their fathers, a lamb for an house.

...and the whole assembly of the congregation of Israel shall kill it in the evening. And they shall take of the blood, and strike it on the two side posts and on the upper door post of the houses, wherein they shall eat it. —Exodus 12:3,6,7

In 1 Corinthians 5:7, Jesus Christ is called our Passover: "For even Christ our passover is sacrificed for us." Passover was instituted back in the Old Testament. And if we can find out what Passover did for people back then, we can find out what Jesus, *our* Passover, did for us in the New Testament.

The children of Israel had been slaves in Egypt for hundreds of years. God told them, "Take a lamb—one per family. Kill the lamb and put the blood on the doorpost. Roast the lamb, eat the flesh and then get out of Egypt."

So the people obeyed the Lord's instructions. The lamb was slain and the blood applied. And once the atonement was made, the people went free, not only spiritually but physically.

The Passover lamb is a picture of the new birth. You see, when Jesus, the Lamb of God, was slain on the Cross, the way was opened for us to live free from Satan's dominion. Now the moment we receive Jesus as our Savior and Lord, we are redeemed, saved and set free from bondage!

Confession:

Because of Jesus, the Lamb of God, I am set free from the devil's dominion. I've been removed from the kingdom of darkness and placed in the kingdom of light. Thank You, Father!

The next day John seeth Jesus coming unto him, and saith, Behold the Lamb of God, which taketh away the sin of the world. —John 1:29

Behold the Lamb of God

When God gave the instructions for the Passover, He gave very specific instructions about the lamb:

> **Your lamb shall be without blemish, a male of the first year: ye shall take it out from the sheep, or from the goats: and ye shall keep it up until the fourteenth day of the same month: and the whole assembly of the congregation of Israel shall kill it in the evening.**
>
> **Exodus 12:5,6**

Jesus fit every one of these qualifications. He was a Lamb without blemish, for He had never sinned. He was the firstborn in his family, "a male of the first year." There was even a particular time this Lamb had to die: "in the evening." The very hour Jesus died on the Cross was the time when the Passover lambs were being sacrificed.

Who killed the Passover lamb? "The whole assembly of the congregation of Israel." In Acts 2:23, Peter preached to the Jewish multitude about who was responsible for Jesus' death: "Him, being delivered by the determinate counsel and foreknowledge of God, ye have taken, and by wicked hands have crucified and slain."

Jesus Christ was condemned by the Romans and crucified by Israel, but He laid down His life for you and me. He took *our* sin and *our* sickness on Himself. Just as the whole congregation of Israel had a part in the slaying of the lamb, we all had a part in the slaying of the Lamb of God. Yet Jesus laid His life down willingly. He knew it was the only way we could be delivered out of "Egypt"—the bondage of sin, sickness and disease.

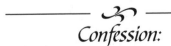

Confession:

I believe Jesus was the Lamb slain to take away the sin of the whole world. Jesus died for me. Through Him I receive all the benefits salvation includes. I am saved, healed and delivered!

MARCH 15

And they shall take of the blood, and strike it on the two side posts and on the upper door post of the houses, wherein they shall eat it.

–Exodus 12:7

Covered by the Blood

God instructed His people to apply the blood of the lamb to the two side posts and on the upper doorposts of their houses. Thus, they would make a type of a Cross and be covered by the blood of the Passover lamb that had been slain for their deliverance.

God was giving His people a portrait of their redemption, pointing ahead to the time when Jesus would come and shed His blood on the Cross of Calvary. God told them, "The blood shall be to you for a token upon the houses where ye are: and when I see the blood, I will pass over you, and the plague shall not be upon you to destroy you, when I smite the land of Egypt" (Ex. 12:13).

That night, death struck the firstborn of every household in Egypt where the blood was not applied. Wherever the blood *was* applied to the doorpost, death passed over. Judgment didn't fall on those residing within; instead, they went free. In the same way, when Jesus' blood is applied to us as we make Him our Lord and Savior, final judgment passes over us, and we step into eternal glory.

We know from Hebrews 9:22 that without the shedding of blood, there is no remission of sins. The blood of the lamb was the sacrifice that allowed the children of Israel to walk out of Egypt's bondage. And it is the blood of the Lamb of God, Jesus Christ, that enables us to walk free of every demonic bondage—including the bondage of sickness and disease.

Confession:

I have applied the blood of the precious Lamb of God to my life. Therefore, I am set free from every yoke of bondage, including sickness and disease. I now step into the provisions of healing and health that God has prepared for me through the blood of His Son.

And they shall eat the flesh in that night, roast with fire, and unleavened bread; and with bitter herbs they shall eat it.

And thus shall ye eat it; with your loins girded, your shoes on your feet, and your staff in your hand; and ye shall eat it in haste: it is the Lord's passover. —Exodus 12:8,11

Redeemed— Spirit, Soul and Body

The Lord said to His people, "On the same night you apply the blood of the Passover lamb to your doorpost, eat its flesh." Notice that God gave specific instructions about how the lamb was to be eaten. He said, "When you eat that lamb, put your belts on, put shoes on your feet and be ready to go." (v. 11.) It's significant that God *didn't* say, "And thus shall ye eat it, with your loins girded and your wheelchairs, stretchers, crutches and pills all ready to go. And with all your aches and pains you shall go forth."

Among the two to three million Israelites God was talking to, there had to be plenty of people who were too sick or too old to travel. But the Lord told them all to eat and be ready to go.

You see, God wasn't satisfied with a partial redemption. Not only would His people go out, but they would go out *well.* Not only would they be set free from Egyptian bondage, but they would also be set free from the bondage of sickness and disease.

What did the Passover do for the Israelites when they applied the blood of the lamb? It spared them from judgment and set them free from bondage. What happened when the Israelites ate the lamb's flesh? They went out *healthy.*

That's why the Passover lamb is a portrait of our full redemption in Christ. When man fell in the Garden of Eden, he fell in spirit, soul and body. When God redeems man, He redeems his spirit, soul and body. Jesus died to make us completely whole, not only in spirit and soul, but in our physical bodies as well.

Confession:

As the Israelites ate of the lamb, they were to be ready to go forth out of Egypt in health. Now I partake of the Lamb of God and go forth in newness of life, receiving healing as part of my redemption package!

MARCH 17

A New and Better Covenant

He brought them forth also with silver and gold: and there was not one feeble person among their tribes. —Psalm 105:37

God gave us a portrait of the new birth when He delivered Israel from Egypt's bondage. This biblical event is a picture of our coming out of Satan's bondage into new freedom in Jesus Christ.

The way Israel looked when they came out of Egypt is a picture of the way you and I should look the minute we're born again. How did Israel look? They came out of the darkness of bondage into the light of freedom. Not only that, but Psalm 105:37 says, "He brought them forth also with silver and gold."

The Israelites didn't take silver and gold out of Egypt because they were wealthy. No, they'd been nothing but Egyptian slaves for centuries. *God* was the source of Israel's sudden wealth. The first thing He did when He brought them out of bondage was to abundantly meet their needs. He turned them from slaves into free people of substance, abundantly taken care of.

Besides material substance, God provided physical health for the Israelites as well. "There was not one feeble person among their tribes." He brought His people out of Egypt free, healthy and abundantly taken care of.

Remember, this is a picture of our redemption. When we were first born again, most of us would have been satisfied just to have our sins forgiven. But that didn't satisfy God. His Son paid the price for a redemption that was meant to affect every part of our lives.

The Passover opened the way to freedom, healing and abundance for the Israelites. Now we live under a new and better covenant established on better promises. (Heb. 8:6.) So if God willed healing and health for His people under the old covenant, we can know without a doubt that He wills healing and health for us under our covenant through Jesus Christ!

Confession:

The Lamb of God opened the way to abundantly supply all my needs— spirit, soul and body. He provided healing for my physical body and peace for my soul. I walk in the fullness of the redemption Jesus purchased for me!

But on the morrow all the congregation of the children of Israel murmured against Moses and against Aaron....

And the Lord spake unto Moses, saying, Get you up from among this congregation, that I may consume them as in a moment....

MARCH 18

Healing in the Atonement

And Moses said unto Aaron, Take a censer, and put fire therein from off the altar, and put on incense, and go quickly unto the congregation, and make an atonement for them: for there is wrath gone out from the Lord; the plague is begun. And Aaron took as Moses commanded, and ran into the midst of the congregation; and, behold, the plague was begun among the people: and he put on incense, and made an atonement for the people. And he stood between the dead and the living; and the plague was stayed. Now they that died in the plague were fourteen thousand and seven hundred. —*Numbers 16:41,44-49*

Numbers 16 gives us another portrait of our redemption. Soon after the Israelites were delivered out of Egypt's bondage, they began to worship idols and criticize the men of God in charge. Their muttering and complaining put them on dangerous territory.

It is clear that God was more than a little upset with these rebellious people. A plague hit the multitude, and more than 14,000 died before anything could be done. Aaron quickly prepared incense to make atonement before all the people died. He ran into the midst of the congregation and stood between the people and the plague. Atonement was made for the people, and the plague was stopped.

This is a portrait of the Atonement Jesus made for us. You see, when Aaron made atonement for the sin of the Israelites, they were not only forgiven, but the sick were healed. Well, if healing was included in atonement under the old covenant, how much more is it included in the Atonement Jesus purchased for us by His blood?

Confession:

Jesus is my Atonement. His sacrifice gives me access to all of God's benefits and blessings. I receive them now by faith in Jesus' name.

MARCH 19

Remember All God Has Done for You

And the soul of the people was much discouraged because of the way. —Numbers 21:4

As the children of Israel made their way toward the Promised Land, they became discouraged because they were looking at the way—the natural hardships of their journey.

But just think what they could have focused on instead. God had brought them out of Egypt with signs, wonders and miracles. When they could go no farther because of the Red Sea, God had worked a miracle, parting the waters so they could cross on dry ground. When the Egyptian army had tried to pursue them, the two walls of water had closed up again and destroyed the Israelites' enemies.

When the Israelites had come to the waters of Marah, where the water was bitter, God had miraculously purified the waters so the people could have water to drink.

God led them with a pillar of cloud by day and a pillar of fire by night. He gave them fresh manna from heaven every night; all they had to do was pick it up. He even gave them water out of a rock. And for the entire forty years that the Israelites wandered through the desert, their shoes and clothes didn't wear out.

But, despite all of these things, the Israelites became discouraged because they looked at the way. We've done the same things at times. "Oh, Lord, things are so hard. The way is so tough. I feel so bad."

We need to look back in our lives and recognize how God has helped us— how He's brought us out of trials and delivered us from bondage. Realizing how much God has already done—and how much more He wants to do—for us, is an instant cure for discouragement!

Confession:

*Through the blood of Jesus, my Father has delivered me,
protected me, provided for me and healed me. Therefore, no matter
what I face, I focus my spiritual eyes on my faithful God.*

And they journeyed from mount Hor by the way of the Red sea, to compass the land of Edom: and the soul of the people was much discouraged because of the way. *–Numbers 21:4*

We Choose What We Look At

Israel is a type of the Church. First Corinthians 10:11 tells us that what happened to Israel was for our admonition. Therefore, we can learn by looking at Israel. When they came out of bondage in Egypt, they headed toward the Promised Land. Now, the Promised Land is not a picture of heaven. (It had giants to overcome, and heaven doesn't.) The Promised Land is actually a picture of the abundant life God has for us while we're here on earth.

Numbers 21:4 says that as the Israelites marched through the wilderness, "The soul of the people was much discouraged because of the way." The Israelites were just like the rest of us; they had a tendency to become discouraged when things got tough. But they got discouraged because they began *looking at the way.*

It's easy to find natural circumstances that will discourage us if we look at them. For example, focusing on symptoms of pain or sickness in our bodies can be very disheartening.

But we choose what we're going to look at. Will we set our eyes on the circumstances we face or on our great God and His ability to take us to our promised land of abundant life?

The Bible says, "According as his divine power hath given unto us *all* things that pertain unto life and godliness, through the knowledge of him that hath called us to glory and virtue" (2 Peter 1:3). Everything God has, everything He is and everything He can do has been made available to us as we look to Him!

Confession:

*I keep my eyes on Jesus and His Word.
He is greater than any problem or sickness
that could ever come against me!*

MARCH 21

Keep Your Mouth out of Trouble

And the soul of the people was much discouraged because of the way. And the people spake against God, and against Moses, Wherefore have ye brought us up out of Egypt to die in the wilderness? for there is no bread, neither is there any water; and our soul loatheth this light bread.
—Numbers 21:4,5

" And the people spake...." When the Israelites got discouraged, the first thing they did was *speak*. And if you'll continue reading this chapter in Numbers you'll notice what happened when they opened their mouths: They got into trouble with their muttering and complaining!

When some people are discouraged, the first One they want to accuse is God. "Oh, God, why did You get me in all this trouble? Why did this disease come on me? God, this is all Your fault. I know I could never get into a mess like this all by myself."

Others get mad at God *and* preachers when things don't seem to work out right. That's what happened in the wilderness: "The people spake against God, and against Moses" (v. 5). The people came against the two men who had delivered them, saying, "Wherefore have ye brought us up out of Egypt to die in the wilderness?"

The Israelites had been led by a pillar of fire by night and a cloud by day. God had protected them every step of the way. Yet still they were discouraged! They complained, "We're going to die out here because we don't have any bread or water." They seemed to forget that God had already given them fresh food from heaven and water out of a rock! Then they admitted the real problem: "Our soul loatheth this light bread." They just didn't like the kind of bread God gave them!

If you need healing in your body, then no matter how long it takes for your healing to manifest, don't let discouragement get *you* into trouble. Keep your mouth from complaining or blaming God. Remember, He's already provided healing for you. Now there's nothing left for your mouth to do but praise Him!

Confession:

I want to please my Father, so I carefully watch the words I speak. Even when I face a trying situation, I'll never blame Him, for He's the One who heals and delivers me!

And the Lord sent fiery serpents among the people, and they bit the people; and much people of Israel died. —Numbers 21:6

MARCH 22

Don't Step out of God's Protection

After the Israelites complained against both Moses and God, an army of fiery serpents crawled into the camp and began biting them. The Isaac Leeser translation says, "The Lord *let loose* fiery serpents."[1]

There's a big difference between *sending* and *letting loose*. Remember, the Israelites were in the wilderness—a place that's full of snakes. So the miracle was not the fact that the snakes started biting them; the miracle was that three million people had been out in the wilderness all this time, and they hadn't been bitten until then!

God had supernaturally surrounded His people with protection and kept the snakes out. But when they broke their covenant through rebellion and complaining, God withdrew His merciful protection. Only then were they bitten. The people got into trouble spiritually when they sinned. As a result, the serpents were able to come in the camp, and the people got into trouble physically as well.

"Therefore the people came to Moses, and said, We have sinned, for we have spoken against the Lord, and against thee; pray unto the Lord, that he take away the serpents from us. And Moses prayed for the people" (v. 7). Isn't it amazing how quickly the people got the revelation that they had sinned! One minute they were complaining about Moses, and the next minute they wanted him to pray for them.

Moses could have said, "I'm not going to pray for you; you got what you had coming!" But he walked in the God-kind of love and prayed for the repentant Israelites. And God not only forgave His wayward people of their sin, but He provided the way for them to be healed of their deadly wounds.

―――――― ∽ ――――――

Confession:

There are forces in this world that want to kill me, but I walk in the protection of my Father God. When I miss it, I run to Him for forgiveness and restoration. I keep my eyes on Him, for He is my Savior, my healer, my provider, my protector.

MARCH 23

Behold Jesus and Live

And the Lord said unto Moses, Make thee a fiery serpent, and set it upon a pole: and it shall come to pass, that every one that is bitten, when he looketh upon it, shall live. And Moses made a serpent of brass, and put it upon a pole, and it came to pass, that if a serpent had bitten any man, when he beheld the serpent of brass, he lived. —Numbers 21:8,9

God told Moses to put a brass serpent on a pole, and He said, "Whoever will look at the serpent will live." Why did God tell Moses to do that? Well, the serpent is a type of Jesus Christ, and brass is a type of judgment. Once again, the Israelites were looking at a portrait of their redemption—a vivid picture of the Atonement.

Some would ask, "How can a serpent be a type of Jesus? Ever since the Garden, a serpent has been a sign of sin."

Jesus never sinned in His life. But when He hung on the Cross, He *became* sin for us and cried, "My God, my God, why have You forsaken me?" (Mark 15:34.) God had to turn His back on His Son because, at that moment, all the sins and sicknesses of the world were nailed to the Cross in the form of Jesus' body. Judgment fell on Him instead of on us.

When Moses held up that serpent, he wasn't showing the people a picture of Jesus as He walked the earth or was raised from the dead. He was showing a picture of Jesus when He hung on the Cross and became the Atonement for all mankind.

So when the children of Israel looked ahead to what Jesus Christ would do for them, they were not only forgiven but healed as well. And God didn't turn anyone down. He said, *"Every one* that is bitten, when he looketh upon it, shall live" (v. 8).

In the same way, every one of us, without exception, can look *back* in faith to what Jesus did for us in the Atonement and receive both forgiveness *and* healing. God didn't turn anyone down under the old covenant, and He certainly won't turn anyone down under the new!

Confession:

*Jesus gave me eternal life and paid the price with His own life.
To free me from the bondage of sickness and disease, He took all the sickness of the world upon Himself. I live free and healed because of Jesus!*

And Moses made a serpent of bronze and put it on a pole, and if a serpent had bitten any man, when he looked to the serpent of bronze [attentively, expectantly, with a steady and absorbing gaze], he lived. —Numbers 21:9 AMP

MARCH 24

In Exchange for a Look Receive Life

When the Israelites were bitten by snakes in the wilderness, they had to *do* something in order to be healed. Just because the bronze serpent was placed on the pole didn't mean the people would automatically be healed. God told Moses to put the bronze serpent on the pole. Then He said, "Every one that is bitten, when he looketh upon it, shall live" (Num. 21:8). The people had to do the looking. The answer was held up before them, but they had to *look* at it.

The Amplified Bible expands that thought. God didn't say, "Once you put the serpent on a pole, you can take a quick glance and head for home." He said, "If you want to live, you'll have to attentively, expectantly and with a steady and absorbing gaze look to that answer."

In essence, God was telling the Israelites, "You can't look at the biting snakes and the serpent on the pole at the same time. It's your choice whether you gaze at the problem or the answer. But if you want to live, you have to look to My answer."

The people received *life* for a *look*. Forgiveness, healing and deliverance were theirs for the taking as they looked at the serpent on the pole.

Today we receive life, forgiveness, healing and deliverance as we set our eyes on Jesus. The Bible says that Jesus took our infirmities and bore our sicknesses. (Matt. 8:17.) It also says we can do all things through Christ, who strengthens us. (Phil. 4:13.) As we fix our eyes attentively, expectantly and with a steady, absorbing gaze on Jesus, we'll receive our healing and begin to live in divine health!

Confession:

When symptoms of pain and sickness attack me, I overlook the circumstances and look to Jesus. Jesus is greater than any sickness or problem I face. He causes me to triumph in every situation as I expectantly look to Him!

MARCH 25

The Divine Exchange

For he hath made [Jesus] to be sin for us, who knew no sin; that we might be made the righteousness of God in him. –2 Corinthians 5:21

When the Israelites were being bitten by snakes, they needed three answers: forgiveness for complaining, deliverance from the snakes and healing of their wounds. However, God gave them only one answer: the serpent on a pole.

How were the people going to be forgiven, healed and delivered by looking at a picture of sin and sickness? Jesus Himself gives the answer in John 3:14: "And as Moses lifted up the serpent in the wilderness, even so must the Son of man be lifted up." Jesus was saying, "That serpent on the pole is a picture of Me when I go to the Cross."

When Jesus went to the Cross, a divine exchange took place. He became what we were and gave us what He is. Jesus became our substitute. He had never sinned, but He became our sin! He was never sick Himself, but He took on our sickness. In exchange, Jesus gave us His right standing with God and His divine health.

So when the people in the wilderness looked at a symbolic image of Jesus Christ going to the Cross, they were forgiven, healed and delivered. When Jesus went to the Cross, He forgave our sins, purchased healing for our bodies and delivered us from all the power of darkness. Then He was raised from the dead so we could become born-again, new creatures in Him.

When we look to Jesus and receive Him as Savior and Lord of our lives, all He did for us on the Cross is ours. Thank God for redemption! Thank God for Jesus' death, burial and resurrection!

Confession:

Jesus took my sin, sickness, failure and spiritual death and gave me back His righteousness, health, success and eternal life. He paid the price for all these benefits, and He freely gives them to me when I ask in faith.

And Aaron shall lay both his hands upon the head of the live goat, and confess over him all the iniquities of the children of Israel, and all their transgressions in all their sins, putting them upon the head of the goat, and shall send him away by the hand of a fit man into the wilderness: and the goat shall bear upon him all their iniquities unto a land not inhabited: and he shall let go the goat in the wilderness.

–Leviticus 16:21,22

MARCH 26

Jesus, Our Scapegoat

The Isaac Leeser translation of Isaiah 53:4 tells us that Jesus took on our sicknesses and pains as our substitute so you and I wouldn't have to carry them: "But only our diseases did he bear himself, and our pains he carried."[1]

But notice that in the *King James Version* Isaiah used the words *borne* and *carried*. Those same words are used in the book of Leviticus when referring to the role of the scapegoat. This scapegoat gives us another portrait of redemption in the Old Testament.

When the nation of Israel sinned, that sin had to be judged. (Remember, Israel was a type of the Church.) But God didn't want the people to suffer judgment; He wanted them to receive mercy. So He told them to find a spotless, perfect goat. The people were to bring this goat to Aaron the priest. Aaron then laid his hands on the goat and confessed the sins of the nation over it. Afterwards, someone took the goat out into the wilderness. The judgment that belonged on the nation of Israel then fell on that scapegoat. In other words, God allowed the sins of the people to be transferred through the hands of Aaron to that goat, and the goat bore the sins of the people and carried them away.

When Jesus went to the Cross, God lay upon Him all the sin, iniquity, sickness, suffering and pain of mankind. Jesus was the ultimate scapegoat—taking our place in judgment, taking the punishment we deserved.

───────── ✌ ─────────

Confession:

Jesus is my substitute. When I was separated from God and deserved to die, He died for me. He bore my sickness and pain so I wouldn't have to bear them. Because of Jesus, I am healed and whole!

MARCH 27

The Year of Jubilee

And ye shall hallow the fiftieth year, and proclaim liberty throughout all the land unto all the inhabitants thereof: it shall be a jubilee unto you; and ye shall return every man unto his possession, and ye shall return every man unto his family.

—Leviticus 25:10

Another portrait of our redemption is found in this Scripture in Leviticus. While talking to Moses on Mount Sinai, God established the Year of Jubilee. According to the instructions He gave to Moses, every fiftieth year would be a special time of setting people free from debt and servitude. (vv. 8-10.)

This wasn't meant to be just an old covenant blessing. When Jesus was just beginning His earthly ministry, He said, "The Spirit of the Lord is upon me, because he hath anointed me to preach the gospel to the poor...to set at liberty them that are bruised, *to preach the acceptable year of the Lord*" (Luke 4:18,19). Jesus said that part of His commission was to preach the acceptable year of the Lord, or the Year of Jubilee.

Jesus came to establish the new covenant through His death, burial and resurrection. So, apparently, the Year of Jubilee was not only meant to be an Old Testament blessing, but also a New Testament blessing. The Old Testament Year of Jubilee was simply a picture of what Jesus Christ would one day do for us when He came to this earth—wipe out our debt of sin and set us free!

Confession:

Jesus is my Jubilee. He bought me back from the power of darkness and translated me into the kingdom of God. Praise God, He has made available everything I could ever need for an abundant life on this earth!

Then shalt thou cause the trumpet of jubilee to sound on the tenth day of the seventh month, in the day of atonement shall ye make the trumpet sound throughout all your land. And ye shall hallow the fiftieth year, and proclaim liberty throughout all the land unto all the inhabitants thereof: it shall be a jubilee unto you; and ye shall return every man unto his possession, and ye shall return every man unto his family.

–Leviticus 25:9,10

MARCH 28

Sounding the Jubilee Trumpet

In the fiftieth year, the Israelites celebrated the Day of Atonement. On this day, animal sacrifices were made to atone for the people's sins.

Every one of those animal sacrifices was simply a picture of Jesus' dying on the Cross for us. Jesus atoned us once and for all when He went to the Cross. He paid for our sins when He laid down His life, shed His blood and rose from the dead on the third day.

After atonement was made for the people's sins, the trumpet of Jubilee was sounded. As part of the body of Christ, we are sounding the trumpets today by preaching and teaching the Word of God and telling others the good news of Jesus' Atonement for them.

After the Jubilee trumpet had sounded, every man went back to his own possessions. If he had debts, his debts were forgiven. If in the past he'd been forced to sell property to pay debts, the property was returned to him. If he had been sold as a servant or a slave, he was set free. The Year of Jubilee, then, was the year of forgiveness, freedom and restoration to one's original position—a beautiful portrait of our new covenant redemption in Christ!

Confession:

I am a trumpet in the hands of my Father. I proclaim liberty to the captives, speaking of God's goodness, mercy and power to heal and deliver them from every bondage of the enemy.

MARCH 29

Returned to Our Original Possession

And ye shall hallow the fiftieth year, and proclaim liberty throughout all the land unto all the inhabitants thereof: it shall be a jubilee unto you; and ye shall return every man unto his possession, and ye shall return every man unto his family.

—Leviticus 25:10

In the Year of Jubilee, every man was to return to his original possessions. Likewise, we're supposed to return to man's original state—to all Adam possessed in the Garden of Eden before he lost everything.

So what was our original possession? When we know that, we'll know what God wants us to return to.

In 1 Corinthians 15:45, God makes a comparison between the first Adam and the last Adam: "The first man Adam was made a living soul; the last Adam was made a quickening spirit." We know who the first Adam was. He was the one who disobeyed God and got mankind in trouble. But who was the last Adam?

Jesus Christ is the last Adam. He made atonement for us when He died on the Cross and God raised Him from the dead. By laying down His life for us, Jesus enabled us to go back to our original possession. That original possession—what Adam had before the Fall—was a family relationship with Almighty God. Adam was in God's family; he was even called the son of God. (Luke 3:38.) But when he sinned in the Garden, he broke that relationship.

Many think that all people are children of God. But Jesus refuted that belief in John 8:44. He told some of the highest religious leaders of the day that they were of their father, the devil. You see, when Adam fell in the Garden of Eden, mankind traded fathers.

So what do we return to? We return to our relationship with the Father God. That's why 1 John 3:1 says, "Behold, what manner of love the Father hath bestowed upon us, that we should be called the sons of God." When we receive Jesus, our Jubilee, He sets us free to become the sons of God!

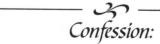

Confession:

When I was born again, Jesus, my Jubilee, gave me back a relationship with my Father. I am privileged to be called a son of God through Jesus' precious blood.

And ye shall return every man unto his possession.

–Leviticus 25:10

Adam's Blessings Restored to Us

What did Adam have before the Fall? He not only had *relationship* with God, but he also enjoyed *fellowship* with God. Adam had walked and talked with God in the cool of the day. But after he fell, God came looking for him, calling, "Adam, where are you?" (Gen. 3:9.)

Adam answered, "I hid myself." (v. 10.) Their fellowship had been broken.

What about *our* fellowship with God? Once we are born again, the Bible tells us to "come boldly unto the throne of grace" (Heb. 4:16). We can talk to God, not just as servants or as friends but as sons and daughters. We are brought back into the fellowship with the Father that Adam lost.

Adam also possessed supernatural intelligence and memory before the Fall. God brought every living creature to him, and Adam named every one of them. (Gen. 2:19,20.) Not only did Adam name the creatures, but he also remembered what he named them!

When you are born again, that capacity for supernatural intelligence is given back to you. First Corinthians 2:16 says, "We have the mind of Christ." God has given you the Holy Ghost, who Jesus promised would "bring all things to your remembrance, whatsoever I have said unto you" (John 14:26).

Adam's needs were abundantly met. God saw that it wasn't good for him to be alone, so He formed Eve. He also showed Adam where all the gold was buried. (Gen. 2:11.) God wanted to make sure Adam was abundantly taken care of.

God wants to meet our needs as well. The Bible says, "Though [Jesus] was rich, yet for your sakes he became poor, that ye through his poverty might be rich [or abundantly supplied]" (2 Cor. 8:9). So through Jesus, we are restored back to our original position in God. There we can enjoy fellowship with the Father, the benefits of a sound mind and every need abundantly met.

Confession:

God wants to restore to me all that Adam possessed before he sinned in the Garden. In Jesus I have fellowship with God, a sound mind and everything I need.

MARCH 31

Our Day of Atonement

And ye shall return every man unto his posses-sion, and ye shall return every man unto his family. —*Leviticus 25:10*

Just as the Year of Jubilee enabled the Israelites to return to their original possessions, salvation through Jesus enables us to return to the original position Adam enjoyed with God.

In that original state, Adam was healthy. No sickness or disease existed in his body, because no sickness or disease existed on earth.

If God had wanted man sick, He would have created sickness. But God never did say, "Let there be cancer." He never said, "Let there be colds and flu." Instead, the Bible tells us God sent His Word to *heal* us. (Ps. 107:20.) Matthew 8:17 says, "Himself took our infirmities, and bare our sicknesses." Referring to Jesus, 1 Peter 2:24 says, "By whose stripes ye were healed."

Adam enjoyed divine health, a sound mind and every need met before he sinned in the Garden. All he had to do was obey God's command and stay away from the Tree of the Knowledge of Good and Evil in the midst of the Garden. But when the serpent said, "Go ahead and eat from it," Adam disobeyed God and chose a new master. (Gen. 3:4-6.) At that moment, he lost all the blessings that had been his to enjoy.

Fear entered in. Adam had never experienced fear before. But after Satan became his legal guardian, Adam told God, "I was afraid" (Gen. 3:10). From that point on, Adam and all his descendants were plagued with hate, murder, poverty and sickness.

But, thank God, then came *our* day of atonement! Jesus became the sacrificial Lamb of God, who takes away the sin of the world. (John 1:29.) He was the last Adam, who redeemed—or purchased back—for us everything the first Adam lost. Through Jesus, we can come into the family of God and have *all* our original possessions restored!

Confession:

Jesus is my Jubilee. He has restored me to all the benefits God originally planned for mankind. Because of Jesus, I walk in divine health. All my needs are met—spirit, soul and body!

And this is the confidence that we have in him, that, if we ask any thing according to his will, he heareth us: and if we know that he hear us, whatsoever we ask, we know that we have the petitions that we desired of him. *—1 John 5:14,15*

APRIL 1

Praying in Faith vs. the Prayer of Faith

Some people think the prayer of faith works for everything, even when they pray for healing for someone else. But there's a difference between *praying in faith* and *the prayer of faith*.

All our prayers must be *in faith*. Hebrews 11:6 says, "For he that cometh to God must believe that he is, and that he is a rewarder of them that diligently seek him." When we go to the Father in prayer, we must believe He hears and answers us when we pray in accordance with His will.

But the prayer *of faith* is what you pray for yourself in order to receive what legally belongs to you according to the will of God. In this prayer, you pray one time; then you believe you receive your answer. You don't request that same petition again in prayer; instead, you thank and praise God for the answer.

But when you pray for someone else, James 5:16 AMP gives you the guidelines: "The earnest (heartfelt, *continued*) prayer of a righteous man makes tremendous power available—dynamic in its working." Your heartfelt prayers for others may have to continue for a time. Don't give up—keep praying until you've seen God's power produce results!

Confession:

When I have a need, I pray to my Father once, believing I receive when I pray. When I pray for another's needs, I continue to pray until I see the answer. My prayers make tremendous power available.

APRIL 2

Jesus Paid for Physical Healing

Who his own self bare our sins in his own body on the tree, that we, being dead to sins, should live unto righteousness: by whose stripes ye were healed. —*1 Peter 2:24*

This Scripture is a New Testament portrait of redemption—a picture of what Jesus did for us. One day when I was teaching on this verse, I made the comment, "To me, this Scripture proves healing belongs to anyone who is saved, because it covers both sides of redemption in one verse."

A person attending the meeting spoke up, saying, "Apparently, you consider this Scripture to be referring to physical healing. But it's talking about *spiritual* healing."

Before I realized what was happening, I heard these words coming out of my mouth: "When you were saved, what happened in your spirit?"

The person replied, "God took out the heart of stone and put in a heart of flesh. He gave me a new spirit."

"Why did you have to be born again?" I asked.

"Because I was spiritually dead."

"Well, why would you need spiritual healing then?" I asked. "You can't *heal* something that's dead—it has to be *reborn.*"

You see, when we're spiritually dead, we don't need to get spiritually healed. That won't do the job. We must be born again. The Bible says, "Therefore if any man be in Christ, he is a new creature: old things are passed away; behold, all things are become new" (2 Cor. 5:17). God gives us brand-new spirits. And our re-created spirits don't need healing—our physical bodies do!

So live in the fullness of your redemption—your spirit man reborn, your mind renewed and your body healed by the power of God!

Confession:

I am born again. I have a brand-new spirit, and my body is healed because of the stripes Jesus bore for me. His sacrifice was more than enough to totally redeem me from the dominion of darkness and bring me into the kingdom of light!

For God so loved the world, that he gave his only begotten Son, that whosoever believeth in him should not perish, but have everlasting life.

—John 3:16

APRIL 3

His Death for Our Life

What is the Atonement? It is the redemptive work Jesus accomplished when He went to the Cross as our substitute and paid the price for our sins with His blood. He was also chastised for our peace and broken in His body for our physical healing. (Isa. 53:5.)

The Atonement is the most basic of all Christian trusts—the very essence of what we believe. It isn't complicated theology or church doctrine. Atonement is His death for our life.

If you don't understand and believe that Jesus Christ shed His blood for your sins and was raised again from the dead so you could be born again, His death won't do you any good. Likewise, if you don't understand and believe that Jesus bore stripes on His back for your physical healing, His broken body won't do you any good.

It all boils down to what you understand. Faith can't operate where the will of God isn't known; neither can the will of God be known about a subject of which you have no knowledge. The only part of the Atonement that will work for you is the part you understand and believe.

Confession:

I believe that Jesus Christ shed His blood for my sins.
I believe He bore stripes for my physical healing.
By faith I take full advantage of the benefits He paid for.

APRIL 4

A Promissory Note on Redemption

That it might be fulfilled which was spoken by Esaias the prophet, saying, Himself took our infirmities, and bare our sicknesses.

–Matthew 8:17

Jesus gave people healing before He ever went to the Cross. At the Cross, healing was provided as part of God's redemption plan, but Jesus proved redemption beforehand by giving people part of it on a promissory note. Every time He forgave people of their sins, in essence He was saying, "I'll pay for it later." Every time He healed the multitudes, He was saying, "I'll pay for it later."

Jesus knew those sicknesses and diseases would be on His own back in a short period of time, but He still let His compassion flow out. He wanted to prove to the world that redemption, freedom, peace and healing belong to everyone.

Jesus didn't turn anyone down. Matthew 8:16 says, "When the even was come, they brought unto him many that were possessed with devils: and he cast out the spirits with his word, and healed *all* that were sick." The people brought the sick, and He healed all who came to Him for help.

Jesus didn't question who the sick people were or where they came from. If redemption belonged to all mankind, it had to be clearly shown that it was available to every person. So to all who came to Him in faith, Jesus delivered a promissory note on God's redemption plan—a promise He knew He would pay for later.

Confession:

Jesus showed us by His life what God's will is. I know God wants me well because Jesus healed all who came to Him and paid the price to make healing available to me.

But he was wounded for our transgressions, he was bruised for our iniquities: the chastisement of our peace was upon him; and with his stripes we are healed. —Isaiah 53:5

APRIL 5

Split the Atonement in Two?

In the past, many in the body of Christ have tried to split the Atonement down the middle. Then they've tried to separate the two halves. They say, "Thank God, salvation is for anyone, anytime. Second Peter 3:9 says, 'The Lord is...not willing that any should perish, but that all should come to repentance.' So whoever wants to be saved may freely come!"

"However," they continue, "healing is *not* for today." Or they say, "God *can* heal, but He normally doesn't do things like that. He heals some, but He doesn't heal everyone." Or perhaps they rationalize, "God has replaced healing with doctors and hospitals."

But no one has a right to split the Atonement down the middle. Jesus paid the price for us—spirit, soul *and* body.

One half of the Atonement is the forgiveness of sin; the other half of the Atonement is healing for the physical body. Jesus Christ not only paid the price for our sins and iniquities, but at the same time He paid the price for our sicknesses and diseases. When the body of Christ grabs hold of that revelation, the sick will be healed, the weak will be made strong and the healthy will stay well!

Confession:

Jesus wants me to be saved and healthy, so He purchased my salvation and healing with His own death on the Cross. His body was broken for me; His blood was shed for me. I receive the salvation and healing He has provided!

APRIL 6

Forever Redeemed

In whom we have redemption through his blood, the forgiveness of sins, according to the riches of his grace.
—Ephesians 1:7

When Jesus shed His blood on the Cross, He redeemed us. *Redeem* means "to purchase or buy back."[1]

For example, several years ago, when you purchased groceries in grocery stores, the store owners gave you green stamps as an incentive to buy at their store. You were supposed to put them in stamp books. After you had filled several books, you went to a "redemption center." The center stocked all kinds of nice gifts: radios, stereos, camping supplies and so forth. But you couldn't buy those items with money. You had to *redeem* them with green stamps.

Well, Jesus redeemed us with His own blood. You see, when Adam sinned, mankind fell into a state of spiritual death, or separation from God. Along with sin came sickness, poverty, fear and failure.

Man was in the grips of sin under Satan's control, but God wanted to buy man back. However, only one price could buy man back from the kingdom of darkness. Silver and gold couldn't do it. The redemption price had to be sinless, spotless blood.

So God sent His only begotten Son to be our sacrifice. Jesus took on flesh and walked sinless among us as "the Lamb of God, which taketh away the sin of the world" (John 1:29). Then He shed His perfect, spotless blood on the Cross, redeeming us from Satan's dominion.

All we have to do is believe in our hearts and confess with our mouths that Jesus is our Lord and that God raised Him from the dead for us. (Rom. 10:9,10.) At that moment, we are translated out of the kingdom of darkness into the kingdom of light—forever redeemed!

Confession:

I've been redeemed from Satan's control. Sickness no longer has jurisdiction over me. Divine health is a benefit of my Father's kingdom, and I walk in all the benefits Jesus purchased for me with His blood!

In whom we have redemption through his blood, even the forgiveness of sins. —*Colossians 1:14*

Jesus Bore the Punishment We Deserved

When Jesus finished the earthly ministry God had given Him, He was about thirty-three years old. Only one thing was left to do. Jesus, the Son of God—the One who never sinned, who never made a mistake in His life, who never hurt anyone and always helped everyone—had to die on the Cross.

The cross was a death reserved for criminals. If anyone belonged on that cross, it was you and I—not Jesus.

The Bible says, "All have sinned, and come short of the glory of God" (Rom. 3:23). We were the ones who sinned, made mistakes, hurt people. We deserved to go to the place of judgment. But Jesus took our place. He is "the Lamb of God, which taketh away the sin of the world" (John 1:29).

The Bible says, "Without shedding of blood [there] is no remission" (Heb. 9:22). Someone had to die for us. We deserved death, but Jesus took our death on Himself so we can walk in newness of life.

Confession:

Jesus, my Savior, redeemed me. With the price of His own blood, He became the way for me to be reconciled to the Father. He took my sickness and my spiritual death so I could have His health and His eternal life.

APRIL 8

We're Already Delivered!

Who hath delivered us from the power of darkness, and hath translated us into the kingdom of his dear Son. —Colossians 1:13

When Jesus redeemed us, He delivered us from the power of darkness. That means every Christian is already delivered. But Christians still run around trying to get delivered all the time.

For instance, one evening a lady came over to me in a meeting and said, "I need to be delivered."

I replied, "Ma'am, you came to the right place. I have good news for you!" Her eyes lit up. Then I asked, "Do you have a Bible?"

She gave me a wary look and said, "Yes."

I told her to open to Colossians 1:13 and read it, which she did: "Who hath delivered us from the power of darkness, and hath translated us into the kingdom of his dear Son."

I instructed the woman to read the first part again several times: "Who hath delivered us from the power of darkness...." I could tell she was getting angry with me. Then I said, "Well, did Jesus deliver us from the power of darkness, or did He not? Either the Bible is true, or it isn't."

She replied, "I know the Bible says that, but you're not getting rid of me that easy! I want some help, and I want something that works."

I said, "Ma'am, you'll never find anything that works any better than that."

Christians who are running around trying to get delivered ought to read the Bible. If they would, they'd realize He already delivered them from the power of darkness.

When we start praising and thanking God for delivering us, there isn't a devil in hell that can stay around us. The first words out of our mouths when we get up in the morning should be, "Thank God, I'm delivered! Oh, it's so good to be free!" If we would do that, we'd be amazed at how quickly we'd begin to walk in our freedom!

───── ✌ ─────

Confession:

My God has delivered me from the power of darkness. Sickness and pain have no control over me, because Jesus took my sickness and carried my pain. Thank God, I'm free!

Giving thanks unto the Father, which hath made us meet to be partakers of the inheritance of the saints in light. —Colossians 1:12

APRIL 9

He Already Paid the Price

Jesus went to the Cross and shed His blood for us. Through His death, burial and resurrection, He forgave our sins, redeemed us, delivered us from the power of darkness and enabled us to become partakers of God's inheritance.

Yet most Christians have had a very low opinion of what redemption really is. They will say, "Well, Jesus redeemed me from sin."

That's true, but there's so much more to it. Thank God, we've been redeemed from every curse in the Old Testament—and that includes sickness!

Now, Jesus didn't redeem us from all the Old Testament blessings. For instance, healing was a blessing back then, so it's still a blessing today. Jesus didn't do away with any blessings; He just added to them.

Look at Isaiah 53:5: "But he was wounded for our transgressions, he was bruised for our iniquities: the chastisement of our peace was upon him; and with his stripes we are healed." Jesus not only redeemed us from our sins, but He also redeemed us from torment and oppression so we could have peace. He redeemed us from sickness so we could have health.

God's report says we were forgiven, delivered and healed. Now we can just reach out in faith to receive any of these covenant blessings. They all belong to us because Jesus already paid the price.

Confession:

I am free from sin and all its effects—from worry, anxiety and fear, from sickness, disease and pain. God's inheritance affects all areas of my life—spirit, soul and body.

APRIL 10

Saved and Healed

Being justified freely by his grace through the redemption that is in Christ Jesus.

–Romans 3:24

Once believers receive a revelation of the redemption Jesus purchased on the Cross, it changes them. Nothing can stop them anymore! I'm not talking about a mental assent to the truth. I'm talking about people who say from their hearts, "Yes, that's the truth, and the truth is setting me free!"

Consider how a person is adopted into God's family. The minute a person finds out Jesus' blood was shed for the forgiveness of his sins, he can confess Jesus as his Savior, and not a devil in hell can stop him from getting born again! Peace and fellowship with God are available to anyone who receives Jesus in faith.

The same thing happens in the area of healing when people discover the truth that healing is included in the Atonement. Miracles abound when people act on that revelation. As believers proclaim that Jesus redeemed mankind from both sin and sickness, people jump up to get saved and healed at the same time!

As believers, we have to establish the truth in our hearts that just as Jesus' blood was shed for us, His body was broken for us. Then we will not only be saved, but we will also rise up healed!

Confession:

Jesus gave Himself as the sacrifice for my total redemption from the kingdom of darkness. Therefore, I receive healing from the Father as freely as I received salvation!

Christ hath redeemed us from the curse of the law, being made a curse for us: for it is written, Cursed is every one that hangeth on a tree: That the blessing of Abraham might come on the Gentiles through Jesus Christ; that we might receive the promise of the Spirit through faith.

–Galatians 3:13,14

APRIL 11

Redeemed From the Curse of the Law

J esus has redeemed us from the curse of the Law, which is given in Deuteronomy 28:15-68. The Lord told the children of Israel if they didn't obey Him, all the terrible curses listed in this passage would come upon them.

Spiritual death is a part of the curse. So are poverty and every kind of sickness and disease. Verse 61 says, "Also every sickness, and every plague, which is not written in the book of this law, them will the Lord bring upon thee." These are the curses that result from breaking God's laws.

But Galatians 3:13-14 tells us the good news: Believers have been redeemed from the curse of the Law through the death, burial and resurrection of Jesus. That curse doesn't exist anymore for the believer. Deuteronomy 28:15-68 doesn't apply to God's children, because Jesus took that curse upon Himself when He went to the Cross. That's the Good News!

In Deuteronomy 28:1-14, the Lord gives us the blessing of Abraham. That blessing includes divine health. We have been redeemed from the curse of *every* sickness and *every* plague—even those not mentioned in the Law. We have been redeemed from cancer, arthritis, colds and flu. If we can name it, we have been redeemed from it!

Confession:

When I received Jesus as my Savior, He freed me from the curse of the Law. Because He took the curse upon Himself as my substitute, I am now redeemed from every sickness and disease and I walk in divine health!

APRIL 12

Don't Carry the Devil's Burden

But Christ being come an high priest of good things to come, by a greater and more perfect tabernacle, not made with hands, that is to say, not of this building; neither by the blood of goats and calves, but by his own blood he entered in once into the holy place, having obtained eternal redemption for us.

–Hebrews 9:11,12

Some people think Jesus came to help us carry our burdens. "Oh, Lord," they pray, "if You could just help me bear this disease until the end, I'd sure appreciate it. Maybe if You carry half, I could carry the other half."

These people don't realize what actually took place in redemption. They may understand that Jesus took their sins to the Cross and paid the price for their slate to be wiped clean. They may even realize that God doesn't want them to take the condemnation for those sins back on themselves again.

But people need to realize that Jesus completed a full redemption for them. Not only did He take on Himself their sin, but their sickness and disease as well.

Just as we have known God doesn't want us to live in sin, we ought to know God doesn't want us to live in sickness and disease. Jesus paid the price to redeem us from both sin and sickness. He already carried it all for us. So He doesn't want us to carry the burden of our sicknesses any more than He wants us to carry the burden of our sins. Sin and sickness are a part of the devil's kingdom, and we are citizens of the kingdom of light!

Confession:

I've been redeemed from the curse of the Law. I refuse to carry the burden of sickness, because Jesus already bore my sicknesses and carried my pains. By His stripes, I am healed!

And it shall come to pass, that whosoever shall call on the name of the Lord shall be saved.

—Acts 2:21

APRIL 13

The Same Price

Who does redemption belong to? It belongs to "whosoever" will call on the name of the Lord Jesus Christ.

It's all through the Bible. God is "not willing that any should perish, but that all should come to repentance" (2 Peter 3:9). In John 6:37, Jesus said, "Him that cometh to me I will in no wise cast out." And John 1:12 tells us, "As many as received him, to them gave he power to become the sons of God."

Jesus died on the Cross for every person. Anyone who believes in Him can freely come into God's family through His blood. But not only did He provide salvation for all mankind; He also provided peace of mind and physical healing to anyone who wants to receive it. He paid the same price for it all.

Because of Jesus' resurrection, your spirit can be born again. You can also enjoy peace of mind and a healthy body. First you receive the healer; then you receive His healing touch (although sometimes God does supernaturally heal the lost to get their attention.)

You see, salvation results from accepting the spiritual side of redemption. Then it's up to you to walk in the soulish and physical sides of Jesus' redemptive work. All of it has already been provided for you. Jesus paid the price.

Confession:

I am redeemed, for I have called on the name of the Lord. I am healed. I am peaceful. And I'm so grateful for all my Lord has done for me!

APRIL 14

Healing Is Simple

And Jesus went about all the cities and villages, teaching in their synagogues, and preaching the gospel of the kingdom, and healing every sickness and every disease among the people.

–Matthew 9:35

God's Word is simple and easy to understand. He didn't make it complicated, because He didn't want anyone left out of His blessings.

Yet some people are deceived into thinking it's hard to receive from God, especially in the area of divine healing. They beg, plead, cry, bawl and squall to be healed, but to no avail.

However, it's easy to receive healing. Why would it be hard to obtain something that already belongs to us? Jesus purchased healing for us with the stripes on His back. We just have to reach out and take what is already ours!

The only reason it has seemed difficult to receive healing is that we've lacked a thorough understanding of Jesus' work on the Cross. Thank God, what Jesus provided for us in the Atonement is simple to receive. Think about it: Was it difficult to get saved? No, we simply found out God loved us, believed in our hearts Jesus was raised from the dead and confessed Him as our Savior. Well, healing is received the same way. We find out healing is God's will for us, believe in our hearts we receive our healing and confess Jesus as our healer.

It's as simple as that. We are healed by faith just as we are saved by faith. As we learn to appropriate what already belongs to us, we will walk in blessings far beyond what we can ask or think!

Confession:

Healing is simple. I know God wants me well. I know Jesus' body was broken for me so I could have His health. So right now I believe I receive my healing.

If thou shalt confess with thy mouth the Lord Jesus, and shalt believe in thine heart that God hath raised him from the dead, thou shalt be saved. —Romans 10:9

APRIL 15

Confess, Believe, Receive

It's so easy to receive from God. God made it easy. He purchased everything we could ever need and then told us, "Just take it."

Someone may say, "But believing God for healing is so hard." Do you know you're saved? Isn't becoming a new creation in Christ the biggest miracle there is?

Well, notice that you don't *hope* you're saved—you *know* you are. One day you said, "Lord, I believe in my heart Jesus was raised from the dead for me. I receive Him as my Lord and Savior. I'm a new creature in Christ!"

You didn't have to labor and strain and stand on the Word of God for years to get saved. Neither do you have to get up every morning to see if you still feel saved. You *know* you're saved, because the Bible tells you so!

Well, if getting saved is the biggest miracle and yet the easiest thing you ever did, would a lesser miracle, such as healing, be more difficult to receive?

No, we receive salvation and healing the same way. They are both part of God's redemption plan.

You'd be amazed at your results if you simply received healing by faith the same way you once received your salvation. Just say, "Lord, I know in my heart that by Jesus' stripes I was healed. I receive You as my healer now. Thank God, it's done!"

Now, don't check to see if you feel healed. You aren't healed because you feel better. You're healed because the Bible says you're healed. And if you hold fast to your faith, your healing *will* come to pass!

Confession:

I confess from a believing heart that Jesus is my Savior.
I also confess from a believing heart that Jesus is my healer.
Thank God, I receive my healing now!

APRIL 16

Head Faith
vs.
Heart Faith

Wherefore, sirs, be of good cheer: for I believe God, that it shall be even as it was told me.

–Acts 27:25

How can we know if we're really in heart faith and not just head faith, or mental assent? That's an important question. We have to learn how to locate ourselves in our faith. If we can do that, we can make the necessary adjustments to receive from God.

Head faith says, "I believe the Word—but look at the size of that problem!" Or it says, "I believe by Jesus' stripes I was healed—but I feel so sick! And let me tell you what the doctors told me…"

Head faith is really "billygoat" faith—it likes to "but"! "I believe the Bible, *but…*" And, of course, your loved ones will help you with some of their own "buts"— "Now, I know you're believing for your healing, *but* how do you *really* feel?"

On the other hand, heart faith says, "Yes, I see the problem. I see the symptoms of sickness. But I'm looking to the Bible! I found my answer there!"

Heart faith fixes its attention on the Word. Heart faith always finishes with this statement: "I believe God. I don't care what it looks like."

Faith doesn't deny the symptoms or the circumstances. It doesn't bury its head in the sand and hope the problem will go away. Faith faces the problem and says, "I know it looks bad, but I have inside information! I'm coming through this as an overcomer in Jesus Christ!"

During a storm when the apostle Paul was in a boat that was about to sink, he said, "I believe God, that it shall be even as it was told me" (Acts 27:25). That's what we have to do as well. Sure, the storms will come. We don't deny the wind, the waves, the symptoms. But we have something better, something bigger, something higher to believe. We have the Word of God!

───────── ✺ ─────────

Confession:

God's Spirit-breathed words are greater than any symptom or circumstance. The Word says I'm healed, and I believe it: I am healed, just as He has told me!

For unto us was the gospel preached, as well as unto them: but the word preached did not profit them, not being mixed with faith in them that heard it. For we which have believed do enter into rest. —Hebrews 4:2,3

APRIL 17

The Rest of Faith

See if this sounds familiar: You're facing a situation where everything looks bad, sounds bad and feels bad. There seems to be no way out. But for some reason, you can't work up a good worry about it! People ask you, "Don't you know how serious this is?" But you walk around with this silly grin on your face, saying, "I just can't seem to get concerned. Everything will be all right."

"How do you know it's going to be all right?" they ask.

"I just know."

That's called *the rest of faith*. Everything looks bad on the outside. But on the inside, you sense only a velvety, peaceful rest.

Hebrews 4:3 talks about the rest of faith: "We which have believed do enter into rest." Now, God isn't talking here about physical or mental rest. Your mind will probably give you fits when you face a bad situation. But when you enter the rest of faith, a quiet peace prevails deep down inside.

Now consider this second scenario: You're in a situation that looks bad, sounds bad and feels bad, and you're endeavoring to believe God. You pray, "Oh, God, this better work!" You scrunch up your face in your intense effort and say, "God, I'm trying to believe, but if You don't come through, I'm sunk!"

That is definitely *not* the rest of faith! Well, what's the difference between the first and the second responses to a bad situation? The difference is in *what you believe*.

So if you need healing in your body but you haven't yet entered into rest, make the necessary adjustment. Start feeding on healing Scriptures and build up your faith. Then, no matter what the situation looks like in the natural, you can peacefully rest in God.

───────── ✌ ─────────

Confession:

*I believe God and His Word, so I enter into rest.
I am confident that I am healed, for I know
my God has already won my victory*

APRIL 18

Enter Into Rest

For only we who believe God can enter into his place of rest.

–Hebrews 4:3 TLB

When you're in a difficult situation and you need a miracle, locate what you believe. Do you believe what God's Word says? Or do you believe what people or circumstances say?

Hebrews 4:3 says, "We which have believed do enter into rest." Belief produces rest, and what you hear determines what you believe.

So if you see you haven't entered into the rest of faith, don't waste your time feeling condemned, discouraged or upset about it. Just realize your belief isn't yet strong enough to produce rest.

What do you do? Find out what the Word of God says about your situation. Search for Scriptures that cover your case. Feed on the Word at every opportunity because *hearing produces belief.*

Some people say, "Well, when I have time, I'll do that." But if you maintain that attitude, you'll never have time.

If you need healing, listen to good healing tapes again and again. Read good books on healing, such as *Christ the Healer* by F. F. Bosworth. Don't just read the books once and set them down; read them from cover to cover several times until you are full of the Word on healing. Then out of the abundance of your heart, your mouth will speak. (Matt. 12:34.) You'll find yourself saying, "It's so good to be healed!"

And when someone asks, "Do you feel better? Are the symptoms gone?" you'll say "I haven't checked yet, but I know I'm healed because the Bible said it. I don't care what anybody says. God says healing is mine, and I have whatever God says!"

Remember, hearing produces belief, belief produces rest and the rest of faith produces *results!*

Confession:

The Word of God is firmly lodged down in my heart, and I enter into rest. God's Word is greater inside me than what I see with my natural eye. It's so good to be healed!

But the manifestation of the Spirit is given to every man to profit withal. For to one is given by the Spirit the word of wisdom; to another the word of knowledge by the same Spirit; to another faith by the same Spirit; to another the gifts of healing by the same Spirit; to another the working of miracles; to another prophecy; to another discerning of spirits; to another divers kinds of tongues; to another the interpretation of tongues. —1 Corinthians 12:7-10

APRIL 19

Manifestations of the Spirit

This is a list of the nine gifts, or manifestations, of the Spirit. In the past, people have sometimes thought this passage of Scripture was just talking about *natural* abilities that God gives people. But God calls them supernatural manifestations of the Spirit or sudden actions of the Holy Ghost.

Within this list of spiritual gifts, healing is included. The phrase "gifts of healing" refers to supernatural manifestations of the Holy Ghost to produce physical healings in the physical body. God works many kinds of miracles on the earth, but this Scripture proves He performs *healing* miracles.

Now notice verse 11: "But all these worketh that one and the selfsame Spirit, dividing to every man severally as *he* will." Not as we will, but as *He* wills. Many times we wish we could control the gifts of the Spirit. But we don't control them; they operate as *God* wills. The gifts are given to the Church, but the manifestations are controlled by the Holy Ghost.

This is the mysterious side of God. We don't know how or when the gifts are going to manifest, and we don't know for whom they will manifest. We just know that at times "the manifestation of the Spirit is given to every man to profit withal" (v. 7).

Confession:

My God is a mighty God. Because of His goodness and mercy, He manifests His power through the nine gifts of the Spirit. I thank God for the gift of healing manifesting in the body of Christ today.

APRIL 20

The Sovereign Side of God

Thus saith the Lord the King of Israel, and his redeemer the Lord of hosts; I am the first, and I am the last; and beside me there is no God.

Is there a God beside me? yea, there is no God; I know not any. —Isaiah 44:6,8

Let's talk about the sovereign side of God. Sometimes I hesitate to use that terminology, because the sovereignty of God is a subject that has caused great wars throughout the body of Christ.

But God *is* the sovereign Creator of the universe, the God of heaven and earth! He does have a sovereign side. He can work miracles within the boundaries of His Word anytime and anyplace He wants to—even without our approval.

Just think about your own life. Have you ever received something from God that you weren't believing for? You probably have more times than you can count.

Most of us wouldn't have lived this long if God hadn't sovereignly done some things for us along the way. His love goes a long way.

For instance, look at Saul of Tarsus on the road to Damascus. He was on his way to persecute more Christians when "suddenly there shined round about him a light from heaven" (Acts 9:3). Jesus appeared to Saul that day on the road to Damascus, and Saul was born again.

I wasn't saved that way. I heard the Gospel preached, believed it in my heart and confessed Jesus as Lord of my life. I never saw a bright light from heaven.

But God has left Himself room to sovereignly intervene in a person's life, as He did with Saul. Why did God do it that way with Saul? I don't know, but it sure paid off, because the apostle Paul wrote half the New Testament!

Confession:

Sometimes my Father moves in miraculous or unusual ways to help people. But I don't have to wait for that to happen. I come to Him in faith, believing His Word, and He takes pleasure in prospering me—spirit, soul and body.

A certain man had two sons; And the younger of them said to his father, Father, give me the portion of goods that falleth to me. And he divided unto them his living. And not many days after the younger son gathered all together, and took his journey into a far country, and there wasted his substance with riotous living.

And when he came to himself, he said.... I will arise and go to my father, and will say unto him, Father, I have sinned against heaven, and before thee.

And he arose, and came to his father. But when he was yet a great way off, his father saw him, and had compassion, and ran, and fell on his neck, and kissed him.

—Luke 15:11-13,17,18,20

APRIL 21

The Father's Love

God performs miracles in two different ways: (1) by sovereignly initiating a miracle at His own will and (2) in response to our faith, initiating a miracle at our will. For the next few days, we'll see this principle clearly illustrated in Jesus' story of the prodigal son.

This is the account of the younger of two sons, who left his father's house to indulge in sin and wrongdoing, wasting his entire inheritance. Later he came to himself and realized the pleasures of sin weren't worth the price he was paying. He decided he'd be better off back in his father's house, even if only as a servant. But when this prodigal son returned home, he found his father waiting for him with open arms of love. And the father didn't stop there. He sovereignly went out of his way to do things for him to prove that he loved him. (vv. 22-24.)

This is really a picture of our loving heavenly Father. Certainly He is always ready to welcome the person who has never known Him. But He also desires to welcome back into fellowship His repentant children who at one time walked away from Him. And often He will sovereignly perform miracles in their lives to show them just how much He loves them.

Confession:

My Father's compassion toward me moves Him to work on my behalf.
I'm so grateful for those times when He works miracles in my life.
But I know I can always depend on my Father to perform
His Word in me as I walk by faith, because He loves me.

APRIL 22

The Elder Son's Inheritance

Now his elder son was in the field: and as he came and drew nigh to the house, he heard musick and dancing.

And he was angry, and would not go in: therefore came his father out, and entreated him. And he answering said to his father, Lo, these many years do I serve thee, neither transgressed I at any time thy commandment: and yet thou never gavest me a kid, that I might make merry with my friends: but as soon as this thy son was come, which hath devoured thy living with harlots, thou hast killed for him the fatted calf.

And he said unto him, Son, thou art ever with me, and all that I have is thine. It was meet that we should make merry, and be glad: for this thy brother was dead, and is alive again; and was lost, and is found.

—Luke 15:25,28-32

The prodigal son is a picture of the person who has broken fellowship with God, but what about the elder son? He was upset. He'd stayed home with the father and worked in the fields while his younger brother had wasted his inheritance through riotous living. Now his brother had returned home, and his father had gone out of his way to prove his love for his younger son, clothing him with luxurious clothes and killing the fatted calf for a celebration feast in his honor. (vv. 22,23.)

Sometimes Christians feel like that elder son. They see God miraculously heal a backslider who doesn't have an ounce of faith. This proves to the backslider that God loves him and receives him back into fellowship. But sometimes other believers get upset and say, "Why did God heal that person? I've never backslidden, but He didn't heal *me.*"

In essence, this is what the older son said. He had worked and been faithful, yet he'd never had a big celebration held in his honor. But the elder son could have whatever he desired at any time. His father told him, "Son, all I have belongs to you!" And your heavenly Father is saying the same thing to you.

———— ✍ ————

Confession:

Because I'm a child of God, everything my Father has is mine. Healing is mine. By faith, I accept my healing now!

And he said unto him, Son, thou art ever with me, and all that I have is thine. It was meet that we should make merry, and be glad: for this thy brother was dead, and is alive again; and was lost, and is found. —Luke 15:31,32

Everything God Has Is Yours

"All that I have is thine." This is what God says to His faithful children. So often believers ask, "God, why don't You work a miracle for *me?*" But God responds, *Child, you are with Me. Everything I have is yours. Healing is yours. Don't wait for Me to sovereignly step out and do something for you. Come get it anytime you want. Receive it by faith!*

So often we've wanted God to do something special for us, but He expects more out of us as His children. He didn't say, "The just shall live by the gifts of the Spirit or the sovereignty of God." He said, "The just shall live by *faith.*" (Rom. 1:17).

By faith we find in the Word what belongs to us through God's plan of redemption. Then we take hold with the hand of faith because everything He has is ours. It belongs to us!

Confession:
Everything my Father has is mine. He has provided everything I could ever need, and I joyously receive from Him!

APRIL 24

God Limits Himself to His Word

I will worship toward thy holy temple, and praise thy name for thy lovingkindness and for thy truth: for thou hast magnified thy word above all thy name. —Psalm 138:2

I've heard people say, "God is sovereign. He can make you sick if He wants to." But God gave us His Word, which says He is our healer, and promised He'd never go outside its boundaries.

I've heard other people say, "I know what His Word says, but God is still God and He can do anything He wants." In other words, they're saying, "God's Word is one thing, but He is *God.* He has a title, and that title enables Him to do anything He wants."

But the Word says, "Thou hast magnified thy word above all thy name." God is the sovereign God of the universe, but He has elevated His Word above His name. He has limited Himself within the boundaries of His Word.

God is saying He can sovereignly manifest anything promised in His Word through signs, wonders, miracles and gifts of the Holy Spirit, But He *cannot* sovereignly steal, kill and destroy. That's the work of the devil. (John 10:10.) But by the decree of His own Word, God is a merciful, loving Father who has only *good* gifts to give. (James 1:17.)

Confession:

My God is my healer, and He has magnified His Word above His own holy name. So according to that Word, I believe I receive my healing now!

As ye have therefore received Christ Jesus the Lord, so walk ye in him: Rooted and built up in him, and stablished in the faith, as ye have been taught, abounding therein with thanksgiving.

–Colossians 2:6,7

APRIL 25

Learning To Walk by Faith

We are well equipped to walk in the blessings of God. Therefore, after we've had time to grow spiritually, God usually doesn't move on our behalf with sovereign miracles or manifestations of the Holy Spirit that require no faith on our part.

You see, God holds us responsible to learn how to believe His Word. He expects us to switch over from the natural realm and begin operating in the realm of faith.

When I started to hear and apply the truth of God's Word, it changed my life. I started receiving answers to my prayers according to my own faith.

You see, the Word sets our doctrines straight. God won't force His truth on us. But if we're willing to learn, He will show us how to rightly divide His Word. (2 Tim. 2:15.) His truth will set us straight and put us on a new course to victory!

Confession:

I spend time with my heavenly Father and grow up in Him. I walk by faith, depending on Him to perform His Word in my life. It's a great privilege to walk by faith!

APRIL 26

Initiating
Your Miracle

How shall we escape, if we neglect so great salvation; which at the first began to be spoken by the Lord, and was confirmed unto us by them that heard him; God also bearing them witness, both with signs and wonders, and with divers miracles, and gifts of the Holy Ghost, according to his own will? —Hebrews 2:3,4

Sometimes people just get healed out of the clear blue. It doesn't look as if they did a thing to receive their healing. They weren't standing in faith; they were just healed.

For instance, I heard about one fellow who was walking past a church meeting and decided to step into the church to get a drink of water. (He was inebriated at the time.) He left the church and walked about a block down the street. Suddenly he realized he'd been healed of a condition he'd been suffering with for a while. He returned to the meeting and was saved!

That man wasn't believing for his healing. He wasn't using any faith. He wasn't expecting anything. He just got healed according to God's own will.

God's power is released in two different ways. First, He sometimes releases His power by His own sovereign will, allowing His love and compassion to flow forth to set people free. Second, He responds to our faith with His power.

We can move over into the realm of faith to receive our answer. When we exercise our faith in God's Word, we release the same power and get the same results as when God moves sovereignly. We don't have to wait for God to pass by to see if He just might do something, because "we walk by faith, not by sight" (2 Cor. 5:7). We can have a miracle at our own will.

God wants you healed. But don't sit back and wait for Him to give you a miracle. God expects you to use your faith to initiate one. Go to His Word and find His will; then stand on His promises by faith. Reach out and take hold of what belongs to you!

Confession:

*My God is so good to me. He shows me in the Word
how to receive the blessings He's provided.
I receive by faith the healing I desire!*

God is not a man, that he should lie; neither the son of man, that he should repent.

—Numbers 23:19

APRIL 27

God Is True to His Word

When we talk about God's sovereignty, we aren't talking about the religious world's viewpoint of sovereignty. Religious people who don't know the Word say, "God is a sovereign God. If He wants you healed, you'll get healed. If He wants you sick, you'll stay sick. If He wants you prosperous, He'll take care of you financially. But God may want you sick and broke. Whatever will be will be."

According to that way of thinking, it doesn't do you any good to believe God's Word, because you will get whatever God wants you to have. He is sovereign, and most likely, He will take your money, steal your health and knock you in the head three or four times a week to keep you in line. That's just the kind of mood God is in most of the time!

One thing is certain—religious people who think that way don't know God *or* His Word!

No, when we say God does something sovereignly, we simply mean God does something according to His Word at His own discretion. *He* initiates it. But God cannot sovereignly do anything outside the boundaries of His Word, because He has bound Himself to His Word.

Titus 1:2 and Hebrews 6:18 say God cannot lie. He doesn't have the capacity to lie, be dishonest or fail to keep His Word. So just as surely as you can trust that "whosoever shall call upon the name of the Lord shall be saved" (Rom. 10:13), you can believe that "by [Jesus'] stripes ye were healed" (1 Peter 2:24)!

Confession:

God's Word is truth. He says I am healed by the stripes Jesus bore. That healing Word is truth in my life because I believe it and act upon it. I am healed!

APRIL 28

Follow the Holy Ghost

And I, brethren, when I came to you, came not with excellency of speech or of wisdom, declaring unto you the testimony of God.

And my speech and my preaching was not with enticing words of man's wisdom, but in demonstration of the Spirit and of power: that your faith should not stand in the wisdom of men, but in the power of God.

—1 Corinthians 2:1,4,5

Sometimes God wants to come in and demonstrate His love and compassion for us. He knows we will retain and understand a greater percentage of what we both hear *and* see.

God will also go out of His way to demonstrate to us that the Holy Ghost flows in many different directions. You see, in John 7:37-38, Jesus likens the Holy Spirit to a river of living water: "If any man thirst, let him come unto me, and drink. He that believeth on me, as the scripture hath said, out of his belly shall flow rivers of living water."

Just as no two rivers are alike, neither are any two flows of the Holy Spirit alike. Sometimes God will almost give us a spiritual "jerk," demonstrating His power in a new way just to show us that He is a God of variety. We need every one of His different directions because we are creatures of habit, who easily get into ruts.

Someone once said, "A rut is nothing but a grave with both ends kicked out of it." We want to make sure we don't get into a rut. The best way to do that is to follow the Holy Ghost, because He's *never* in a rut!

Confession:

My God moves in many different ways as He leads me into healing and whatever else I need. I stay sensitive to His Spirit so that wherever He leads, I follow His flow!

*Nay, in all these things we are more than
conquerors through him that loved us.*

—Romans 8:37

APRIL 29

Build Your Spiritual Muscles

E ven though you are not *of* this world, you still
live *in* this world; therefore, tests, trials and
temptations are bound to come your way.

Many people think, *Well, tests and trials only come to make me strong.* Some
have even written songs with that message! These people may have been taught
that sickness and disease come in their lives to teach them something or to make
them more pious.

But sickness, disease, tests, trials and temptations will never make you strong.
If they did, you'd be Mr. or Mrs. Universe by now! It's what you do with the tests
and trials you face that makes the difference.

Think of this principle in terms of weight lifting. A weight lifter wants to develop
his muscles, but he'll never reach that goal unless he lifts some weights. He certainly
won't turn into Charles Atlas if he just sits in an easy chair reading weight lifting
books and thinking, *I'm going to be strong!* And when he lies on the workout
bench, the 100-pound weight lying across his chest won't help his muscles gain
strength unless he lifts up the weight and starts pushing it away from himself.

The same principle is true with tests and trials. You have the capacity to
believe God's Word, but you won't be strong in faith unless you exercise your
spiritual muscles. How do you do that? Every time you push your problems away
in the name of Jesus, you gain strength.

People say, "I want strong faith." But strong faith only comes by exercising the
faith you have against something that's contrary to the Word of God.

We normally don't look forward to tests and trials. But every time a problem
arises, we can say, "Glory to God, here's just one more opportunity for me to
develop my faith muscles and prove that the Word of God works!"

Confession:

*I develop my spiritual muscles by using God's Word every time problems
come against me. When my body says, "I'm sick," I say, "By Jesus' stripes,
I'm healed!" The Word works for me because I work the Word.*

APRIL 30

Let Patience Have Her Perfect Work

My brethren, count it all joy when ye fall into divers temptations; knowing this, that the trying of your faith worketh patience. But let patience have her perfect work, that ye may be perfect and entire, wanting nothing.

–James 1:2-4

Notice in verse 4 that James *didn't* say, "Let those *tests and trials* have their perfect work." He said, "Let *patience* have her perfect work...."

You see, tests and trials don't perfect you. It is what you do with them that counts. You are not perfected because a bunch of problems come along. You are perfected because you stick with the Word of God in the midst of those problems and patiently endure. That's when patience has its perfect work.

Patience is consistent endurance. When you walk in patience, you remain consistent all the way through situations, no matter what comes along. You aren't up and down like a yo-yo. You base everything on God's Word. You don't get up in the morning and ask yourself how you are. You get up in the morning, open your Bible and *tell* yourself how you are according to the Word!

I've seen people grow in their spiritual walks as a result of using their faith against tests and trials. I've seen other people go under when they faced the same tests and trials. It's what people do with their problems that makes the difference.

Faith thrives in the midst of a trial. That doesn't mean we enjoy the trial. But when it comes our way, we don't shrink away from it either! We stand on God's Word and say, "Thank God, I know and trust the One whom I have believed!" Even when the going gets tough, we just dig our heels in and say, "I don't care what it looks like, seems like, sounds like or feels like. I believe what the Word of God says!"

Confession:

My faith thrives in the midst of a trial. When symptoms come, I tell my body, "You're healed because Jesus bore your sickness!" I'm not the sick trying to get healed. I am the healed, and in Jesus' name the symptoms have to leave!

Now thanks be unto God, which always causeth us to triumph in Christ, and maketh manifest the savour of his knowledge by us in every place. —2 Corinthians 2:14

Conquer Sickness With Your Faith!

A few years ago, my father decided he didn't want to get "soft," so he started lifting weights. As Dad worked out every morning with those weights, he became stronger and stronger. He'd say, "I don't like lifting these weights, but I'm going to conquer them. If it takes the rest of my life, I'm going to conquer them!"

It's the same way with tests and trials. You can either let them plant themselves in your life and put pressure on you, or you can use your faith muscles to push those trials out of your life. You can decide, "Bless God, I'm going after those tests and trials, and I'm going to conquer them!"

I remember when it used to take me two weeks to get rid of a cold. But I didn't just sit back and say, "Well, I'm going to learn from this cold." (I don't know what you could learn from a cold anyway—except that you don't want another one!) I kept using my faith muscles to push off those cold symptoms. After a while, the symptoms only lasted one week instead of two. Then they lasted three days instead of a week. Soon the cold symptoms just started falling off before they could hook on to my body!

The more you push off the enemy's attacks—the symptoms, the tests, the trials, the temptations—the stronger your faith muscles will get and the quicker the problems will leave. So don't forget—sickness doesn't come to make you strong; it comes to *defeat* you. Just keep using your faith muscles to push those symptoms out of your body. Soon your faith will be so strong that the sickness won't even bother trying to return!

─── ✣ ───

Confession:

I look at God's Word to find truth, and I believe that truth is manifested in my life. The fact may be that symptoms are affecting my body, but the truth is that I am healed!

MAY 2

Come Out of the Trial Stronger!

Fight the good fight of faith, lay hold on eternal life, whereunto thou art also called, and hast professed a good profession before many witnesses.

—1 Timothy 6:12

Someone said, "I thought when a person operated in faith, he wouldn't have any problems." No, that's what faith is for—to help you overcome the enemy when he attacks you with problems.

A man came to one minister and said, "I want you to pray I'll never have any more trouble with the devil."

The minister said, "Do you want me to pray you will die?"

You can count on it—the enemy *will* come with tests and trials. He is trying to steal, kill and destroy everything good in your life. (John 10:10.) As long as we live down here, we will have trouble with the devil.

What does the devil do? He tries to stir up negative circumstances, symptoms, thoughts, imaginations and trials. He does anything he can to discourage us and make us quit. I'm not preaching doom and gloom; I'm just saying we may as well face the fact that life on this earth won't be "a bed of roses."

Even though we are Christians, problems will come to us in life. But we aren't supposed to hide, bury our heads in the sand or run in fear and cry, "Oh, God, what am I going to do now?"

We just need to stay scriptural. Then every time symptoms, temptations, tests or trials come along, we'll get a silly grin on our faces and say, "Glory to God! Here's one more chance for me to flex my faith muscles. I'll come out of this stronger. The next time the devil comes, he'd better have some bigger guns because whatever he throws against me, I'm throwing back in his face with the Word of God! And in the name of Jesus, I'll grow as a result of it!"

Confession:

I overcome every test, every trial and every symptom with God's Word and the name of Jesus. I will not be discouraged, I will not fear and I will not quit. I come out of every test stronger because I am growing in faith!

*The thief cometh not, but for to steal, and to
kill, and to destroy: I am come that they might
have life, and that they might have it more
abundantly.* —John 10:10

God's Kind of Life

Where does sickness come from? I was taught for years that it came from God. I was told He used sickness to teach us and to make us pious and more "Christ-like."

However, if we look in the Word, we definitely see that sickness comes from the enemy and not from God. Jesus certainly didn't get Christ-like through sickness and disease, so I don't know why *we* should have to do it that way! Sickness is a satanic force. God called it a *curse* in Deuteronomy 28:59-61. In Luke 13:16, Jesus called it a *bondage.* And by the inspiration of the Holy Ghost, Peter called it *satanic oppression* in Acts 10:38.

God doesn't like sickness; He is totally and completely against it. He has done, and is still doing, everything in His power to get healing and health to His children.

The thief—the devil—is the one who comes to steal, kill and destroy. Jesus gives only abundant life. (John 10:10.)

So where do sickness and disease fit into that equation? Well, do sickness and disease steal, kill and destroy, or do they give abundant life?

Sickness steals money; it steals families; it steals homes. It steals everything it can steal. Sickness kills and destroys. The thief comes to kill, steal and destroy, and one way he does that is through sickness and disease.

Jesus said, "I have come that you might have life and have it more abundantly." The word *life* in the Greek is "zoe," and it refers to life as God has it.[1] Jesus was saying, "I have come that you might have the life of God."

Was God ever sick? No! Sickness and disease don't come from God; otherwise, Jesus would have given sickness to us as part of the "abundant life" package. Remember, He was the will of God in action. But Jesus didn't come to bind us in chains of bondage and oppression. He came to set us free!

Confession:

*Jesus gives me abundant life—life as God has it.
God doesn't get sick, so I don't allow sickness to stay
in my body either. God's divine health belongs to me!*

MAY 4

Fill Your Mind With the Word

For this purpose the Son of God was manifested, that he might destroy the works of the devil.
—1 John 3:8

Where does sickness come from? We have to find the source of the problem before we can get rid of it. So let's look at the reason Jesus came to earth. First John 3:8 says He came "to destroy the works of the devil." What are the works Jesus came to destroy? Sin, poverty, sickness and disease.

I know people who are just beginning to walk by faith. But even though they are learning to believe and confess the truth of God's Word, they still have that old, doubt-filled thought following them around: *God may want me sick for a purpose. This sickness may be sent from God to teach me something.*

If that's what you're thinking, you won't be healed. Your faith will never operate beyond your knowledge of God's will. You have to know healing is God's will before you can believe for it.

So feed your spirit on healing Scriptures that tell you God wants you healthy and whole. Fill your mind with the Word so those old, doubt-filled thoughts can't even find a way to get in! Your faith can make you whole—*if* you know what you believe!

Confession:

It's God's will for me to be healed and live in health. Sickness doesn't come from God, and He doesn't use sickness to teach me. Jesus destroyed the works of the devil, so I live free of sickness and disease!

He that wavereth is like a wave of the sea driven
with the wind and tossed. For let not that man
think that he shall receive any thing of the Lord.
A double minded man is unstable in all his
ways. —James 1:6-8

MAY 5

Don't Be Double-Minded

Whenever sickness or disease attack our bodies, everything in us wants to be free of it. It's uncomfortable. It is "dis-ease," and we automatically want to get rid of it as quickly as we can.

But if we think sickness is from God for any reason—whether we think it's commissioned by Him, sent by Him or allowed by Him—we're in trouble. We become double-minded. One side of our mind thinks, *I don't want this;* but the other side thinks, *If God wants me to have this sickness, it must be good for me, and I should keep it. I want whatever God wants for me. I want to obey God.*

If sickness is a blessing from God, we should never be found fighting against it. We shouldn't fight it with medical science, with prayer, with the laying on of hands or anything else. If our sickness is from God, we should keep it and pray for the rest of the family to get sick!

But if sickness is *not* from God, then as God's children, redeemed by the blood of Jesus, we shouldn't have any part of it.

You can walk free of sickness. So don't be double-minded about it—refuse to accept it when it comes. If symptoms attack your body, attack those symptoms with the Word of God! You are God's child, and you don't have to keep one thing that doesn't come from Him!

Confession:

I am single-minded and stable in all my ways.
I know God's will for me is healing and good health.
Sickness has no place in me, and I refuse to let it stay!

MAY 6

Does Sickness Come From God?

He sent his word, and healed them, and delivered them from their destructions.

–Psalm 107:20

If sickness or disease comes from God, how does He give it to us? Does He reach out and touch us, giving it to us by His own hand?

Jesus was the express image of God—the will of God in action. He said, "If you've seen Me, you've seen the Father." (John 14:9.) So if it were true that God gave us sickness by His hand, then Jesus would have given sickness to people instead of taking it away from them.

But when Jesus touched people, they were healed. He lived on this earth thirty-three-and-a-half years and ministered for three-and-a-half of those years. In all that time, Jesus never gave sickness or disease to anyone. He acted out the will of God, taking sickness away from people.

Well, then, does God give us sickness by His Word? Does He speak it on us? No, Psalm 107:20 says, "He sent his word, and *healed* them." So God doesn't put sickness on us with His hands nor by His Word.

Where would God get sickness to put on us anyway? He doesn't have sickness in heaven. And when sickness entered this earth through the fall of man, Jesus paid the price to send it to the depths of hell, where it belongs.

So there's only one conclusion to make: God doesn't have any sickness to give us. *Therefore, sickness and disease are not from God.*

Confession:

*Father, let Your will be done in my life, as it is in heaven.
Because there is no sickness in heaven, sickness must leave
my body! I receive God's healing Word now in Jesus' name.*

Do not err, my beloved brethren. Every good gift and every perfect gift is from above, and cometh down from the Father of lights, with whom is no variableness, neither shadow of turning.

—James 1:16,17

MAY 7

The God Who Never Changes

Every good and perfect gift comes from God, who never changes. So when we find out that something is good and perfect, we know it comes from God. And if it isn't good or perfect, we know it doesn't come from above.

What about sickness? Well, if sickness came from God, it would have to be good. But we know sickness *isn't* good, because it steals, kills and destroys. It doesn't come from God.

I like the last part of verse 17, where James describes God as "the Father of lights, with whom is no variableness, neither shadow of turning." God never changes. This verse says He doesn't even have a *shadow* of turning! There isn't even a trace of change in God.

Jesus doesn't change either. He is the express image of the Father, and He's the same yesterday, today and forever. (Heb. 13:8.) And Acts 10:38 says Jesus "went about doing *good,* and healing all that were oppressed of the devil; for God was with him."

God didn't send sickness and disease to the earth in the beginning; He didn't send sickness and disease during the time of Jesus' earthly walk, and He doesn't send sickness and disease to the earth today. Rather, God made a way to *deliver* us from sickness and disease when He sent the living Word, Jesus Christ.

Confession:

My Father and His Word never change. He sent His Word to heal His people under the old covenant, and He sends His Word to heal me today. I receive my healing by faith in God's Word!

MAY 8

Was Sickness Part of God's Creation?

And God saw every thing that he had made, and, behold, it was very good. And the evening and the morning were the sixth day.

–Genesis 1:31

God had just finished Creation. He said, "That's it. I'm through!" His finished creation displayed His perfect will for Adam and all his descendants. That was the way He wanted everything to be.

But what was *not* in God's creation on that sixth day? Well, you'll never find a Scripture that says, "On such-and-such a day, God created sickness and disease." You'll never read, "And God said, 'Let there be cancer! Let there be pneumonia!'" No, God looked at His creation, and "behold, it was very good" (Gen. 1:31). That means sickness and disease were absent in the original creation.

When Adam sinned and fell spiritually in the Garden of Eden, he chose a new master to serve. He turned creation over to the enemy. At that moment, Satan became the god of this world with a long-term lease on creation.

When Satan entered into his new domain, he brought all his goods with him— sickness, disease, fear, poverty, depression, oppression, death and everything else that's evil. Someone once said, "Sickness is the foul offspring of its father, Satan, and its mother, sin."

You don't find sickness and disease anywhere in the Bible until after Satan became the god of this world. Then you find sickness running rampant throughout the earth.

Satan is the author of sickness. He brought it into the earth with him. And only through the redemptive work of Jesus Christ on the Cross would life ever again become "very good" on this earth.

Confession:

Sickness doesn't come from God. Satan is the father of all diseases, but I've been delivered from his kingdom. I walk in health and healing because my Father wants me well!

God anointed Jesus of Nazareth with the Holy Ghost and with power: who went about doing good, and healing all that were oppressed of the devil; for God was with him. —Acts 10:38

MAY 9

Healing Is Good!

The Bible doesn't say, "God anointed Jesus of Nazareth with the Holy Ghost and power: who went about making people sick everywhere He went." No, Jesus went about doing *good*. What "good" did Jesus do? This Scripture says He "went about doing good, and *healing.*" Whom did He heal? Those who were oppressed.

Who oppressed them? The devil. That's pretty plain. God tells us in this Scripture where sickness and disease come from—the devil.

God also tells us what "good" is: Good is *healing*. Sickness isn't good, because Jesus healed those who were sick and oppressed of the devil. "Good" is setting people free from sickness and disease.

Sickness isn't a blessing from God. It's a curse, a satanic oppression and a bondage that the enemy places in the body of Christ to slow us down or stop us from preaching the Gospel to all the world.

God wants us well so we can fulfill the Great Commission. He wants us not only to preach the Gospel, but to lay hands on the sick to set them free. (Mark 16:18.) Why? Because sickness is bad, and healing is *good!*

Confession:
My Father says healing is good. He willingly heals me.
And as I lay hands on the sick, God's power causes them to recover!

MAY 10

Rightly Discerning Jesus' Body

But let a man examine himself, and so let him eat of that bread, and drink of that cup. For he that eateth and drinketh unworthily, eateth and drinketh damnation to himself, not discerning the Lord's body. For this cause many are weak and sickly among you, and many sleep.

—1 Corinthians 11:28-30

Writing to the believers at the Corinthian church, Paul says, "Many in the church are weak, sickly and sleeping."

What does Paul mean? Some definitions will help us understand. The word *weak* indicates being without strength, infirmed, feeble, impotent, diseased and sick. A *sickly* person is one whose strength has failed through disease. Paul is talking about physical problems in this Scripture. And when he refers to those who are *sleeping,* he is talking about the "sleep" of death.

So Paul is actually saying in this verse, "For this reason, many are physically sick and even dying early."

What is the reason Paul is referring to? He's discussing the Lord's Supper. In verse 29, he says, "For he that eateth and drinketh unworthily, eateth and drinketh damnation to himself, *not discerning the Lord's body."* Weymouth's translation says, "...if he fails to estimate the body right." *Wuest's* translation says, "...if he does not properly evaluate the body." *The Living Bible* puts it this way: "...not thinking about the body of Christ and what it means." Finally, *The Modern Language Bible* says, "...without due appreciation of the body."

This is the only place in the Bible where Paul says, *"For this cause* many are weak and sickly among you, and many sleep." Apparently, it's important to understand how to rightly discern, estimate, evaluate and appreciate the body.

Confession:

I rightly discern Jesus' body, broken for my physical healing.
I appreciate and appropriate the healing Jesus purchased for me.

For he that eateth and drinketh unworthily, eateth and drinketh damnation to himself, not discerning the Lord's body. For this cause many are weak and sickly among you, and many sleep. —1 Corinthians 11:29,30

MAY 11

Don't Judge Others

One way we can look at Paul's warning about "not discerning the Lord's body" is as it refers to our discernment of others in the body of Christ.

Some Christians say, "We have more revelation than anyone else in the body of Christ. If you aren't one of us, you don't have anything." These people want to criticize others and put themselves on a level above everyone else. That's a bad position to be in. A church like that is not rightly discerning the body of Christ and will be full of sick people who don't receive their healing.

Those of us who have received the fullness of the Holy Spirit have to be careful about this kind of prideful attitude. We aren't on a level above anyone else. We only have more responsibility. You see, when we understand what God's Word says about healing, faith and confession, the way is opened for us to receive more benefits.

We need to walk in love toward fellow Christians who haven't received as much revelation of the Word as we have. When we look down on other believers, we do not rightly discern the body of Christ. Judging others will always give us trouble, because everyone in the body of Christ is important.

Confession:

Jesus' blood was shed and His body was broken for all people. Each person is important to the Lord! I will not judge another in the body of Christ. I will pray and intercede so that we all may be healed.

MAY 12

Understand Why Jesus' Body Was Broken

For he that eateth and drinketh unworthily, eateth and drinketh damnation to himself, not discerning the Lord's body. For this cause many are weak and sickly among you, and many sleep.
—1 Corinthians 11:29,30

Let's look at another meaning of the phrase "not discerning the Lord's body." In Communion, the cup is the symbol of Jesus' blood, which was shed for us. We've preached about the blood of Jesus for years. Most people have a revelation of the blood of Jesus Christ. They know His blood was shed for our sins.

But what about those who don't understand or believe in the blood of Jesus? A person who takes Communion without understanding the purpose of the blood may think, *I don't know why Jesus went to the Cross. I don't believe His blood has anything to do with me.*

What blessings will such a person receive? Someone who doesn't understand or believe in the blood of Jesus will not partake of salvation. He is walking in spiritual death because he doesn't know why Jesus shed His blood.

In the same way, the bread is the symbol of Jesus' body, which was broken for us. But many Christians haven't been taught *why* the body of Jesus was broken. They don't know His body was broken for their physical health. Therefore, they remain sick.

A person can partake of the symbol of Jesus' broken body in Communion for years and still say, "I don't believe healing is for today." If people don't understand, believe and act on the truth that Jesus' body was broken for their physical healing, then Jesus' redemptive work won't help them. They are likely to be weak and sickly, and they may die prematurely because they don't rightly discern the Lord's body.

Don't make that mistake. Believe Jesus' body was broken for you, and enjoy walking in health!

Confession:

*Jesus' body was broken for my physical healing
just as surely as His blood was shed for my sins.
I rightly discern His body, so I walk in divine health!*

For my thoughts are not your thoughts, neither are your ways my ways, saith the Lord. For as the heavens are higher than the earth, so are my ways higher than your ways, and my thoughts than your thoughts. —Isaiah 55:8,9

MAY 13

Choose God's Higher Thoughts

People say, "I believe God wants to use sickness to teach me." But is that in the Bible?

All of us have probably held theories and beliefs at one time or another that have messed up our thinking. Perhaps Satan's biggest lie is that sickness and disease are from God. When we fall for that lie, we stop resisting the devil's attacks on our bodies and open the door for him to walk right in and strap sickness on us. Then we wonder why we can't get rid of the sickness!

We might receive temporary relief from sickness or pain if people lay hands on us and pray. But often the symptoms come right back. We won't find permanent relief until we make sure that the door giving the enemy access is closed and locked. How do we lock the door? By getting a strong revelation in our hearts that healing is God's will.

You see, we open the door to sickness through wrong thinking. Wrong thinking produces wrong believing, and wrong believing produces wrong speaking. When all those factors are put together, we experience only bad results.

When faced with symptoms of sickness, we should immediately say, "The Bible is God talking to me. What does God think? What does the Bible say?"

God's thoughts are higher than our thoughts. (Isa. 55:9.) Thank God, He wrote down His thoughts and ways in sixty-six books and gave them to us! And in those books, He tells us that *healing is His will!*

Confession:

I don't allow the devil's doubt and unbelief to keep me from receiving my healing. I choose God's higher thoughts and ways, and they produce healing in me!

MAY 14

Act Like the Word Is True

Giving thanks unto the Father, which hath made us meet to be partakers of the inheritance of the saints in light: who hath delivered us from the power of darkness, and hath translated us into the kingdom of his dear Son.

—Colossians 1:12,13

Why do people get sick? Well, we know why people in the world get sick: Sometimes their father, the devil, gives sickness to them. But what about Christians? Our Father God doesn't have any sickness to give to us, and we don't have to take it from the world's father anymore. He doesn't have rule or authority over us. We've been delivered from the power of darkness.

But because of a lack of knowledge, Christians often don't realize sickness comes from the devil. Therefore, they don't resist the symptoms when they show up. Or they may think the sickness is a blessing from God and therefore want to keep it.

When these Christians start feeling symptoms, they just say in resignation, "Well, I guess I'm sick." They don't know the enemy is trying to bind them up, cause them problems and keep them from obeying God. They're ignorant of the devil's efforts to hinder them from doing the work of the ministry and fulfilling the Great Commission. Therefore, they don't resist the devil. When symptoms come, they "sign for the package," receive them and get sick.

Amazingly enough, another major reason many Christians are sick is that they haven't obeyed James 4:7: "Submit yourselves therefore to God. Resist the devil, and he will flee from you." They just haven't had the spiritual energy or intestinal fortitude to resist the symptoms and act like the Word of God is true!

If you're going to live in divine health as God intended, you first have to know that sickness comes from the devil. Then you have to act on the Word. When symptoms come, resist them in the name of Jesus! Act like the Word is true in your life—because it is!

Confession:

*I am delivered from the power of darkness.
I submit to God and resist the devil, and the devil
has to go and take his symptoms with him!*

*Out of the abundance of the heart the mouth
speaketh.*   *—Matthew 12:34*

Be a Person of Your Word

Vou cannot separate yourself from your word, for you are only as good as your word.

I heard one minister say, "Sometimes a person's faith doesn't work because his word is no good." After hearing this probably 100 times, I finally realized that if our word isn't any good, our faith will never work.

Sometimes people aren't used to believing their own words. If they don't believe their words in certain natural areas of their lives, they'll have a hard time believing their words when they're standing in faith for something.

Faith is believing that what you say according to the Word *will* come to pass. Mark 11:23 says, "For verily I say unto you, that whosoever shall *say* unto this mountain, Be thou removed, and be thou cast into the sea; and shall not doubt in his heart, but shall believe that those things which he *saith* shall come to pass; he shall have whatsoever he *saith*."

If you are going to be a person of faith whose faith works, you have to be a person of your word. Stick to your word. Keep your word. Honor your word. Watch over your word.

As you do, people may start talking about you, saying, "Boy, I'm telling you, if that person says something, you can just count on its coming to pass. You can count on him to back up his word." When you gain a reputation like that, your faith will skyrocket!

Confession:

*My words create God's realities in my life. I watch
my words carefully and speak only truth and life. As I walk
in faith according to God's Word, I shall have whatever I say.
So right now I say, "By Jesus' stripes, I am healed!"*

MAY 16

The Miracle at the Pool of Bethesda

Now there is at Jerusalem by the sheep market a pool, which is called in the Hebrew tongue Bethesda, having five porches. In these lay a great multitude of impotent folk, of blind, halt, withered, waiting for the moving of the water. For an angel went down at a certain season into the pool, and troubled the water: whosoever then first after the troubling of the water stepped in was made whole of whatsoever disease he had.

—John 5:2-4

This account gives us a picture of God's sovereign side. Five sheds full of people sat by that pool. The people didn't know when the angel was coming; they just knew he was coming. They didn't know who would be healed; they just knew *someone* would be healed. And afterwards, the rest of the people would have to sit and wait for the next time the angel came to trouble the water.

Now let's look at verses 5-9:

And a certain man was there, which had an infirmity thirty and eight years. When Jesus saw him lie...he saith unto him, Wilt thou be made whole?

The impotent man answered him, Sir, I have no man, when the water is troubled, to put me into the pool....

Jesus saith unto him, Rise, take up thy bed, and walk. And immediately the man was made whole, and took up his bed, and walked....

Obviously, the impotent man wasn't healed on his own faith. "Well, then," someone may say, *"Jesus'* faith healed the man." But Jesus never once said in the Bible, "My faith made you whole." If Jesus' faith had healed that man, He would have healed everyone else there too. But after healing this one man, Jesus disappeared into the crowd.

So what healed the man? The sovereignty of God. Why did God single that one man out? I don't know; that's God's business. God did it, and He knows what He's doing.

Confession:

God reaches out to heal people as He wills. He also made a way for me to receive my healing by faith in His Word. I exercise that faith, and I receive my healing now!

[Jesus] saith unto him, Wilt thou be made whole? The impotent man answered him, Sir I have no man. —John 5:6,7

MAY 17

Keep a Watch on Your Words

*T*he Living Bible puts it this way: "When Jesus saw him and knew how long he had been ill, he asked him, 'Would you like to get well?'"

"'I can't,' the sick man said...."

Just as we can locate this man's faith by his words, "I can't," we can locate our faith by *our* words. You see, many of us have been taught a great deal about faith and confession (or saying what the Word says) and can "talk a good talk." But when no one is listening and the pressure is on, we need to pay attention to what comes out of our mouths. We don't need to be "confession monitors" for other people; we can stay busy just checking up on ourselves!

When many of us first heard the teaching, "You can have what you say," we were dangerous. We'd say, "Don't say that!" to people who had no idea what we were talking about. Hopefully we've learned better by now. But we still need to locate *ourselves* with our words. It's easy to keep a good confession when things are going well. But when pressure comes and no one is listening, we may discover some adjustments we need to make!

When you get into a tight spot while standing in faith for something, you may say words of doubt and unbelief. Don't let that put you under condemnation. Don't say, "Oh, dear God, I thought I was in faith, but now I've completely blown it by spewing out all kinds of unbelief!" No, all isn't lost. Just make the adjustment, and feed on the Word for a while. Get full of the Word, for "out of the abundance of the heart the mouth speaketh" (Matt. 12:34)!

Confession:

The words I speak control the circumstances of my life.
God's Word in me drives out sickness and disease.
I can have what I say, and I say I'm healed!

MAY 18

Don't Wait for the Water To Move

When Jesus saw him lie, and knew that he had been now a long time in that case, he saith unto him, Wilt thou be made whole? —John 5:6

Notice Jesus went to this pool where a great multitude of sick people gathered. They were all waiting for the water to be troubled. They knew that when the water moved, the first person who stepped in would be healed. Everyone else had to wait for the next visitation. And they'd wait and wait and wait...

The situation was a little like a person who decides to stand out in a field and wait for lightning to strike. Maybe it will strike; maybe it won't. There are no guarantees.

Unfortunately, most of the church world is in that state of wishful thinking. Most Christians would like healing to just hit them. But they won't do their part to take hold of their healing by faith.

"Wilt thou be made whole?" That's a good question.

Some Christians would protest, "But if healing were for today, everyone would be healed." No, not everyone even wants healing! Some folks would rather stay sick. For example, Janet and I know a lady who has been sick for thirty-five years, and she's become accustomed to it. If some people were healed, they wouldn't have anything to talk about. It would cut their vocabulary about 95 percent! If other people were healed, they wouldn't get any attention.

I don't mean that unkindly, but that kind of situation is a reproach to the body of Christ. We ought to love people and give them the attention they need when they're well so they don't have to be sick to receive it.

At the same time, we ought to examine ourselves. Are we "waiting for the water to move"? Or are we doing our part to receive our healing by faith?

Confession:

I am whole. I don't use sickness as a way to get attention, and I don't just wait for the "water to move." Healing is mine, and I receive it now by faith!

And a certain man was there, which had an infirmity thirty and eight years. When Jesus saw him lie, and knew that he had been now a long time in that case, he saith unto him, Wilt thou be made whole?

The impotent man answered him, Sir, I have no man, when the water is troubled, to put me into the pool: but while I am coming, another steppeth down before me. —John 5:5-8

MAY 19

Put Your Trust in Jesus, Not Man

Jesus walked directly to the man and asked, "Is it your will to be healed?"

The man replied, "But I have no man...."

That was this man's first problem. *He was looking to man.* In other words, he was saying, "Yes, I'd like to be healed, but I can't. I'm too slow. I've been here too long. I don't have any friends. No one will help me, so I can't be healed."

Apparently, some of the sick around the pool were prosperous enough to hire a man to stay with them. When the water was troubled, the hired man would pick up the sick person, run to the pool and put him in the pool. And if that person was first, he'd be healed. But evidently this crippled man didn't have any money, because he told Jesus, "I have no man."

We must not make the mistake this man did by keeping our eyes on what we lack. We have a man—*the* Man Jesus—and in Him there is *no* lack. If we focus on what we don't have, we miss our answer when it stands before us.

When you look to man, you will always be sadly disappointed. Some believers even go to a specific healing evangelist, expecting him to heal them. But no man can heal anyone.

Regardless of what kind of anointing someone operates in, no man is a healer. Jesus alone is the healer. So trust in Him alone for your healing. Jesus is all you need!

Confession:

I focus my spiritual eyes on Jesus, with whom there is no lack.
No man is my healer—Jesus is my healer!

MAY 20

When God Is Moving, Enter In

Now there is at Jerusalem by the sheep market a pool, which is called in the Hebrew tongue Bethesda, having five porches. In these lay a great multitude of impotent folk, of blind, halt, withered, waiting for the moving of the water.

—John 5:2,3

Let's talk about the Holy Ghost. This incident occurs, of course, under the old covenant, but moving waters are always a type of the flow of the Spirit of God—the move of the Holy Ghost. When sick people come into the flow of the Holy Ghost, that is the easiest time for them to be healed.

Many times as we endeavor to receive our healing, we do all we know to do. We hear the Word of God, act on the Word, hold fast to our confession of faith and stand fast. (Heb. 4:14; 10:23.)

The best thing to do at that point is to get into the move of the Holy Ghost. Wherever God is moving, whether it's in our prayer closets or in a church service, we must do everything we can to enter in. It's much easier to receive the manifestation of what we're believing for when we're in the flow of the Spirit.

You see, the Holy Ghost is the One who causes our answers to come. He's the One who confirms the Word. I like what someone said: "When the Holy Ghost starts moving, your manifestation will catch up with your confession."

Confession:

I know my Father wants me well, so I enter into the flow of His Spirit when He's showing Himself strong. I take every opportunity for the Holy Ghost to move in my life!

And when Jesus was entered into Capernaum, there came unto him a centurion, beseeching him, and saying, Lord, my servant lieth at home sick of the palsy, grievously tormented.

And Jesus saith unto him, I will come and heal him.

MAY 21

Take God at His Word

The centurion answered and said, Lord, I am not worthy that thou shouldest come under my roof: but speak the word only, and my servant shall be healed. For I am a man under authority....

When Jesus heard it, he marvelled, and said to them that followed, Verily I say unto you, I have not found so great faith, no, not in Israel. —Matthew 8:5-10

The Roman centurion had great faith because he understood Jesus' words had authority over sickness and disease. The centurion was willing not only to believe the words of Jesus, but to act on them as well.

The centurion didn't say, "Jesus, I need You to come to my house." He said, "You just speak the Word, Jesus, and I'll take that Word and act on it!" In verse 13, Jesus responded to the centurion's faith: "Go thy way; and as thou hast believed, so be it done unto thee. And his servant was healed in the selfsame hour." The centurion didn't need a special manifestation or special feeling. He just heard the incorruptible seed of Jesus' words, and said, "I believe what You say." And when the centurion acted on the Word he heard, his servant received his healing.

That's what God expects us to do. He doesn't expect us to wait for some special manifestation, even though that may happen at times. God expects us to simply take Him at His Word, believe we receive His promises and boldly act on them in faith.

Confession:

Jesus responds to faith. The servant was healed because the centurion believed the words Jesus spoke would come to pass. I am healed because I believe God's healing promises will come to pass in me!

MAY 22

You Can Do Something About the Devil!

And when Jesus was entered into Capernaum, there came unto him a centurion, beseeching him, and saying, Lord, my servant lieth at home sick of the palsy, grievously tormented.

And Jesus saith unto him, I will come and heal him.

The centurion answered and said, Lord, I am not worthy that thou shouldest come under my roof: but speak the word only, and my servant shall be healed. For I am a man under authority.

–Matthew 8:5-9

There's a connection between understanding authority and having great faith. Sometimes a believer's faith doesn't operate because he doesn't understand his authority in Christ. Every time he starts to receive something from God, the devil steals it away, and he doesn't realize he can do something about it.

So we must develop an understanding of the authority God has given us. Authority is not our own power or strength. The best term to explain authority is "delegated power." Jesus delegated authority to His disciples and to the Church: "Verily I say unto you, Whatsoever ye shall bind on earth shall be bound in heaven: and whatsoever ye shall loose on earth shall be loosed in heaven" (Matt. 18:18). Jesus said, "Whatever you forbid on earth, heaven will forbid. Whatever you allow on earth, heaven will allow."

Jesus is the Head of the Church. We are His body on this earth with the right to use the authority vested in His name. The body has the same authority as the Head.

God is waiting for us to give orders to the enemy so He can legally enforce those decisions. We are the ones with the authority to do something about the devil. Whatever we forbid on earth, heaven forbids. Whatever we allow on earth, heaven allows!

Confession:

Jesus has spoken healing to me through His Word.
Now I have authority on earth to keep the devil from
stealing my healing from me. In the name of Jesus, I am healed!

And when Jesus was entered into Capernaum, there came unto him a centurion, beseeching him, and saying, Lord, my servant lieth at home sick of the palsy, grievously tormented.

And Jesus saith unto him, I will come and heal him.   *–Matthew 8:5-7*

MAY 23

Jesus' Will Is the Father's Will

When the centurion asked Jesus to come heal his servant, Jesus responded, *"I will."* Jesus was saying, "My will is to heal him because My will is the Father's will. And the Father's will is to heal *everyone* who allows Him to. Therefore, I will come heal him."

Jesus didn't know and had never before seen the centurion's servant. Jesus wasn't even in the servant's presence. But Jesus knew the will of the Father.

Then the centurion said, "You don't need to come to my house, Lord; I'm not really worthy of that. But if You will just speak the word, my servant will be healed." Jesus commended the centurion for his faith and sent him home. There the centurion found his servant healed and set free!

Healing the servant was God's will. Jesus had probably never seen the centurion or the servant before; He didn't know them. But Jesus knew the will of the Father—*healing for all!*

Confession:

Like the centurion, I believe in the power and authority of Jesus' words.
I know God's will is that I be healed and walk in health.
So I ask in faith for my healing, and I believe I receive my answer.

MAY 24

A Crippled Man Walks

And [throughout Lycaonia] they preached the gospel. And there sat a certain man at Lystra, impotent in his feet, being a cripple from his mother's womb, who never had walked: the same heard Paul speak: who stedfastly beholding him, and perceiving that he had faith to be healed, said with a loud voice, Stand upright on thy feet. And he leaped and walked.

–Acts 14:7-10

Paul and Barnabas were preaching the Gospel, the Good News, in the cities of Lycaonia. Good news to a sinner is that he can be saved, good news to a poor man is that his needs can be met and good news to a sick man is that he can be healed. Therefore, healing must have been part of the Gospel Paul and Barnabas were preaching.

As they preached in Lystra, a crippled man who had never walked sat in the crowd. Suddenly, something radically changed his condition. What was it that changed the course of his life? "The same *heard* Paul speak." The man heard the Gospel. Then Paul "stedfastly beholding him, and *perceiving that he had faith to be healed,* said with a loud voice, Stand upright on thy feet. And he leaped and walked."

A miracle happened that day. Yes, the man leaped and walked and praised God for his healing. But the first step he took that set a new course in his life was to *hear.* He tapped into the connection between *hearing* and *healing.*

Confession:

Hearing God's Word produces faith in me.
Therefore, as I continually hear the Word,
I walk in divine health, peace and abundance.

And there they preached the gospel. And there sat a certain man at Lystra, impotent in his feet, being a cripple from his mother's womb, who never had walked: the same heard Paul speak: who stedfastly beholding him, and perceiving that he had faith to be healed, said with a loud voice, Stand upright on thy feet. And he leaped and walked. —Acts 14:7-10

MAY 25

A Miracle Received Through Faith

That crippled man had never taken a step in his life. Then suddenly, he was up leaping and praising God! How did that happen? He received through faith. Where did he get his faith? "The same *heard Paul speak."* What did Paul speak? Verse 7 says, "And there they preached *the gospel."* So the man put his faith in the Gospel message and received a miraculous healing!

You hear some people say, "Well, Brother, we don't preach healing around here; we just preach the Gospel." That's amazing. When Paul preached the Gospel, people had faith to be healed! A person can't preach the whole Gospel without preaching healing.

"The same heard Paul speak: who stedfastly beholding him, and *perceiving that he had faith to be healed...."* Did Paul perceive that someday the man would get faith? No, Paul perceived that the man had faith right then. The man hadn't taken a step yet, but he had faith to be healed. However, his faith didn't work until he stepped out and acted on it.

It isn't right to say to someone, "Well, if you had faith, you'd be healed." Sometimes people just haven't come to the point of stepping out and acting on their faith to get results.

And you can't say, "Well, then, so-and-so is not healed because he isn't *acting* on his faith." No, a number of things can keep faith from working.

The bottom line is that we can't judge another person's faith. However, we *can* know that it's God's will to heal every person every time, because we have His Word on it!

Confession:

I hear the full Gospel of salvation and healing, and faith rises in me to be healed. I act on my faith in God's Word, and it produces what I desire. God's Word works!

MAY 26

God Is Willing To Heal

And, behold, there came a leper and worshipped him, saying, Lord, if thou wilt, thou canst make me clean.

And Jesus put forth his hand, and touched him, saying, I will; be thou clean. And immediately his leprosy was cleansed. —Matthew 8:2,3

This leper is the only person recorded in the New Testament to have questioned God's will to heal. This man is also the first in the four Gospels whom Jesus heals. So the first thing God does through Jesus is to clear up this question: Is it God's will to heal?

A major obstacle standing between Christians and miracles today is that they know God is *able* to heal, but they don't know whether He's *willing*. Many in the church world say, "Lord, heal this person, if it be Thy will."

Under the Levitical law, a leper was unclean and had to live in the wilderness away from civilization. This particular leper, however, had apparently heard that Jesus was healing people. He wanted to be healed so much that he took risks to be well.

The leper fell before Jesus and said, "Lord, if it is Your will, You can make me clean." He came to Jesus desiring to be healed. But desire wasn't enough. The leper didn't receive anything until Jesus cleared up his question, "Is it Your will to heal me?"

This is a guideline for the Church today. People say, "I saw people in the prayer lines who weren't healed" or "I prayed, and I wasn't healed." But so many of these people didn't *expect* to be healed; they only *hoped* they would be. They couldn't expect healing, because they didn't confidently know that God's will is healing every time.

One translation of verse 3 says, "Jesus stretched out his hand and placed it on the leper saying, 'Of course I want to. Be clean!'" (PHILLIPS). The man didn't get healed until Jesus answered that question for him.

So we can see the importance of knowing God's will. When Jesus answered the leper, He also gave that answer to all mankind—including *you*. God is able *and* willing to heal you!

✌ Confession:

With two words, "I will," Jesus showed me beyond a doubt that God's will for me is divine health. If sickness shows up, God wants me well. Therefore, according to Your will, Lord, I accept my healing!

And there came a leper to him, beseeching him, and kneeling down to him, and saying unto him, If thou wilt, thou canst make me clean.

And Jesus, moved with compassion, put forth his hand, and touched him, and saith unto him, I will; be thou clean. And as soon as he had spoken, immediately the leprosy departed from him, and he was cleansed. —Mark 1:40-42

It's God's Will To Heal You

The average Christian is in the same position as this leper was—not knowing whether it is God's will to heal or not. The believer may think, *I know God is able to heal. I just don't know whether or not it's His will to heal me.*

The leper knew the ability of Jesus. He came to Jesus and said, "Lord, if You will, You can make me clean." I've heard the same thing from people in prayer lines. They stand there praying, "Oh, Lord, I know You're able to heal me."

But knowing God is able isn't enough; it's just a starting point. Knowing God's *ability* is about 25 percent of the answer. The other 75 percent is knowing His *will*.

The one hindrance that stood between the leper and his miracle was revealed in his statement: "If thou wilt, thou canst make me clean." The same is true for people all over the world. They are trusting God for healing. But if you were to ask them if they are convinced that it is God's will to heal them, they would probably answer, "I sure hope so." They are operating in strong hope, but they haven't stepped over into the realm of faith yet.

Faith always begins where the will of God is known. "I know God heals some people," you may say. But only when you know that it's God's will to heal *you* do you reach the beginning point of faith.

Confession:

*I know without a doubt that it is my Father's will to heal me.
I come to Him with confident assurance that He desires
my healing even more than I do. Healing is mine!*

MAY 28

Taking the "If" Out of Healing

And Jesus put forth his hand, and touched him, saying, I will; be thou clean. And immediately his leprosy was cleansed. —Matthew 8:3

What did Jesus do when this leper said, "I know You are able to heal me, Lord, but I don't know if You are willing"? Did Jesus say, "Now, Brother, I'll have to fast and pray first to see if it is God's will to heal you"? No, Jesus answered the question for all mankind right there. He turned to that man and said, *"I will; be thou clean."* In other words, Jesus was saying, "Why in the world would you doubt a thing like that? If I'm able, surely I am willing."

We shouldn't have any question in our hearts about God's will to heal. Jesus certainly didn't. He didn't hesitate when the leper said to Him, "If You will." Immediately Jesus turned to the man and said, "Of course, I will. That's part of My commission. That's part of the reason I came. Of course it's My will for you to be whole."

Jesus took the "if" out of the healing issue. He didn't have to beg, plead or spend three days finding God's will about healing. He just automatically said, "I will heal you." Why? Because Jesus was the will of God in action.

Jesus was the expression of the will of God to Adam's race. Jesus didn't say, "I heal on My own." He said, "The Father that dwelleth in me, he doeth the works" (John 14:10). Therefore, for Jesus to heal the leper, it had to be God's will because it was the Father, dwelling inside Jesus, who did the work!

Confession:

I read and meditate on God's Word, and it builds an unshakable confidence in me that God wants me healthy and whole. So I boldly say, "I am healed," and the Holy Spirit, who lives in me, does the work!

And Jesus, moved with compassion, put forth his hand, and touched him.   *–Mark 1:41*

MAY 29

God's Compassion To Heal

"M oved with compassion," Jesus touched the leper. This may have been the first time in years that someone touched this man. No one wanted to touch him. He wasn't even supposed to come near people.

In Luke 17:12, Jesus came to a place where ten lepers cried unto Him from afar. Why didn't these ten lepers walk over to Jesus? Because it was illegal. If a leper came within 100 paces of a healthy human being, he had to get out of the way and call out, "Unclean! Unclean!"

So these ten lepers, knowing they couldn't legally come within 100 paces of Jesus, cried to Him from some distance away. Jesus told them to go show themselves to the priest, and they were healed as they went. (v. 14.)

Yet this one leper came close to Jesus. Though he could have been stoned for being there, he had the tenacity of someone who wanted healing so badly that he was willing to take a risk for it.

The leper fell down before Jesus and said, "Lord, if You will, You can make me clean." Jesus immediately settled that question. Moved with compassion, He put forth His hand and touched the leper, saying, "I will; be thou clean."

You see, *God's ability shows His power, but His willingness shows His compassion.* In the Word, God's compassion is magnified above His power. The Bible says, "God is love" (1 John 4:8), but it never says, "God is power."

So trust in your heavenly Father's love for you. As you come to Him in faith, His compassion will flow freely to you to heal you and make you whole.

Confession:

God's love and compassion reach out to me and heal me of every sickness and disease. He is not only able, but willing to make me whole. I am healed and whole!

MAY 30

"I Will"

And, behold, there came a leper and worshipped him, saying, Lord, if thou wilt, thou canst make me clean.

And Jesus put forth his hand, and touched him, saying, I will; be thou clean. And immediately his leprosy was cleansed. —Matthew 8:2,3

Jesus did two things when He was moved with compassion: First, He touched the leper. Second, He said something to him.

I always thought that the moment Jesus touched someone, that person was healed. But this man's leprosy didn't depart until Jesus *said* something. Apparently, His words were as important as His touch.

What did Jesus say to the leper? "Be thou clean." He gave the command for the leprosy to depart. But He also said something else—the phrase most Christians are looking for—*"I will."*

Notice what Jesus *didn't* say. He didn't say, "I won't" or "Later." He didn't say, "This disease is good for you" or "You deserve this" or "God sent this leprosy to teach you something."

Jesus didn't have to fast and pray to find out God's will. He just said, *"I will."* He knew God's will. He also knew one of His purposes for coming to earth was to destroy all the works of the devil (1 John 3:8), including sickness and disease. Part of Jesus' commission was to heal the sick, cleanse the lepers, raise the dead, cast out devils and bring deliverance to all mankind—spirit, soul and body.

God never told Jesus to just seek out a few here and there who needed healing. Jesus was sent to heal *all!* So when that man said, "If You will," Jesus responded, "Of course I will! Why shouldn't I heal you? God's will is healing for all mankind!"

───────── ✌ ─────────

Confession:

My Father sent Jesus to destroy the works of the devil, including sickness. Sickness isn't in God's plan for me. Therefore, by faith I receive my healing!

And as Jesus passed by, he saw a man which was blind from his birth.

[Jesus] spat on the ground, and made clay of the spittle, and he anointed the eyes of the blind man with the clay, and said unto him, Go, wash in the pool of Siloam, (which is by inter- pretation, Sent.)

He went his way therefore, and washed, and came seeing. —*John 9:1,6,7*

MAY 31

Step Out on the Word

Here was a man who had been blind from birth. Jesus walked over to him, spit in the dirt, made clay of the spittle, smeared the clay on the man's eyes and said, "Go, wash in the pool of Siloam."

That man could have said, "What do You mean, 'go wash in the pool of Siloam?' Look, Jesus, I don't need a bath—I need my sight! What is mud in my eyes going to do? Everyone will laugh at me. I'm waiting for You to work a miracle. I'm waiting for a feeling."

Instead, the Bible tells us that the blind man submitted himself to Jesus and went to the pool of Siloam and washed the mud off his eyes. He had to obey what Jesus told him to do with no feeling and no manifestation. Every symptom was still there; his eyes were still blind. The only difference was that he now had mud in his eyes! There was no physical change at all.

But Jesus said, "Go," and the blind man went. Jesus gave him an opportunity to walk by faith. The blind man took off for the pool of Siloam on the Word of God alone. That was his faith in operation. He went, he washed and he came again seeing. But he had to step out on the word Jesus spoke before he saw results.

Sometimes people say, "I wish Jesus would speak a word to me so I'd have something to believe." But God *has* given them something to believe—His Word!

So find out in God's Word what He has said about your situation. Then step out on that Word, believing what He said. Let your faith take hold of your answer. Release God's power in your life!

Confession:

Jesus has spoken to me in His Word. I choose to take Him at His Word, even when I'm not able to see my answer yet. Jesus says I'm healed, so I am healed!

JUNE 1

Jesus Is the Healer

And when they were come to the multitude, there came to him a certain man, kneeling down to him, and saying, Lord, have mercy on my son: for he is lunatick, and sore vexed: for ofttimes he falleth into the fire, and oft into the water. And I brought him to thy disciples, and they could not cure him.

Then Jesus answered and said, O faithless and perverse generation, how long shall I be with you? how long shall I suffer you? bring him hither to me. And Jesus rebuked the devil; and he departed out of him: and the child was cured from that very hour.

–Matthew 17:14-18

Some people have said, "I've been to every preacher in the country, and I couldn't get healed. It must not be God's will to heal me." The father in this account in Matthew 17 could have come to that same conclusion. After all, he'd taken his son to Jesus' own personal trainees! All of the disciples had prayed for his son, but the boy wasn't healed.

However, instead of concluding that it wasn't God's will to heal his son, the father took the boy to Jesus and explained, "I brought my son to Your disciples, and they couldn't heal him."

Jesus didn't turn to the man and say, "Well, it must not be the will of God then." He said, "Bring the boy to Me." You see, the man had taken his son to the wrong person to begin with. He'd tried to get the disciples to heal the boy, when *Jesus* is the healer.

I believe this proves something to the Church today. Jesus was the will of God in action. And when no one else could help that boy, Jesus revealed God's will by setting him free. Jesus didn't say, "Take him to My disciples." He said, "Bring him to *Me.*"

Some people don't receive their healing because they are trying to find some man to heal them. No man has the power to heal. Thank God for the ministry gifts and special anointings that operate in the Church today. But Jesus is the power behind those ministry gifts. He alone is the healer!

Confession:

Jesus is my healer. I come to Him in faith, and I am confident that I am healed!

And one of the multitude answered and said, Master, I have brought unto thee my son, which hath a dumb spirit; and wheresoever he taketh him, he teareth him: and he foameth, and gnasheth with his teeth, and pineth away: and I spake to thy disciples that they should cast him out; and they could not.

But if thou canst do any thing, have compassion on us, and help us. —Mark 9:17,18,22

JUNE 2

Call On the Mercy of God

In this Scripture passage, a man brought his son to Jesus' disciples and asked them to deliver his son from the seizures he was experiencing. The father said to Jesus, "An evil spirit is causing my son's condition. I asked Your disciples to cast it out, but they couldn't."

Then the disciples brought the boy to Jesus, and the man said, "If You can do anything, have compassion on us and help us."

The man called on the compassion, or the mercy, of God. When you call on the mercy of God, you are calling on His very nature. He is the God of mercy. He is the God of compassion.

In Matthew 20:30, two blind men called on Jesus. They cried out, "Have mercy on us, O Lord, thou son of David." The disciples and the people in the crowd tried to quiet them down, but they kept crying, "Have mercy on us, O Lord, thou son of David."

Jesus didn't say, "Do you want your sight?" He didn't say, "Do you want your healing?" He just asked, "What would you have Me do?" You see, the blind men in Matthew 20 and the father in Mark 9 called on God's nature. So Jesus responded, "I'm at your disposal. You called on the nature of God. Whatever you need, want or desire is yours because you've called on His nature to receive your answer. I'm here to meet your needs." And the blind men received their sight!

Confession:

My God is full of mercy and compassion. His nature is to give life, to save, to heal, to help, to deliver. I call upon His compassion and mercy and by faith receive the healing He has provided for me.

JUNE 3

A Withered Hand Becomes Whole

And it came to pass also on another sabbath, that he entered into the synagogue and taught: and there was a man whose right hand was withered. And the scribes and Pharisees watched him, whether he would heal on the sabbath day; that they might find an accusation against him.

But he knew their thoughts, and said to the man which had the withered hand, Rise up, and stand forth in the midst. And he arose and stood forth. Then Jesus said unto them, I will ask you one thing; Is it lawful on the sabbath days to do good, or to do evil? To save life, or to destroy it?

And looking round about upon them all, he said unto the man, Stretch forth thy hand. And he did so: and his hand was restored whole as the other. And they were filled with madness....

—Luke 6:6-11

Jesus was in the synagogue teaching, and a man with a withered hand was present. The scribes and Pharisees watched closely to see whether Jesus would heal on the Sabbath day. They wanted to accuse Jesus of breaking the law of the Sabbath.

Meanwhile, Jesus was looking for a way to show the goodness of God, the Lord of the Sabbath! Jesus called the man forward and said, "Stretch forth thy hand." The man stretched forth his hand, and immediately his hand was restored.

That made the religious leaders angry.

Jesus asked them, "What's better on the Sabbath day? To do good, or to do evil? To save life, or to destroy it?" While the scribes and Pharisees associated doing good with obeying man-made Sabbath traditions, Jesus associated doing good with healing and saving life.

Acts 10:38 says Jesus "went about doing *good....*" What good did Jesus do? *"...healing* all that were oppressed of the devil; for God was with him." Obviously, healing is good in God's sight!

Confession:

Jesus healed all who came to Him in faith, and He's still the same today. It's good in His sight when I come to Him and by faith receive my healing.

And it came to pass also on another sabbath, that he entered into the synagogue and taught: and there was a man whose right hand was withered.

And looking round about upon them all, he said unto the man, Stretch forth thy hand. And he did so: and his hand was restored whole as the other.   *—Luke 6:6,10*

JUNE 4

The Making of a Miracle

A man with a withered hand was in the synagogue, and Jesus called him forth. He said, "Stretch forth your hand," and He made the man's hand as whole as the other. A miracle had just occurred. However, that miracle wasn't just something that fell on this man; his faith worked.

How do we know that? Well, remember the man had a withered hand. Jesus called him forward and said, "Stretch out your hand." If that man had just been waiting on a miracle, he might have said, "What do you mean, stretch it forth? That's why I'm here—it doesn't stretch! I'm waiting for You to heal me so I *can* stretch it!"

But this man's faith was in operation. You see, faith *always* does what it can do. But if it stops there, it isn't real faith. Real faith does what it can do and then attempts to do what it cannot do.

So when Jesus said, "Stretch out your hand," the man stretched it out. A person can't stretch a hand that doesn't stretch, so the man wouldn't have even tried to stretch his withered hand if he weren't expecting something to happen.

Why did the man expect something to happen? Because he was in faith. How did he get in faith? Verse 6 says that Jesus "entered into the synagogue and *taught.*" The man had heard Jesus teach.

That was the way it usually happened in Jesus' ministry. Before most of the major miracles occurred, the people first heard Him teach. Then after they had heard the Word, they were healed. And the same is true today!

Confession:

*Faith comes by hearing, and hearing by the Word of God.
I hear the Word on healing and act on what it says to me,
and I confidently believe I receive my healing!*

JUNE 5

Partaking of the Ministry of Jesus

And again he entered into Capernaum after some days; and it was noised that he was in the house. And straightway many were gathered together, insomuch that there was no room to receive them, no, not so much as about the door: and he preached the word unto them.

And they come unto him, bringing one sick of the palsy, which was borne of four. And when they could not come nigh unto him for the press, they uncovered the roof where he was: and when they had broken it up, they let down the bed wherein the sick of the palsy lay.

When Jesus saw their faith, he said unto the sick of the palsy, Son, thy sins be forgiven thee.
                                                                    —Mark 2:1-5

Let's look at this miracle a little at a time. First, verse 1 says, "And again he entered into Capernaum." The word *again* indicates that Jesus must have been there before. Mark 1 mentions the first time He went to Capernaum. Many sick were healed, many devils were cast out and Jesus performed miracles all over the city. So when Jesus returned to Capernaum, the word got around. Soon the house where He was staying was packed to overflowing.

That's the way it's supposed to happen. As more and more people are healed, delivered and set free through the preaching of the Word, churches won't have buildings big enough to hold all the people. Word gets out when Jesus shows up!

We're about to see Jesus' ministry go forth through the Church as we've never seen it before. Of course, no one person will ever stand in the same anointing Jesus did. Jesus had the Spirit *without measure,* whereas each believer has the anointing *by measure.* But as the body of Christ, we are learning how to rise up in unity, and that same powerful anointing is beginning to sweep the earth again!

Confession:

Every time Jesus preached the Word, miracles began to happen.
The Holy Spirit teaches me that same living Word,
which produces miracles in my life each day!

And again he entered into Capernaum after some days; and it was noised that he was in the house. And straightway many were gathered together, insomuch that there was no room to receive them, no, not so much as about the door: and he preached the word unto them.

—Mark 2:1,2

JUNE 6

Hearing and Miracles Go Hand in Hand

Jesus gave the people something to believe. He preached the Word to them. He didn't tiptoe from town to town, healing a leper over here and a blind man over there and then teaching on the Beatitudes for a while. There was a method to what Jesus did.

In about 70 percent of His ministry, Jesus either stated or implied that *the people's faith* had made them whole. But if most people were healed through their faith, where did they get their faith? Did God lean over the balcony of heaven and zap them with a faith gun? No, they obtained faith the same way we do today: "Faith cometh by hearing, and hearing by the word of God" (Rom. 10:17).

Matthew 4:23 says, "And Jesus went about all Galilee, teaching in their synagogues, and preaching the gospel of the kingdom, and healing all manner of sickness and all manner of disease among the people." The healing came *after* the teaching and preaching.

Jesus had to teach the people the Word so they'd have faith to be healed. When they heard, the Word built their faith; then Jesus would tell them to act. When they acted on their faith, they were healed.

So often today, people are not healed because they aren't taking time to hear God's Word. They want a miracle, but they don't want to hear.

But as we feed on God's Word, miracles will begin to occur more and more in our lives. Hearing and miracles go hand in hand.

Confession:

*Faith comes when I hear God's Word.
I read and meditate upon the Word, and
my faith grows to receive the miracle I need.*

JUNE 7

God's Power To Heal

And it came to pass on a certain day, as he was teaching, that there were Pharisees and doctors of the law sitting by, which were come out of every town of Galilee, and Judaea, and Jerusalem: and the power of the Lord was present to heal them. —Luke 5:17

This verse says, "The power of the Lord was present to heal *them*." Who is "them"? The Pharisees and doctors of the law. Was it God's will to heal them? Well, it must have been His will. He wouldn't have sent His power to heal them if He hadn't wanted them healed. God isn't confused, and He doesn't waste His power.

How many of them were healed? One man, who was lowered through the roof, was healed. But to the best of our knowledge, not one of the Pharisees or doctors of the law received their healing.

Jesus said, "My meat is to do My Father's will." (John 4:34.) So it must have been God's will for Jesus to go to Capernaum and teach the Word. It also must have been God's will for the Pharisees and doctors of the law to be healed, because God sent His power. When God's power is present to heal, anyone who will receive that power by faith can be healed.

But if that's true, why are so many of us not getting healed? Our problem hasn't been a lack of power, but a lack of knowledge. God gave us the power when He gave the Holy Spirit. We just haven't known how to tap into it.

So make it a priority to learn how to receive from God. First, get the revelation that it's God's will to heal you. Second, act on that revelation—receive by faith God's power to heal you. Third, hold fast to your confession that the power of God is working in you, effecting a healing and a cure!

Confession:

God's power is available to me through the Word and the Holy Ghost. I tap into His power by believing, confessing and acting on the Word. God's Word works!

And it came to pass on a certain day, as he was teaching, that there were Pharisees and doctors of the law sitting by, which were come out of every town of Galilee, and Judea, and Jerusalem: and the power of the Lord was present to heal them. —Luke 5:17

JUNE 8

Don't Just Listen—Hear

The power of the Lord was present to heal the Pharisees and doctors of the law, but not one of them was healed. The Bible says Jesus was teaching, but how many present were actually hearing?

Someone may say, "Well, all of them must have been hearing; they were sitting right there in the room with Jesus."

Not necessarily so! Did you know you can be listening without hearing? I know that from experience. I've been in numerous conversations with my wife, Janet, where she suddenly stopped talking and said, "Mark, you haven't heard a word I've said!"

"I've been listening!" I always protest. But then I think, *Have I really been listening?* Although I can remember what Janet said five minutes earlier, my mind has been on something else. I've been listening; I know she's been talking. But I haven't heard what she's said.

Also, as a child growing up in church, I'd sit at the end of the family pew. Sometimes I'd prop one elbow on that arm rest and go to sleep during the sermon. Other times I'd stay awake. But awake or asleep, I didn't hear one thing that was said in the services from ages six to sixteen! Yes, it *is* possible to listen to people and still not hear a thing.

The Bible never said a word about the scribes, Pharisees and doctors of the law hearing. In fact, those religious leaders weren't hearing Him so faith could grow in their hearts; they were listening to find something to accuse Jesus with. Yet, despite the fact that this group was there for the wrong reason, God still sent His power to heal them. All they had to do was receive it by faith.

Confession:

I don't just listen; I hear the Word of God concerning healing. Then faith rises up in my heart to receive my healing, and I am healed!

JUNE 9

And they come unto him, bringing one sick of the palsy, which was borne of four.

–Mark 2:3

Get Tired of Being Sick!

This man who had palsy, or paralysis, apparently found four friends to pick him up and carry him to Jesus. But notice the way verse 3 is worded: "And they come unto him, bringing *one sick of the palsy.*" The man was sick of the palsy—sick *with* it and sick *of* it. He was tired of the whole mess.

I don't blame him. That's actually a good state of mind to be in. People will go after their healing when they're sick of being sick. They've had it; they're finished with it; they're tired of being sick! *No more!*

Janet and I were in a service where a man greatly used of God in the gifts of the Spirit was ministering in a healing line. At one point, he called a woman to the front and told her, "The Spirit of God is showing me right now exactly what is wrong with you." Then he proceeded to tell her exactly what her problem was.

The woman replied, "No, that's not it—and besides, I can live with it!" She probably will, too, bless her heart. She wasn't sick of being sick yet!

But this man in Mark 2 was. He was tired of being sick; he wanted to get rid of the palsy. So when Jesus spoke out his miracle, he was ready to receive! (vv. 11,12.)

That's when things happen—when we get tired of being dominated, depressed and overrun by the devil. That's when we're in for some blessings. That's when we jump out in faith and refuse to give up until we receive the miracle we need!

Confession:

I won't allow sickness or disease to remain in my body.
I don't put up with any illness or pain, because
God's Word is medicine to my flesh.

And they come unto him, bringing one sick of the palsy, which was borne of four. And when they could not come nigh unto him for the press, they uncovered the roof where he was: and when they had broken it up, they let down the bed wherein the sick of the palsy lay.

When Jesus saw their faith, he said unto the sick of the palsy, Son, thy sins be forgiven thee.

–Mark 2:3-5

JUNE 10

Determined Faith

Jesus had been in Capernaum before. (Mark 1:21-34.) During His first visit, the entire city had gathered around the door of the house where He was staying and had healed many sick and cast out many devils.

This time, the place filled up again, but with a different crowd—Pharisees and doctors of the law. These religious leaders didn't want healing or miracles. They came to try to catch Jesus saying something wrong so they could accuse Him. They were listening with their ears but resisting everything He said.

So the first time Jesus visited Capernaum, people came to be healed. The second time, many came to *stop* folks from being healed.

Sometimes doubt and unbelief are so strong in a place that it's difficult for anyone to receive from God. Jesus was in a situation like that on this second visit to Capernaum. God's power was present in the midst of a room packed with people. But there was so much unbelief in the room that no one was receiving healing.

So what did Jesus do? Luke 5:17 tells us, "And it came to pass on a certain day, *as he was teaching...."* Jesus knew the unbelief was strong, but He just kept on teaching. He knew that someone in the crowd would hear and that when that person heard, he'd be healed.

Suddenly, four men came carrying a man on a stretcher. The place was so full of people *not* getting healed that the one who wanted healing couldn't even squeeze in! So the man's friends found another way into the building. And when Jesus saw the determined faith of these four men, their paralyzed friend was healed.

Confession:

Those who won't receive God's goodness and mercy aren't going to keep me from receiving all that God says is mine. I will enjoy salvation, healing and every other blessing God has provided for me!

JUNE 11

Bring Them to Jesus

And they come unto him, bringing one sick of the palsy, which was borne of four. And when they could not come nigh unto him for the press, they uncovered the roof where he was: and when they had broken it up, they let down the bed wherein the sick of the palsy lay. —Mark 2:3,4

Here we see four men bringing a paralyzed man to Jesus. I can't prove this, but I wouldn't be surprised if those four men were some of those who had been healed the last time Jesus had been in town. They seemed so convinced that if they could get their friend to Jesus, he would be healed.

These four men had to take the roof apart to get the paralyzed man down in the middle of the room! And they must have been convinced that Jesus wouldn't turn anyone down who came for healing. They didn't say, "Lord, heal him, if it be Thy will." No, the four men were sure their friend would receive his healing.

Matthew 8:16 talks about others who brought the sick to Jesus: "When the even was come, they brought unto him many that were possessed with devils: and he cast out the spirits with his word, and healed all that were sick." Notice the verse says, *"They* brought unto him." That phrase is used several times in the Gospels. (Matt. 9:32; Mark 1:32.)

Did you ever wonder who "they" were? Did Jesus have His own healing teams? No, "they" are people who don't need anything themselves but go out and find folks who do need something and bring them to Jesus. They bring people because they're fully convinced that the people's needs will be met.

The truth is, "they" are the body of believers! People sometimes say, "What if I invite someone to church, and God doesn't do anything spectacular?" Yes, but what if He does? And if God doesn't do anything miraculous, the people we bring to church will still hear His Word.

So fulfill your part of the "they" work of this world: Go out and find folks who need help, and bring them to Jesus!

Confession:

I can do the "they" work! I've experienced the healing power of Jesus, and I know without a doubt that when I bring others to Him, they will be healed.

And they come unto him, bringing one sick of the palsy, which was borne of four. And when they could not come nigh unto him for the press, they uncovered the roof where he was: and when they had broken it up, they let down the bed wherein the sick of the palsy lay.

When Jesus saw their faith, he said unto the sick of the palsy, Son, thy sins be forgiven thee.

–Mark 2:3-5

JUNE 12

Faith Won't Quit

You can see in this passage of Scripture one of the differences between faith and hope. Four men carried this man to where Jesus was. But the building was so full that they couldn't get him in.

Now, hope would have said, "Well, we tried, but we couldn't get our friend to Jesus. We might as well go home." Hope will go just so far and quit. It says, "Well, I tried that faith business, but it didn't work." Then it will give up and throw in the towel.

But faith won't quit! It has tenacity. It says, "Let's go up on the roof. We aren't quitting now!"

Faith digs its heels in and says, "I know whom I have believed, and am persuaded that he is able to keep that which I have committed unto him against that day" (2 Tim. 1:12). It says, "I'm not moving! I know what the Word says. I know healing belongs to me, and I'm not going without it! I believe the Word of God. Who cares what I feel like?"

So the four men took the roof apart, probably making a big hole in it. Then they lowered the man into the room right in front of Jesus. Jesus had been teaching for some time and hadn't yet seen a spark of faith. But now He was seeing faith come through the roof! And when Jesus saw the men's faith, their friend was healed.

No one likes tests and trials, but that's the atmosphere in which faith thrives. In the midst of a trial, faith has to flex its muscles and grow. Our heads may give us trouble during those hard times. But if we're really in faith, we won't quit!

Confession:

Jesus bought and paid for my healing, and I have it by faith. I persistently walk by faith regardless of my feelings or circumstances. In Jesus' name, I am healed!

JUNE 13

Forgiveness and Healing–A Package Deal

When Jesus saw their faith, he said unto the sick of the palsy, Son, thy sins be forgiven thee.

But there were certain of the scribes sitting there, and reasoning in their hearts, Why doth this man thus speak blasphemies? who can forgive sins but God only?　　　*–Mark 2:5-7*

The paralyzed man needed to be healed, but Jesus didn't say, "Get up and walk." Instead, He told the man his sins were forgiven. That presented a problem to the religious leaders sitting there in that house. They didn't believe that Jesus was God manifest in the flesh, so they didn't believe He could forgive sins.

But Jesus was proving something to us through this incident. He was making the point that *forgiveness and healing go hand in hand.* When we receive one, the other belongs to us as well.

Mark 2:8 says, "Jesus perceived in his spirit that they so reasoned within themselves." Then Jesus asked the religious leaders, "Which is easier to say: 'Your sins are forgiven,' or 'Take up your bed and walk'?"

That didn't make sense to me for a long time. Then I saw it. It's so simple. Jesus was saying, "It doesn't matter which one I say. If I say, 'Get up and walk' that means you're forgiven. If I say, 'You're forgiven,' that means 'Get up and walk.' The two always go together. Once you have one, the other automatically belongs to you. It's a package deal!"

Confession:

I'm forgiven! I'm healed! Healing belongs to me as surely as forgiveness does. Both are included in my covenant with my heavenly Father.

When Jesus saw their faith, he said unto the
sick of the palsy, Son, thy sins be forgiven thee.

—Mark 2:5

Healing Comes With Forgiveness

J esus wasn't known for being a diplomat. He wasn't on the earth to please man; He was here to please God. He really didn't care what men thought, as long as He was pleasing to God. So, knowing He would be in trouble with the religious leaders, He looked at the paralyzed man and said, "Son, your sins are forgiven."

All through the Bible, forgiveness of sin and physical healing have always been a package deal. Jesus wasn't trying to make those religious leaders angry; He was trying to prove a point to them. So Jesus gave them an illustrated sermon. He preached, and then He demonstrated His point. He said, "If I say you're forgiven, it means you're also healed."

Back then, people thought Jesus could heal but couldn't forgive sins. Today most people believe Jesus can forgive sins but can't heal! The truth is that during Jesus' ministry on earth He could do both, and today He can do both. He never turns anyone down for either forgiveness or healing.

Some people ask, "If I'm sick in my body, does that mean I'm not forgiven of my sins?" No, if you've made Jesus Lord of your life and received forgiveness for your sins, then healing belongs to you whether you know it or not. You may as well reach out and take hold of the blessing that's rightfully yours!

Confession:

God has provided forgiveness for my sins and healing
for my physical body. As surely as I know
He wants me forgiven, I know He wants me well.

JUNE 15

Healing–Proof of Jesus' Power To Forgive

Whether is it easier to say to the sick of the palsy, Thy sins be forgiven thee; or to say, Arise, and take up thy bed, and walk? But that ye may know that the Son of man hath power on earth to forgive sins, (he saith to the sick of the palsy,) I say unto thee, Arise, and take up thy bed, and go thy way into thine house.

–Mark 2:9-11

What proof could Jesus give the religious leaders that the paralyzed man's sins were forgiven? Jesus knew exactly what proof to give them. He said, "When I finish here, you'll know the Son of Man has power on earth to forgive sins."

Jesus wasn't just speaking to the man on the stretcher; He was talking to the whole group. Then He told the paralyzed man, "Arise, and take up thy bed, and go thy way into thine house. And immediately he arose, took up the bed, and went forth before them all; insomuch that they were all amazed" (vv. 11,12).

Jesus said, "I'll prove to you that I have the power to forgive sins: I'll tell this man to get up and walk, and he *will* do it!" He did, and they were all shocked!

If the religious leaders had been as knowledgeable about the Scriptures as they were about their traditions, they would have jumped up and exclaimed, "Jesus is the Messiah! He is the One we are looking for!" Remember, these were the Old Testament scholars—Pharisees and doctors of the law. They should have known that every time God gave them a picture of the Messiah's crucifixion in the Old Testament, two things happened: People were forgiven of their sins and healed of their diseases.

How does that help us? Well, we know forgiveness and healing were always given together under the old covenant. That assures us that as children of God under the new covenant, physical healing automatically belongs to us!

Confession:

Under the old covenant, healing and forgiveness were connected. I live under a better covenant based on better promises, so forgiveness and healing are still available to me. I am both healed and forgiven!

Whether is it easier to say to the sick of the palsy, Thy sins be forgiven thee; or to say, Arise, and take up thy bed, and walk?

–Mark 2:9

JUNE 16

Two Inseparable Blessings

Forgiveness of sins in the new birth belongs to everyone. But we've tried to make healing a different matter, saying, "You never know whom God will heal." We've taken what God put together in the Atonement and made them two different subjects.

But when Jesus went to the Cross, He took our sin, iniquity, sickness and disease. Forgiveness and healing were purchased together at the Cross, and we can't take them apart.

Forgiveness and healing are not even two different subjects. Healing is nothing more than the new birth affecting the human body. Certainly, sin takes a toll on the human body. You've probably looked at someone and thought to yourself, *Boy, that person has lived a tough life!* You were saying that the person's sinful lifestyle had an adverse effect on his body.

Well, if sin can have an effect, righteousness can have an effect as well. When the new birth, which takes place in the inner man, works its way to the outer man, the results are strength, healing and health.

You may ask, "Why haven't strength, healing and health worked their way to *my* outer man before now?" Well, perhaps you have not been thinking, believing and talking in line with God's Word.

Jesus told the religious leaders, "I'll prove to you I can forgive your sins by telling a sick man to get up well." Then He turned to the sick man and said, "Get up and walk." The man got up and walked away completely whole! This miracle proved Jesus' case, because forgiveness of sins and healing always go together in the kingdom of God.

Whom does God want healed? Anyone who is forgiven. Who is forgiven? Anyone who has received Jesus as Savior. Healing belongs to every believer because forgiveness and healing always go hand in hand.

Confession:

God's Word says that both forgiveness and healing are available to me through the new birth. I believe the Word, so I walk in the fullness of all its benefits!

JUNE 17

A Gentile Woman's Great Faith

And, behold, a woman of Canaan came out of the same coasts, and cried unto him, saying, Have mercy on me, O Lord, thou Son of David; my daughter is grievously vexed with a devil. But he answered her not a word.

And his disciples came and besought him, saying, Send her away; for she crieth after us.

But he answered and said, I am not sent but unto the lost sheep of the house of Israel.

Then came she and worshipped him, saying, Lord, help me.

But he answered and said, It is not meet to take the children's bread, and to cast it to dogs.

And she said, Truth, Lord: yet the dogs eat of the crumbs which fall from their masters' table.

Then Jesus answered and said unto her, O woman, great is thy faith: be it unto thee even as thou wilt. And her daughter was made whole from that very hour.

–Matthew 15:22-28

If anyone had a right to give up, this woman did. Her daughter was oppressed by an evil spirit and desperately needed to be set free. But this woman was a Syrophenician, a Gentile; she didn't have a covenant with God.

Even so, this Syrophenician woman came to Jesus, the healer and source of power, and cried out for help. At first, Jesus ignored her. Then He turned to His disciples and said, "I'm not sent to help her anyway. I'm sent to the lost sheep of Israel."

I used to read this Scripture passage and think, *Why did Jesus harass that poor woman?* But Jesus didn't harass her; He *located* her to see if she was in faith. Someone may say, "I thought Jesus knew everything." No, Jesus only knew what God showed Him. But Jesus knew that if the woman came in faith, she could get results even though she had no legal covenant with God.

This woman didn't quit. Hope would have given up, but her faith held on. And as a result, her daughter was made whole!

Confession:

I have a covenant with my Father, and healing is included in that covenant. I have confidence in what the Lord Jesus has provided for me, and I will never give up!

Then Jesus answered and said unto her, O woman, great is thy faith: be it unto thee even as thou wilt. And her daughter was made whole from that very hour. —Matthew 15:28

JUNE 18

What Is "Great Faith"?

J esus said the Syrophenician woman had great faith. If she had faith under the old covenant, we surely ought to have faith under the new covenant.

What made this woman's faith great? She put so much confidence in Jesus' Word that she came for healing for her daughter—and didn't even bring the daughter with her! In essence, she said to Jesus, "You just say the word, and my daughter will be healed."

In Matthew 8:6-8, a Roman centurion displayed that kind of great faith. He came to Jesus and said, "My servant is at home sick."

Jesus answered, "I will come and heal him."

He said, "No, I'm not worthy that you should come under my roof. If you'll just speak the Word, my servant will be healed."

Many people in the Bible operated in faith: the ten lepers (Luke 17:12-19), the nobleman at Capernaum whose son was sick (John 4:46-53) and, of course, Abraham (Rom. 4:19). They all operated in faith, saying, "Whatever You say, Lord, we'll believe it. We take You at Your Word. We don't need goose bumps; we don't need burning bushes. You say it, and we'll go our way believing."

Great faith always takes God at His Word. That's why, in Mark 11:24, Jesus said, "When you pray, believe the answer has been granted to you, and you will have it!"

Confession:
The written Word is God's word to me today. I believe, I receive and I go my way praising and thanking God for my answer. I have great faith because I take God at His word!

JUNE 19

It Pays To Persevere

Then came she and worshipped him, saying, Lord, help me.

But he answered and said, It is not meet to take the children's bread, and to cast it to dogs.

And she said, Truth, Lord: yet the dogs eat of the crumbs which fall from their masters' table.

Then Jesus answered and said unto her, O woman, great is thy faith: be it unto thee even as thou wilt. And her daughter was made whole from that very hour. —Matthew 15:25-28

Under similar circumstances most of us would have given up, but not this woman. First Jesus ignored her; then He said to His disciples, "I'm not even sent to help her." Still, "came she and worshipped him, saying, Lord, help me." This Gentile mother wouldn't leave Jesus alone!

Then Jesus told her it wasn't right to take the children's bread and give it to *dogs*. Jesus called her a *dog!* Most of us would have gone home angry. But look what she told Jesus: "Truth, Lord: yet the dogs eat of the crumbs which fall from their masters' table."

You may have thought she responded that way because of her humble attitude. "O Lord, just give me one of the crumbs from Your table!" But she was really saying, "Lord, I don't need the whole loaf. Give that to the children, although most of them won't take it. Just give me a crumb. I know what Your bread will do."

She was not talking about how much humility she had; she was talking about how powerful Jesus' bread is! She was saying, "Call me anything you want to, but heal my daughter."

Then Jesus told her, "With faith like that, you can have anything you want!" Jesus had taken this woman to the limits, and she'd passed the test. He knew her faith would turn His power loose.

Great faith always takes God at His Word, and that's what this Gentile woman did. It paid to hang on and refuse to give up, because she received the answer she'd come for: Her daughter was made whole!

Confession:

I hold fast to God's Word with tenacity until my healing is manifested. I refuse to give up, because I know that God's Word works!

But [Jesus] answered and said, It is not meet to take the children's bread, and to cast it to dogs.

–Matthew 15:26

JUNE 20

Healing–The Children's Bread

The Syrophenician woman wanted healing for her daughter. Jesus called healing "the children's bread." If healing was the children's bread back then, it's still the children's bread today.

Who were the children back then? The lost sheep of the house of Israel. Who are the children today? These Scriptures tell us:

The Spirit itself beareth witness with our spirit, that we are the children of God.

Romans 8:16

Behold, what manner of love the Father hath bestowed upon us, that we should be called the sons of God....

1 John 3:1

But as many as received him, to them gave he power to become the sons of God, even to them that believe on his name.

John 1:12

We are the children! Healing is *our* bread! We have been grafted into God's family through the shed blood of Jesus Christ. Through the new birth, we are now new creatures in Christ, the children of God.

Psalm 37:25 says, "I have been young, and now am old; yet have I not seen the righteous forsaken, *nor his seed begging bread.*" We don't have to beg for bread, because the bread belongs to us through Jesus Christ. It is part of our redemption, our covenant, our inheritance in Christ. God doesn't want us begging for healing, because healing belongs to us!

Confession:

Jesus called healing the children's bread. I qualify for that bread, for I'm a child of God. I don't beg for healing; I receive it now because it already belongs to me!

JUNE 21

"Be It Unto Thee as Thou Wilt"

Then Jesus answered and said unto her, O woman, great is thy faith: be it unto thee even as thou wilt. And her daughter was made whole from that very hour. —Matthew 15:28

Did Jesus say, "Oh, woman, great is thy faith. Be it unto thee as God wills"? No, He said, "Be it unto thee even *as thou wilt*"—and her daughter was made whole. You see, this woman's will was involved.

Sometimes people don't set their wills into action as they try to get healed. They hope and pray that their faith works. But if they don't receive their healing in a certain time frame, they go another direction. They find it easier to keep an alternative route open rather than to hold fast to their stance of faith.

But this woman set her will in motion. She willed to get her daughter healed, and there *was* no alternative way.

She came to Jesus and said, "My daughter is grievously vexed with a devil." Jesus didn't speak a word to her. She fell down and worshiped Him, and He said, "It's not right to take the children's bread and cast it to dogs."

But the Syrophenician woman said, "Well, even the dogs get the crumbs that fall off their masters' tables." She called Jesus her Master. She wouldn't let anything defeat her—not humiliation, pride or anything else. She was going after healing for her daughter no matter what it took!

We need to realize that God has provided healing for us and then make a bold stance of faith. We can set our wills in action by saying, "I'm going after my healing, and I'm not quitting until it's manifested!" When we get that stubborn and tenacious in our faith, we'll see results!

Confession:

Such a high price was paid for my healing that I refuse to go without it. I know what is mine by faith, and I will not quit until it manifests in my life!

And a certain woman, which had an issue of blood twelve years, and had suffered many things of many physicians, and had spent all that she had, and was nothing bettered, but rather grew worse, when she had heard of Jesus, came in the press behind, and touched his garment. For she said, If I may touch but his clothes, I shall be whole.

And straightway the fountain of her blood was dried up; and she felt in her body that she was healed of that plague.   —Mark 5:25-29

JUNE 22

The Touch of Faith

Jesus was walking through the crowd. Everyone in the crowd was pushing toward Him, but no one was being healed. No miracles were occurring, and no power was flowing out of Him.

Suddenly Jesus felt power surge out of Him. (v. 30.) He stopped and said, "Who touched My clothes?" His disciples replied, "Everyone is touching You!" But Jesus recognized a different touch. It wasn't the physical touch He sensed; it was the touch of faith.

Why was this woman the only one in the crowd who was healed? Jesus answered that question in verse 34: "And he said unto her, Daughter, thy faith hath made thee whole; go in peace, and be whole of thy plague."

The rest of the crowd had come wondering what was going to happen and thinking, *Well, I'll give this Jesus fellow a try.* But this woman had come in faith; she had *known* what would happen when she touched the hem of Jesus' garment. She had come believing and expecting—and, therefore, she received!

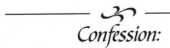

Confession:

I am thoroughly convinced that I can touch Jesus with my faith just as the woman with the issue of blood did. My faith draws that same healing power out of Him, and healing is what I receive!

JUNE 23

Our Faith Releases God's Power

And Jesus, immediately knowing in himself that virtue had gone out of him, turned him about in the press, and said, Who touched my clothes?

And he said unto her, Daughter, thy faith hath made thee whole; go in peace, and be whole of thy plague.   *–Mark 5:30,34*

Jesus didn't deliver healing to this woman with the issue of blood. He didn't sovereignly walk up to her and say, "God has chosen to make you well." No, the woman crept up behind Jesus in the crowd, touched the hem of His garment and was healed. And her great faith drew so much healing power out of Jesus that it stopped Him in His tracks!

Jesus asked, "Who touched Me?" I'm sure everyone thought His question was a little strange because *everyone* was trying to touch Him. His disciples exclaimed, "The multitude is thronging You! How can You ask, 'Who touched Me?'"

Then Jesus looked around to find the person who had touched Him in faith. The woman returned to Him, trembling with fear, and told Him what had happened to her. Jesus didn't rebuke her; instead, He praised her faith.

You see, the woman's faith released Jesus' power. And if faith released His power 2000 years ago, our faith still releases God's power today!

Confession:

God's power heals all who come to Him in faith.
My faith releases His healing power in my life.
My faith and His power make me whole!

And he said unto her, Daughter, thy faith hath made thee whole; go in peace, and be whole of thy plague. —Mark 5:34

You Can Believe for Your Miracle!

If this woman's faith made her whole, our faith can make us whole as well.

Sometimes folks say, "Oh, but it was easier for her. Jesus was standing right there!" No, not a chance. You see, this woman wasn't born again. The new birth wasn't available until the death, burial and resurrection of Jesus.

Therefore, the woman was under the old covenant. She wasn't alive unto God. She wasn't filled with the Holy Ghost. She wasn't a temple of the living God. Her redemption hadn't been purchased yet.

This woman received her blessings on a promissory note. Jesus was saying, "I'll give them to you now, and I'll pay for them later."

Some say, "Yes, but it was still easy for her to believe for her healing because Jesus was standing right there." Well, where is Jesus today? He said, "My Father and I will come and make our abode with you. Where two or more are gathered in My name, there I am in their midst." (John 14:23; Matt. 18:20.)

Jesus is *in* us through the person of the Holy Spirit. We live under a new and better covenant established upon better promises. We should not only be able to do the same things this woman did, but it should be a lot easier! We're full of the life, nature and ability of God. We're born-again, new creatures in Christ Jesus. We're not just friends of God; we're part of His *family*—faith sons and daughters of a faith God. We *can* receive our miracle by faith!

Confession:

I am the child of a healing God. My healing has already been bought and paid for, and I receive it by faith!

JUNE 25

Our Faith Plus God's Power Equals Healing

And Jesus, immediately knowing in himself that virtue had gone out of him, turned him about in the press, and said, Who touched my clothes?

And he said unto her, Daughter, thy faith hath made thee whole; go in peace, and be whole of thy plague. —Mark 5:30,34

What was it that made this woman whole? The Bible says Jesus sensed "virtue," or power, go out of Him at the same time that she felt in her body that she was healed of the issue of blood. (vv. 29,30.) But then Jesus said, "Daughter, your faith made you whole." So which was it? Did Jesus' power heal her, or was it her faith?

It was a combination of the two. If He'd said, "Daughter, My power has healed you," everyone in the crowd could have asked, "Why did Your power heal her and not me? I need a miracle too."

Jesus answered that question before it was asked. He said, "Daughter, your *faith* made you whole." Then everyone knew why she'd gotten healed and they hadn't.

Jesus' healing power would have gone into anyone in that crowd who had come in faith. But no faith was involved when the others touched Jesus. Therefore, God's power wasn't released on their behalf, and the woman was the only one healed.

Even today we need a combination of faith and power. God's power performs the miracle, but our faith releases His power to work in our lives.

Jesus was anointed with the Holy Ghost and with power. (Acts 10:38.) By His power, Jesus healed the woman with the issue of blood 2000 years ago, and His power is still the same today. He will heal us of any sickness, disease or infirmity the enemy tries to throw our way. God's power is always available to us as His children. It's just a matter of learning how to tap into that divine source of power by faith!

Confession:

The woman with the issue of blood released God's power with her faith. By faith I release that same power into my life. God's power works in me and makes me whole!

When she had heard of Jesus, came in the press behind, and touched his garment. For she said, If I may touch but his clothes, I shall be whole.

—Mark 5:27,28

Make Your Miracle Happen!

There are three kinds of people in the world: those who watch things happen, those who make things happen and those who wonder what is happening.

Similarly, we have three kinds of people in the body of Christ. First, we have folks who wonder what's happening most of the time. Then, we have another group of believers who watch things happen. In other words, they watch folks get healed and receive miracles and think, *Man, I'd like to get in the middle of that! Oh, I wish God would do something like that for me!*

But then there's the third kind of Christian. These believers are the bunch who make things happen. I don't know about you, but that's the group I want to be part of! I don't want to wait for anything to happen; I want to be out there making it happen!

Some folks say, "Well, that's pushing God." No, we don't push or control God. No one does. We just act on what He has already said in His Word.

This woman with the issue of blood didn't wonder what was happening or wait for something to happen. She *made* something happen with her faith. She didn't say, "Oh, I wish Jesus would come to my house." No, she went to find *Him.*

Everyone else in the crowd was touching Jesus, and power wasn't flowing into any of them. But this woman didn't touch Him with her hand only; she touched Him with her *faith.* Power flowed out of Him into her, and she was instantly healed.

And notice, Jesus not only turned around and commended the woman, but He had her testify before the entire crowd to show how faith works. He tried to help some of the other folks get into faith. If they'd done the same thing this woman had, they would have received their own miracles.

Confession:

I receive from God just as this woman did. I find in the Word that Jesus healed all kinds of sickness and disease. I ask for my healing, touching Jesus with my faith, and I believe I receive my miracle!

JUNE 27

Change the Course of Your Life

And a certain woman, which had an issue of blood twelve years...when she had heard of Jesus....
—Mark 5:25,27

The woman with the issue of blood had been sick for a very long time. She'd seen every doctor in the country and spent everything she had trying to get better. She desired healing with all her heart, but nothing had helped; she'd only grown worse.

What was the first step this woman took that totally changed her condition? What did she do that set her on a new course toward healing? Mark 5:27 gives us the answer: "When she had *heard....*"

Nothing happened in this woman's life until she heard. That may sound like a small thing, but hearing is the biggest factor in changing the course of a person's life. All through the Bible, we find a direct correlation between hearing and healing.

What did she hear? "When she had heard of Jesus...." In John 1:1, Jesus is called *the Word.* So when the Bible says, "She had heard of Jesus," it could just as well say, "She heard *the Word.*" Psalm 107:20 says, "He sent his word, and healed them...."

Jesus doesn't dwell among us today in the flesh, but we still have the written Word. As we set ourselves to continually hear the Word, our faith will grow. That's the first step to changing the course of our lives!

Confession:

Jesus, the Word made flesh, was sent to heal me.
The power in God's written Word heals me as
I hear it, believe it and act upon it in faith.

> *And a certain woman, which had an issue of blood twelve years, and had suffered many things of many physicians, and had spent all that she had, and was nothing bettered, but rather grew worse.* —Mark 5:25,26

JUNE 28

Get Tenacious in Your Faith

This woman had *tenacity.* Tenacity means stubbornness. We have to be stubborn if we are going to walk in God's best. That doesn't mean we are to be stubborn with other people, but we must be stubborn in our stand on God's Word.

Now, tenacity could also be said to mean "resistance to flow." Many people "flow" with whatever word or wind of doctrine comes along. They say, "The Word says I'm healed, but the doctors tell me there is no hope." These people are double-minded, flowing back and forth between God's promises and man's opinions.

But this woman got tenacious about her healing. She heard of Jesus, and she decided to go the faith route. She'd been to every doctor in the country, and they had probably pronounced her incurable. She didn't have any natural hope left.

So she decided to flow against natural circumstances. It wasn't easy to do that, because she was weak, sick and broke. Besides that, she had to flow against a multitude of people crowding around Jesus. She had to press through that crowd until she finally reached Him.

The flow of the natural realm was telling her, "Give up, lady. This won't work. You've tried everything. Remember, the doctor said you can't make it."

But the woman got stubborn about it. She wouldn't flow with what the doctors said. She was tenacious, resistant to flow. She pressed through the crowd, touched Jesus' garment and was healed.

Thank God for good doctors. But we have the Word of God, which is higher than any other belief, thought or expert opinion. And we need to get stubborn about holding fast to that anointed Word, no matter what it looks like in the natural!

Confession:

*I'm stubborn about standing on the Word of God.
Circumstances don't move me. I don't walk by sight—
I walk by faith in God's Word!*

JUNE 29

Take a Stand!

And a certain woman, which had an issue of blood twelve years...came in the press behind, and touched his garment. —Mark 5:25,27

The more you consider this woman with the issue of blood, the more you understand that she had to be stubborn. Under the Jewish law, she was considered unclean. When a woman with an issue of blood came out in public, she risked being stoned.

As if that weren't bad enough, notice whom Jesus was walking with at the time: "And, behold, there cometh one of the rulers of the synagogue, Jairus by name" (v. 22).

Jesus was on His way to Jairus' house to heal his daughter when He perceived that power had flowed out of Him and stopped to find out who had touched Him. As a ruler of the synagogue, Jairus had authority to have this woman stoned.

This woman had to be tenacious, stubborn, resistant to flow. She had to overcome her fear and go against religious leaders.

You know, some ministers say, "Well, you just can't be healed. God doesn't do that anymore." When that happens, people have to override what those ministers are saying about healing in order to receive their healing.

This woman had to overcome unbelief, fear and weakness. She had to decide that no matter what came against her, she was going to receive her healing.

We have to get to that same point and make the same decision: "I don't care what anyone says. I don't care what it looks like, seems like or feels like. I'm taking a stand on God's Word, and that's all there is to it!"

Confession:

I will not be moved by circumstances or by what others say about my situation. I am moved only by what God's Word says. No sickness is too hard for my Father to heal. I receive my healing today!

And [Jesus] was teaching in one of the synagogues on the sabbath. And, behold, there was a woman which had a spirit of infirmity eighteen years, and was bowed together, and could in no wise lift up herself.

And when Jesus saw her, he called her to him, and said unto her, Woman, thou art loosed from thine infirmity. And he laid his hands on her: and immediately she was made straight, and glorified God. —Luke 13:10-13

JUNE 30

"Thou Art Loosed!"

This woman had been bowed over for eighteen years. That's a tough condition—eighteen years of looking at your shoestrings! The woman couldn't straighten her back and stand straight. She must have been in tremendous pain.

But then Jesus touched her and said, "Woman, thou art loosed from thine infirmity." Immediately, she was made straight, and she glorified God!

Jesus got her attention with His first words to her: "Woman, you are loosed." In other words, "You were set free a long time ago. Now you just need to get rid of the symptoms." She was the daughter of Abraham. She was loosed, but she didn't know it.

It's the same thing with Christians today. The Bible says those whom the Son sets free are free indeed. (John 8:36.)

We're loosed from all the works of the enemy, whether we realize it or not. But it's time to *act* loosed. We were re-created in Jesus to walk free of all sickness and disease, so let's do that today!

Confession:

Because of Jesus, I am loosed from any infirmity. I am free from all circumstances and symptoms, because I hear, believe and act on the Word.

JULY 1

Don't Miss an Opportunity To Act

And [Jesus] was teaching in one of the synagogues on the sabbath. And, behold, there was a woman which had a spirit of infirmity eighteen years, and was bowed together, and could in no wise lift up herself.

And when Jesus saw her, he called her to him, and said unto her, Woman, thou art loosed from thine infirmity. And he laid his hands on her: and immediately she was made straight, and glorified God. —Luke 13:10-13

Jesus called the woman who was bowed over to come to Him. He didn't walk back to her in the crowd and deliver her miracle to her. Why didn't He? Why did Jesus make that poor woman come hobbling to Him? It would have been easier for Him to walk to her than for her to walk to Him. After all, she'd been bowed over for eighteen years, and He was healthy.

But Jesus was giving the woman an opportunity to act in faith. How do we know her faith was in operation? Because faith always acts on the Word, and the woman had been hearing the Word.

Look back at verse 10: "And he was *teaching* in one of the synagogues on the sabbath." Jesus was always putting something into people to believe. And when they believed and acted on it, they got results.

If the woman had told Jesus, "No, I can't come to You," it would have been evident that she wasn't expecting anything. She wouldn't have made the difficult effort to come forward if she hadn't expected to walk back healthy. But this woman was in faith. And when Jesus called her to come forward, she acted on her faith and received her miracle!

Confession:

Jesus calls me to Himself through the Word. He gives me opportunity to believe Him and to receive from Him all I need. Through Jesus, I am delivered from every yoke of bondage. I am free!

And he laid his hands on her: and immediately she was made straight, and glorified God. And the ruler of the synagogue answered with indignation, because that Jesus had healed on the sabbath day....

The Lord then answered him, and said, Thou hypocrite, doth not each one of you on the sabbath loose his ox or his ass from the stall, and lead him away to watering? And ought not this woman, being a daughter of Abraham, whom Satan hath bound, lo, these eighteen years, be loosed from this bond on the sabbath day?

–Luke 13:13-16

JULY 2

Loosed From the Devil's Bondage

When Jesus healed this woman, the religious people got angry. Isn't it amazing how religious people never change? They still get angry when people are healed today. Often people are angry when someone else is healed and they're not.

This story proves something else to me. The Bible says over and over again that the majority of Jesus' healings took place on the Sabbath, the Jews' sacred day. To me, this proves that healing is a sacred thing to God. However, the ruler of the synagogue didn't think healing was sacred at all. Jesus rebuked him, saying, "You'd water your animals on the Sabbath, but you wouldn't let this little woman get healed!"

Also, notice what this woman did as soon as Jesus healed her: "Immediately she was made straight, *and glorified God."* Some people say, "Well, God is getting glory through my sickness." But the Bible says that God got the glory when the sick woman was *healed.* She wasn't glorifying God much while she was sick. But as soon as she was healed, she glorified God with all her heart! If you'd been bowed over for eighteen years and suddenly stood up straight—healed and whole, delivered from the devil's bondage—you'd glorify God too!

Confession:

My Father has set me free from the kingdom of darkness.
I am loosed from all bondage, and I give all the glory to God!

JULY 3

Sickness— Bondage or Blessing?

And ought not this woman, being a daughter of Abraham, whom Satan hath bound, lo, these eighteen years, be loosed from this bond on the sabbath day? —Luke 13:16

Let's see what we can learn from this verse. First, Jesus called sickness *bondage*. We don't know the specific disease this woman had. It could have been crippling arthritis. The Bible called it a spirit of infirmity. But whatever it was, Jesus never called her sickness a blessing. Nor did He say, "Ought not this woman whom Satan hath *blessed* these eighteen years be loosed?" He also didn't say, "Whom *God* hath blessed these eighteen years." No, God's blessing was in sending Jesus to loose the woman from her infirmity.

God never had anything good to say about sickness. In fact, He detested it so much that He sent His own Son to bear all the sickness of the world upon Himself. Sickness was never called a blessing in the Bible, and anyone who calls it a blessing today doesn't know what the Bible says.

If sickness and disease are from God, then Jesus was fighting against God when He healed people. If sickness and disease are from God, then Jesus robbed God of His glory when He called sickness a bondage of Satan.

Thank God, the Bible sets us free from wrong thinking and wrong believing so we can enjoy the blessings of healing and health!

Confession:

I'm not confused about where sickness came from. Sickness is a bondage from Satan. God wants me to live free of sickness and pain, so I choose to walk in health today!

And ought not this woman, being a daughter of Abraham, whom Satan hath bound, lo, these eighteen years, be loosed from this bond on the sabbath day?   *–Luke 13:16*

JULY 4

Satan Is the Author of Sickness

We see from this Scripture that (1) sickness is a bondage and (2) Satan is the author of sickness.

For years, I've heard people say, "God chose to have me sick." But Jesus said *Satan* bound the woman; God didn't.

The truth is that God detests sickness as much as He detests sin, because sickness is a result of the original sin. Sickness didn't come into the world until sin did. When God ruled and reigned on the earth through Adam, there was no sickness on the earth. But Adam gave Satan his authority and a long-term lease on creation, and Satan brought sickness with him.

Yet people still blame God for sickness. God had nothing to do with it! It just doesn't make any sense to call God the author of sickness.

For instance, 1 John 3:8 says, "...For this purpose the Son of God was manifested, that he might destroy the works of the devil." But if God made anyone sick under Jesus' ministry, then Jesus was destroying the works of *God* when He healed people! If Jesus destroyed God's works, then we're in trouble because the Bible says a kingdom divided against itself cannot stand. (Matt. 12:25.)

No, Jesus never destroyed one work of God. He only "went about doing good, and healing all that were oppressed *of the devil"* (Acts 10:38).

Confession:

Any sickness that attacks my body is a bondage of Satan. No sickness is from God. Jesus came to set me free from every sickness and disease, so I accept my healing now!

JULY 5

Be Loosed!

And ought not this woman, being a daughter of Abraham, whom Satan hath bound, lo, these eighteen years, be loosed from this bond on the sabbath day? —Luke 13:16

We've learned from this Scripture that sickness is bondage. Next, we saw that sickness came from Satan. Now let's look at Jesus' question: "Ought not this woman...be loosed?"

Satan had kept this woman in bondage for eighteen years. But, thank God, Jesus said she ought to be loosed!

Jesus was also saying that *any* person whom Satan has bound with sickness and disease ought to be loosed. And Jesus is in the business of loosing people!

What qualified this woman to be loosed from this satanic bondage? Was she a real saint? Had she done something special? No, Jesus said she ought to be loosed because she was "a daughter of Abraham."

"Well, where does that leave me?" you may ask. Galatians 3:7 says, "Know ye therefore that they which are of faith, the same are the children of Abraham." According to this Scripture, we are sons and daughters of Abraham. We have been grafted into his family through the blood of Jesus Christ.

Galatians 3:29 says, "If ye be Christ's, then are ye Abraham's seed, and heirs according to the promise." What is that promise? Well, one of the promises is that we can be loosed from every bondage of the enemy!

Confession:

Because I'm a child of Abraham, I am loosed from every satanic bondage.
I not only enjoy the same rights and privileges as Abraham did, but I also
live under a new and better covenant, established on better promises—
including the promise that by Jesus' stripes I am healed!

And said, If thou wilt diligently hearken to the voice of the Lord thy God, and wilt do that which is right in his sight, and wilt give ear to his commandments, and keep all his statutes, I will put none of these diseases upon thee, which I have brought upon the Egyptians: for I am the Lord that healeth thee. —Exodus 15:26

"The Lord That Healeth Thee"

This was God's first healing covenant with His people. Some Hebrew scholars say this verse should be translated in the permissive tense—"I will *allow*" instead of "I will *put,*" in which case it would read, "I will allow none of these diseases upon thee, which I have allowed upon the Egyptians."

God finishes by saying, "For I am the Lord that healeth thee." The Hebrew says, "I am Jehovah Rapha."[1]

Two or three million children of Israel had left Egypt believing God. They went out of Egypt with silver and gold, and the Bible says there wasn't one feeble person among them. (Ps. 105:37.)

But God put a few conditions on this covenant between Himself and His people: "If thou wilt *diligently hearken* to the voice of the Lord thy God, and wilt do that which is right in his sight, and wilt *give ear* to his commandments...." You see, even back then in the first healing covenant, there was a correlation between hearing and being healed. One of the conditions for receiving the healing benefits of Jehovah Rapha is giving ear to His commandments. There is a direct connection between hearing and being healed.

Also, notice God didn't say, "I *will be* the Lord that healeth thee," or "I *was* the Lord that healed thee." He said, "I *am* the Lord that healeth thee."

We find in James 1:17 that God never changes. James said there is "no variableness, neither shadow of turning" with God. If He was the Lord who healed His people back then, He is the Lord who still heals His people today. He is still saying, "I am the Lord who heals you. I am Jehovah Rapha."

───── ✽ ─────

Confession:

*I am in covenant with Jehovah Rapha,
the God who heals me.
Therefore, I live in divine health!*

JULY 7

The Arm of the Lord Revealed

Who hath believed our report? and to whom is the arm of the Lord revealed? —*Isaiah 53:1*

Did you ever wonder, *To whom does God reveal His arm?* In other words, to whom does God show His strength? For whom does He work miracles? People say, "Well, you never know for whom God will use His power. God works in mysterious ways." But that isn't the way it works.

If someone starts to reveal his arm—to roll up his sleeves—he is getting ready to use some strength. If some big guy is rolling up his sleeves, you can know he is either about to work or he is getting ready to fight. Well, God reveals His arm—His strength and power—for His people.

For whom does God reveal His arm? Does He have favorite children, or are there some He doesn't like? Does He look at some people and say, "I don't know what it is, but something about you bothers me. I just don't like you, and I don't even know why. I think I will take all My blessings away from you and give them to someone else"?

No, God is no respecter of persons. God doesn't have favorite children. What He does for one, He does for anyone. He loves the whole world equally. God loved us while we were yet sinners to the extent that He sent His own Son to die for us.

God doesn't reveal His arm, use His strength or exert His power for everyone. God's arm, His power and His strength are revealed to people who will believe God's report—His Word. It's so important to believe what God says.

So really, the choice isn't God's; it's yours. If you want God's power revealed to you, then you must believe His report.

Confession:

God's report says by Jesus' stripes, I am healed.
I choose to believe and receive that report. Therefore, God reveals
His healing power to me, and His report comes to pass in my life.

Surely he hath borne our griefs, and carried our sorrows: yet we did esteem him stricken, smitten of God, and afflicted. —Isaiah 53:4

He Carried the Curse Away

Isaiah is called "the Gospel of the Old Testament." Hundreds of years before Jesus Christ ever took on flesh and dwelt among us, God gave the prophet Isaiah a vision. Isaiah saw into the future, when Jesus would go to the Cross and die for mankind. The prophet told us not only what the Crucifixion looked like, but he told us what Jesus purchased and why He went to the Cross.

Let's look at this verse carefully: "Surely he hath *borne* our griefs, and *carried* our sorrows." A lot of people think that means Jesus just helped us along with our burdens. But *borne* means to lift up, bear away, convey or remove to a distance.[1] When Jesus bore our sins, our sicknesses and our pains, He bore them away, or removed them. Both these words, *borne* and *carried* imply substitution, or bearing another's load.[2]

Now look at this: "Surely he hath borne *our* griefs, and carried *our* sorrows." Jesus didn't have any griefs or sorrows of His own. He didn't have any sickness, pain, sin, iniquity or disease—*we* do.

We live in this world; we're under the curse of the Law. But Jesus bore it all for us. He came in as our substitute and took the curse away from us. He didn't have to do that; He *chose* to do it. He carried our sickness and pain on Himself; died on the Cross; paid the price; descended into the depths of hell; left the sin, sickness and disease there; and arose three days later. He knew we couldn't carry that burden, but He could.

Jesus became sin for us; He became sickness for us. Jesus took *our* sickness, took *our* disease and carried *our* pain. We deserved the curse; but, as our substitute, Jesus carried it away.

Confession:

Jesus, the perfect, sinless Lamb of God, took upon Himself my pain, sickness and disease because He loves me. By faith I receive the healing and divine health His sacrifice provides for me.

JULY 9

Jesus Purchased Our Physical Healing

Surely he hath borne our griefs, and carried our sorrows: yet we did esteem him stricken, smitten of God, and afflicted. —Isaiah 53:4

Let's take this Scripture apart word by word and examine it closely. "Surely he hath borne our *griefs,* and carried our *sorrows."* Isaac Leeser's respected translation of the Old Testament—the only English translation of the Bible accepted by the Jewish council—translates the words *griefs* and *sorrows* as "sicknesses" and "pains."[1] So in the Hebrew, it actually says, "Surely He has borne our sicknesses [or our diseases], and carried our pains." That puts a little different light on this Scripture.

Of course, griefs and sorrows are really the same as sickness and disease because sickness and disease *cause* grief and sorrow. Anyone who says that sickness, disease and pain are blessings from God doesn't understand God's nature.

If we want an accurate translation of what this Scripture says, we can go to where it was fulfilled in the New Testament: Referring to Jesus' healing the multitudes, Matthew 8:17 says, "That it might be fulfilled which was spoken by Esaias the prophet, saying, Himself took our infirmities, and bare our sicknesses."

So Isaiah 53:4 was fulfilled during Jesus' ministry as He healed people physically. Isaiah's prophecy, therefore, looked ahead to the time when Jesus would purchase healing for our physical bodies.

Confession:

Jesus took my sickness and disease and carried my pain. He paid the price so I could be well. I believe what the Word says. I am healed!

But he was wounded for our transgressions, he
was bruised for our iniquities: the chastisement
of our peace was upon him; and with his
stripes we are healed. —Isaiah 53:5

JULY 10

Redeemed– Spirit, Soul and Body

When man fell in the Garden of Eden, his spirit, soul and body fell. God responded with a plan to redeem mankind with the blood of Jesus. God wasn't interested in doing just half a job. He wanted to redeem man's spirit, soul and body.

Man had a threefold problem, and Jesus gave us a threefold answer. He went to the Cross as our substitute, bearing our sins, our chastisements and our sicknesses. He paid the same price for all three dimensions of our being, so apparently all three are equally important.

You may say, "Well, I thought spiritual things were more important." In the realm of eternity, spiritual matters *are* more important. But God thinks spirit, soul *and* body are important.

God never required us to choose whether we wanted our spirits, souls *or* bodies to be taken care of. He said, "I paid the price for all three dimensions. They all belong to you, so receive all three benefits."

The first benefit mentioned in Isaiah 53:5 takes care of the sin problem: "He was wounded for our transgressions, he was bruised for our iniquities." Jesus died on the Cross to pay for our sins. He shed His blood for us because without the shedding of blood, there is no remission of sins. (Heb. 9:22.) He was raised from the dead so we could be born again. Once we receive Jesus Christ as Lord and Savior, God's report is that we are forgiven of sins.

Confession:

Jesus purchased freedom for my spirit, soul and body. He took
my spiritual death so I could have His eternal life. I believe
God's report. I am saved, delivered, healed and full of His peace!

JULY 11

Chastised for Our Peace

But he was wounded for our transgressions, he was bruised for our iniquities: the chastisement of our peace was upon him; and with his stripes we are healed. —Isaiah 53:5

"The chastisement of our peace was upon him." Why was Jesus chastised so much? Think about it: He was beaten. He was whipped until His back was laid open. His beard was plucked out, and a crown of thorns was placed on His head. Then, finally, He was nailed to the Cross.

But none of Jesus' suffering was without purpose. Everything that happened to Him was substitutionary. Jesus wore a crown of thorns so we could be crowned with glory and honor. Because He bore our chastisement, we can now live in peace, free from depression and mental anguish.

When you go into any church in this nation and ask, "How many would like more peace?" most of the people raise their hands. Why? Because most Christians don't know that peace already belongs to them.

Jesus didn't have to put up with all that His tormenters did to Him. He said, "No man can take My life; only I can lay it down. No man has any authority or power over Me unless it comes from above." (John 10:18.) But Jesus paid that price willingly, bearing our chastisement and shedding His blood to give us peace of mind.

Confession:

*Jesus was chastised for my peace; therefore,
I am forever free from depression and mental anguish.
I live in the peace of God!*

But he was wounded for our transgressions, he was bruised for our iniquities: the chastisement of our peace was upon him; and with his stripes we are healed. —Isaiah 53:5

JULY 12

Settling the Question of Healing

When Jesus was raised from the dead, was He still sick? No, He was raised with a perfect, glorified body. So where did He leave the sickness and disease? He left them in hell. Jesus was then called the firstborn of all creation. (Col. 1:15.)

Jesus died and descended to the depths of hell, carrying our sickness and disease. But when He—the firstborn among many brethern—was raised from the dead, He came forth as a healed man. Therefore, when we are born again, healing is ours to claim!

Here's another question: If God didn't want us healed, why in the world did Jesus bear those stripes before He went to the Cross? That was one part of the misery Jesus could have bypassed. But He did it by choice.

Healing is a firmly established fact. Now we just need to get the revelation in our own spirits that healing is God's will for *us*. When we do, we will start walking in the divine health Jesus purchased for us with the stripes on His back.

Confession:

Jesus willingly paid the price for me. He took my sickness; He gave me His health. I appropriate what the Lord did for me and receive my healing now.

JULY 13

Do You Believe God's Report?

But he was wounded for our transgressions, he was bruised for our iniquities: the chastisement of our peace was upon him; and with his stripes we are healed. —Isaiah 53:5

Isaiah 53:1 says, "Who hath believed our report?" Believing the right report isn't mind over matter or the power of positive thinking. It's believing God's Word over our problems. This means we have to *choose* whom we will believe. Will we believe God or the world? Will we believe the voice of the Holy Spirit or the voice of the devil?

Once we know what God says, we can choose to believe His report. In Isaiah 53:5, God gives us this report to believe: Jesus was wounded for our transgressions and bruised for our iniquities, so we can be set free from sin. He took the chastisement of our peace upon Himself, so we can have His peace. And He bore stripes upon His back for us, so we can be healed.

In my *King James Version* Bible, a note in the margin states that the Hebrew word for *stripes* literally means "bruise." Now look at Isaiah 53:10: "Yet it pleased the Lord to bruise him...." Apparently it pleased God when Jesus took those stripes for us. Can you imagine our heavenly Father being pleased to bruise His Son?

Jesus was bruised for our sickness and disease; then He died on the Cross because of His love for us. It pleased God to bruise Jesus because God knew the end result. In three days Jesus would be raised from the dead in a glorified, healthy body. Because of the bruises He bore, the body of Christ would go free from sickness and disease. That's the report God wants us to believe!

Confession:

Jesus shed His blood for me so I could be set free from sin. He was bruised for my physical healing. I am saved, healed and delivered because I choose to believe the report of the Lord!

The former treatise have I made, O Theophilus, of all that Jesus began both to do and teach.

—Acts 1:1

JULY 14

Jesus' Ministry—Then and Now

In Acts 10:38, Peter preached about the earthly ministry of Jesus to Cornelius' household: "How God anointed Jesus of Nazareth with the Holy Ghost and with power: who went about doing good, and healing all that were oppressed of the devil; for God was with him." Did poor old Peter get confused? Jesus was already gone. Why preach about His earthly ministry? His earthly ministry was finished, wasn't it?

No, Jesus' earthly ministry was just getting started, because He didn't really leave the earth. He just ascended to the Father's right hand to become the Head over all things to the body. (Col. 1:18.)

Jesus is still here, working in us and through us. His earthly ministry didn't stop or diminish—it multiplied! Jesus told His disciples, "It's better for you if I go. I'll pray to the Father, and He'll send another Comforter to abide with you forever." (John 14:16.)

He also said, "He that believeth on me, the works that I do shall he do also; and greater works than these shall he do; because I go unto my Father" (John 14:12).

The last verse of the book of John says, "And there are also many other things which Jesus did, the which, if they should be written every one, I suppose that even the world itself could not contain the books that should be written" (John 21:25). Then in Acts 1:1, the next verse in the Bible, Luke talks about "all that Jesus *began* both to do and teach." Luke didn't say Jesus had finished His ministry; he said Jesus had just gotten started!

God wants us to know that Jesus' ministry still continues through us. God is the same, Jesus is the same, the Holy Ghost is the same and the Word is the same. Therefore, God's methods of healing and deliverance will be the same as well.

Confession:

While Jesus walked on the earth, He preached the Word and healed the sick. As I hear God's Word, I believe it, act on it and receive my healing because Jesus' ministry is still alive today in me!

JULY 15

Act in Faith
as God
Leads You

When [Jesus] had thus spoken, he spat on the ground, and made clay of the spittle, and he anointed the eyes of the blind man with the clay, and said unto him, Go, wash in the pool of Siloam, (which is by interpretation, Sent.) He went his way therefore, and washed, and came seeing. *—John 9:6,7*

You may wonder, *What should I do to act on my faith?*

Don't do something because it worked for someone else. Let *God* show you how to act in faith.

Jesus spit in the dirt, made clay of the spittle, put it on a blind man's eyes and said, "Go wash in the pool of Siloam." (John 9:6,7.) But He didn't tell anyone else to go dip in that pool. Jesus gave people a whole variety of instructions for acting on their faith.

I had a friend who was waiting for God to heal him from severe sugar diabetes. He heard of someone who had thrown away his insulin, so he thought, *That's my step of faith! If I throw away this insulin, God will have to do something.* But the man almost died! He tried to make something happen instead of acting because he believed God had already healed him.

Another time, I traveled for a summer with a group that included two people who had sugar diabetes. I watched these people throughout the summer. They had to check the amount of insulin they needed every day. Every time they checked, they said, "Thank You, Father. I believe I'm healed by Jesus' stripes. Glory to God!" Then they'd take whatever insulin they needed.

The insulin wasn't healing these two people; it was just keeping them alive. A week or so later, they'd need a little bit less insulin. They'd take whatever insulin they needed, but they'd always say, "Thank God, I believe I'm healed." Over a period of about three months, I watched both of these people get healed of diabetes. By the end of the summer, neither one of them needed any insulin!

So let God teach you what you need to do to act on your faith. Then obey Him, and be healed!

Confession:

*God shows me how to act in faith,
and I follow His instructions and
praise Him because His Word is true!*

He that committeth sin is of the devil; for the devil sinneth from the beginning. For this purpose the Son of God was manifested, that he might destroy the works of the devil.

—1 John 3:8

JULY 16

Sickness Is a Work of the Devil

Why did Jesus become flesh and dwell among us on this earth? Why was He manifested? The main reason He came into this realm was to destroy the works of the devil.

Did Jesus fulfill what God called Him to do, or did He fail? Of course Jesus accomplished what God sent Him to do! He destroyed the works of the devil. So if we want to find out what the works of the devil are, we need to find out what Jesus destroyed.

Acts 10:38 tells us that Jesus "went about doing good, and *healing all that were oppressed of the devil;* for God was with him." What good did Jesus do? He healed people.

Every time Jesus healed someone, He destroyed the works of the devil—sickness and disease. Every time He forgave someone, He destroyed the works of the devil—sin and separation from God. Every time He set someone free, He destroyed the works of the devil—spiritual, mental and physical bondage.

Healing multitudes of people was a major part of Jesus' ministry. In fact, there were times when as many as touched Jesus were made whole! Jesus accomplished the purpose for which He was sent. Whenever He went about healing people, He was destroying the works of the devil.

Confession:

The devil wanted to kill me, but Jesus set me free and gave me eternal life. The devil wanted to make me sick, but Jesus destroyed his efforts. I am the healed of the Lord!

JULY 17

Satan, a Defeated Foe

For this purpose the Son of God was manifested, that he might destroy the works of the devil.
—1 John 3:8

Sickness is not a blessing from God; it's a curse from the enemy from which we've been redeemed. If sickness is from the enemy, we don't have a thing to be concerned about. Jesus was manifested to destroy the works of the devil—and He did what He was sent to do!

And having spoiled principalities and powers, he made a shew of them openly, triumphing over them in it.

Colossians 2:15

We see in this Scripture that Jesus spoiled principalities and powers. He spoiled Satan's army—the beings that back up what little authority Satan had.

Forasmuch then as the children are partakers of flesh and blood, he also himself likewise took part of the same; that through death he might destroy him that had the power of death, that is, the devil.

Hebrews 2:14

So if sickness and disease are from the devil (and they are!), then we're in a good position because Jesus destroyed his works and ruined his army. The Rotherham translation says Jesus defeated Satan so "He might paralyse him that held the dominion of death."[1] Jesus did all of that for us!

Satan has no legal, moral or spiritual authority to put anything on you and make it stick. He can only make you sick if you let him. His works have been destroyed, his army has been beaten and he's been paralyzed by the blood of Jesus, which covers you!

Confession:

Jesus has given me authority over all the devil's works in my life. The devil has no legal authority to put anything on me. I am redeemed from the curse!

I call heaven and earth to record this day against you, that I have set before you life and death, blessing and cursing: therefore choose life, that both thou and thy seed may live.

—Deuteronomy 30:19

Choose Life

A number of years ago I heard a certain minister say, "The person who shuts his spirit away cripples himself in life and becomes an easy prey to selfish and designing people. But the individual who learns to be led by the Spirit of God will rise to the top in life."

Something rose up on the inside of me when I heard that, and I thought, *Well, now I know it's my choice!*

You see, God doesn't just choose who will be successful in life. He is no respecter of persons. He doesn't have favorites. He doesn't pick some to receive His blessings and others to miss out. He isn't in a good mood on some days and in a bad mood on other days. He doesn't look at one person and say, "I like you. You get everything I've got" and then look at someone else and say, "I don't know what it is about you. You just bug me. You just rub my fur backwards. You don't get anything." *No!* God has no favorites. He loves everyone equally.

It is up to us whether or not we rise to the top in life. We are free moral agents. We can live mediocre lives, scraping the bottom of the barrel, or we can rise to the top.

Through His death, burial and resurrection, Jesus purchased for us "all things that pertain unto life and godliness" (2 Peter 1:3). The work is already done; it's already purchased and paid for. The benefits belong to us, but we have to choose to partake of them.

Will you walk in the blessings of God? The choice is yours. So follow God's counsel in Deuteronomy 30:19: "Therefore choose life."

───────── ✌ ─────────

Confession:

*I choose life, blessing, healing and health.
I choose to believe the Word of God
and rise to the top in life!*

JULY 19

Choose you this day whom ye will serve....

–Joshua 24:15

Whom Will You Serve?

Man has always had a choice. God has tried to show us that from the very beginning. He formed man from the dust of the earth and breathed His own life into him. He put man in the midst of the Garden and gave him authority over all the works of His hands. He told him to dress it, keep it and take care of it.

Then God said, "You can eat of anything you want in the Garden. It's good, and it's yours. You will find a tree in the midst of the Garden called the Tree of Life. You can eat of that freely. But don't eat of the Tree of the Knowledge of Good and Evil, for in the day you do, you will surely die." (Gen. 2:16,17.)

God was talking about spiritual death, which is separation from Him. So what happened? Adam ate of that tree, and the next time God came to walk and talk with him in the cool of the day, Adam hid. He had separated himself spiritually from God.

From that time on, mankind was separated from God, except when animal sacrifices were made. Then the Lord Jesus, our sacrificial Lamb, came to earth and brought us back into relationship with the Father.

I used to read the account of Adam and Eve and think, *God, why did You do that? Instead of putting the Tree of the Knowledge of Good and Evil in the midst of the Garden, why didn't You put it on the southern tip of South America, where it would have taken them 5000 years just to find? By that time, Adam wouldn't have wanted it!*

Some folks would say, "God was just testing mankind." No, this wasn't a test. God was allowing man the privilege of being a free moral agent. You see, man could only be a free moral agent if he had choices to make.

God doesn't want us to serve Him because we have to. He wants us to serve Him because we *want* to. He will allow us to go to hell and spend eternity there if we so choose. Or we can choose *life* and spend eternity in His presence—starting here and now!

Confession:

This day I choose to obey God because I want to.
My choices determine the paths I take.
Therefore, I choose life, that I and my seed shall live!

*And Jesus went forth, and saw a great multi-
tude, and was moved with compassion toward
them, and he healed their sick. —Matthew 14:14*

God Heals Because He Loves

Why did Jesus heal the multitudes?
Because He was moved with compassion.

God often demonstrates His power for people who have never had the opportunity to hear His Word. Through these demonstrations, God puts His "seal of
approval" on the Word that has gone forth and manifests His love to the people.

Janet and I were in a church service recently where God demonstrated His
love to some visitors. The Holy Ghost quickened a word of knowledge to me, so
I spoke it out. A woman on the front row came forward and was healed.

Before the service was over, the Holy Ghost had ministered to every person on
that row. We later found out it was the first time those people had been to that church.

The next night, the woman who had been healed gave her testimony. She
explained, "All these years, I didn't think God loved me. But I found out differently last night. God called me out of a whole church full of people and healed
me. This is the first time in my life I've truly known the love of God."

I thought to myself, *God sure knows His business!*

Healing is the dinner bell for the Gospel, and we need to ring that bell! Many
people are tired of religious doctrines and man's ideas. They're looking for something real. God will show Himself real to them by demonstrating His compassion
and power. *Healing shows God's compassion, and miracles show His power.*

Many have the idea that God is a big bully with a baseball bat, sitting on a
cloud, waiting to belt them every time they do something wrong. But God is love,
and He desires to show His nature to the world by *healing people.*

Confession:

*God loves me. He loved me so much that
He sent Jesus to die for me. Because of
His love, I am healed.*

JULY 21

Keep the Law of Love

And hope maketh not ashamed; because the love of God is shed abroad in our hearts by the Holy Ghost which is given unto us. —Romans 5:5

One way for us to stay healthy is to walk in love.

Under the old covenant, God told His people that if they served Him, He would take sickness away from the midst of them. (Ex. 23:25.) Then He gave His people a list of commandments and ordinances to obey, knowing that the Israelites had no power to fulfill them.

In essence, He was saying to them, "Here are all these rules and regulations to follow in order to live holy before Me. However, there's no way you can keep them. So when you break My laws, the blood of an animal sacrifice will cover your sins and iniquities. It will push your sins ahead for a year so you can receive My blessings."

God gave His laws and commandments to His people to prove to them that they needed a Savior. Galatians 3:24 says the law served as a schoolmaster to bring God's people to Jesus. God's people couldn't be perfected through the Law. They needed a Redeemer.

What about us? Are we in better shape today? Are we able to obey Jesus' commandment to "Love one another" (John 13:34) any better than the Old Testament saints were able to keep the Law?

Under the old covenant, God's people possessed the Law but had no power to keep it. Under the new covenant, when we're born again, the Holy Ghost indwells us and imparts the love of God into our spirits. We then have the power to keep the law of love. And as long as we walk in love, we have the power to fulfill the other commandments as well.

So, actually, our job on this earth is to walk in love. As long as we walk in love, we're keeping God's commandments. And as long as we keep His commandments, our God, Jehovah Rapha, will take sickness from the midst of us!

Confession:

God's love is shed abroad in my heart.
God, my healer, heals me and keeps me in divine health
as I follow the ways of His Word and His Spirit.

Charity suffereth long, and is kind; charity envieth not; charity vaunteth not itself, is not puffed up. —*1 Corinthians 13:4*

Judge Your Love Walk

In order to open our hearts to God and allow Him to work in our lives, we need to judge ourselves in our love toward the brethren. First, we have to find out what God's love acts like, and then we have to make sure we are doing the same thing. Sure, it's going to be an effort. Sure, we'll miss it now and then. But if we don't start endeavoring to walk in love, then we never will.

The Amplified Bible says, "Love endures long and is patient and kind; love never is envious nor boils over with jealousy, is not boastful or vainglorious, does not display itself haughtily." Love endures long. Do we endure long with people? The *Phillips* translation says, "This love of which I speak is slow to lose patience." Are we always that way?

"Love envies not, love flaunteth not itself."[1] The *Williams* translation says, "Love never boils over with jealousy." Have we ever been jealous? That's not love. Love doesn't react that way.

The *Phillips* translation says, God's love "is neither anxious to impress, nor does it cherish inflated ideas of its own importance." Love never tries to impress anyone.

When we know what love acts like, we have a goal to reach toward. As we trust the greater One in us and tap into His love, which is poured out in our hearts, God will enable us to walk in love.

Confession:

By the power of the Holy Ghost indwelling me, I walk in love toward people. I endure long and am patient and kind. I don't boil over with jealousy. I'm not boastful or anxious to impress. In every circumstance, I obey the law of love.

JULY 23

Love Always Forgives

[Love] doth not behave itself unseemly, seeketh not her own, is not easily provoked, thinketh no evil.   *—1 Corinthians 13:5*

Love always forgives. Forgiveness is one of the offsprings of love. *The Amplified Bible* says it this way:

[Love] is not conceited (arrogant and inflated with pride); it is not rude (unmannerly) and does not act unbecomingly. Love (God's love in us) does not insist on its own rights or its own way, for it is not self-seeking; it is not touchy or fretful or resentful; it takes no account of the evil done to it [it pays no attention to a suffered wrong].

Galatians 5:6 talks about "faith which worketh by love." Love forgives, so we could say faith works by forgiveness. Isn't that what Jesus was trying to tell us in Mark 11:25? "And when ye stand praying, forgive...." Faith works by love, and love always forgives; therefore, faith works by forgiveness.

First Corinthians 13:5 goes on to say that love "seeketh not her own." The *Revised Standard Version* says, "Love does not insist on its own way." *Goodspeed* says, "It does not insist on its own rights."[1] How often have we said, "I've got my rights!" No, love doesn't insist on its own rights.

Love "is not easily provoked, thinketh no evil." *The New English Bible* says that love is "not quick to take offence." Love keeps no score of wrongs. It never remembers the wrongs done by others. Now, flesh will say, "I remember what that old bat did to me." But love doesn't take any account of the evil done to it, because love always forgives.

———— ✌ ————

Confession:

I walk in love because my Father is love. I am not conceited or arrogant, prideful or rude. I don't insist on my own rights or keep a score of wrongs. I am not quick to take offense, but I am quick to forgive. My faith works because I walk in love.

[Love] rejoiceth not in iniquity, but rejoiceth in the truth; beareth all things, believeth all things, hopeth all things, endureth all things. Charity never faileth.... —*1 Corinthians 13:6-8*

JULY 24

Walking in the God-Kind of Love

*T*he Amplified Bible helps us see what it really means to walk in the God-kind of love:

[Love] **does not rejoice at injustice and unrighteousness, but rejoices when right and truth prevail. Love bears up under anything and everything that comes, is ever ready to believe the best of every person, its hopes are fadeless under all circumstances, and it endures everything [without weakening]. Love never fails [never fades out or becomes obsolete or comes to an end].**

First, this Scripture says that love "rejoiceth not in iniquity." Love is never glad when others go the wrong way in life. On the other hand, your flesh is glad when someone else stumbles, because that elevates you in your own mind.

Love is always glad when truth prevails. It overlooks faults. It's always slow to expose faults or sins and is always eager to believe the best. Love will go a long way to believe the best. It doesn't look for something wrong but always looks for the good in every person.

So how do you measure up to this definition of love? If you find areas where you are lacking in your love walk, ask the Holy Spirit to help you make the necessary adjustments. Remember, your faith only works when love is operating in your life.

Confession:

I walk in love because I'm a child of a loving God. I don't rejoice at injustice or iniquity, but I rejoice in the truth. I believe the best about people and endure everything without weakening. God's love in me never fails!

JULY 25

Keep Your Confidence Toward God

Beloved, if our heart condemn us not, then have we confidence toward God. And whatsoever we ask, we receive of him, because we keep his commandments, and do those things that are pleasing in his sight. And this is his commandment, That we should believe on the name of his Son Jesus Christ, and love one another, as he gave us commandment. —1 John 3:21-23

God said if our hearts don't condemn us, we have confidence toward Him and we receive what we ask for. So if we've been asking for something and haven't received our answer, we need to examine our love walk with others.

We receive what we ask for, because we obey His commandments and do that which is pleasing in His sight. And these are His commandments: first, that we believe on the Lord Jesus; and second, that we love one another.

Walking in love keeps us out of trouble and in the blessings of God. Sure, it's work. It's not easy to put the body under. Most of us have been accustomed to letting the flesh dominate us in certain areas. For instance, the flesh thinks it's fun to criticize and talk about people. It always makes us feel bigger.

But if we walk the love walk, we put ourselves in a position to walk in God's blessings. And I guarantee you, nothing the flesh offers comes close to the blessings of God!

Confession:

I walk in love; therefore, I am confident that God hears and answers my prayers.

> *A new commandment I give unto you, That ye love one another; as I have loved you, that ye also love one another. By this shall all men know that ye are my disciples, if ye have love one to another.* —*John 13:34,35*

JULY 26

The Command of Love

What are God's statutes and commandments under the new covenant? In this Scripture, Jesus gives us one new commandment—that we *love one another.*

Under the old covenant, God said if we would keep His ordinances, statutes and commandments, He would take sickness from our midst. (Ex. 23:25.) Similarly, 1 John 3:22 says that because we keep God's commandments, we receive what we ask of Him. So we see that the same restrictions that applied under the old covenant apply now. Under both covenants, God says, "I'll take care of you and bless you and cause you to walk in health, *if* you will keep My commandments."

In the Old Testament, God's people had many statutes, commandments and ordinances to obey. In the New Testament, God condenses all His statutes, commandments and ordinances into one commandment and calls it *love.* Romans 13:10 says, "…Therefore love is the fulfilling of the law." As we walk in love, we fulfill all of God's other commandments.

Confession:

I will walk in love toward others in every situation. As I obey the commandment of love, my Father takes sickness away from me and I live in divine health.

JULY 27

What Can You Believe?

...but if thou canst do any thing, have compassion on us, and help us.

Jesus said unto him, If thou canst believe, all things are possible to him that believeth.

—Mark 9:22,23

A man brought his demon-possessed son to Jesus and said, "If You can do anything, have compassion [or have mercy] on us and help us."

Jesus said, "It's not a question of what I can do; the question is, What can you believe. If you can believe, all things become possible for you. It's not up to Me; it's up to you. It's not My decision whether or not your son is healed; it's your decision. I have the ability, but it's up to you whether or not My ability is released."

Over and over again in the Scriptures God "puts the ball back in our court." We've been crying out to God, saying, "Oh, God, move. Oh, God, do something!" Meanwhile, He's been saying, "You believe; then I'll move."

God gave us His Word and His faith. After we use the faith He gave us to believe the Word He gave us, it's His turn to move again.

God really gave us the easy part of the covenant. But a lot of times, we've avoided our responsibility. It's easier to just lean back and wait for God to do everything.

But that never would have worked for the people under Jesus' ministry. Jesus always taught the Word to give the people something to believe; then they had to act on their faith in that Word.

Jesus never attributed the resulting miracles to His faith or His disciples' faith. He always attributed them either to the individual's faith or to spiritual gifts. According to Jesus' own words, approximately 70 percent of the people who received healing under His ministry did so as a result of their own faith.

The man said, "Lord, I believe; help thou mine unbelief." (v. 24.) The man had done his part, confessing his faith in Jesus' power to heal his son. Instantly Jesus cast the spirit out of the man's son, setting the boy totally free!

Confession:

Nothing is impossible to me when I know what God has said and I stand in faith on His Word. I believe and act on the Word and receive my miracle today!

...but if thou canst do any thing, have compassion on us, and help us.

Jesus said unto him, If thou canst believe, all things are possible to him that believeth.

And straightway the father of the child cried out, and said with tears, Lord, I believe; help thou mine unbelief. —Mark 9:22-24

JULY 28

"Help Thou Mine Unbelief"

W hen the man in this passage pleaded with Jesus to help his son, Jesus, in essence, said to him, "It's not just up to Me. It's whether *you* can believe that really matters." Instead of getting discouraged, the man caught what Jesus said. He said, "All right, Lord, I believe. Help my unbelief." In other words, he said, "I believe it in my heart, but my head is giving me trouble."

A lot of times people say, "I believe I'm healed, but what about the symptoms? What about the circumstances?" or "I believe I'm healed, but when is this pain going to stop?"

Have you ever been in a spot like that? That's where this father of a demon-possessed son found himself. "I believe my son is free, Lord; I extend my faith. But please help my unbelief." In other words, doubts were trying to crowd into his head.

The minute people say, "I believe, but..." you just know they're looking in the wrong direction. In 2 Corinthians 4:18, Paul said, "While we look not at the things which are seen, but at the things which are not seen...." Too many times, we've dwelt on, thought about and watched the *problem*. Then we've wondered why our faith hasn't worked.

We need to say, "I know the problem is there, but who cares? I'm not looking at what I can see. I'm looking at the unseen—God's Word, the answer, the victory over all my faith challenges."

We have to follow the example of Paul, who said, "I'm not dwelling on the problems; I'm dwelling on the *answer*. I'm keeping my eyes fixed on Jesus, the author and finisher of my faith!" (Heb. 12:2.)

Confession:

I believe God's Word. He speaks to me through the Bible and in my heart, and I choose to believe what He says. The Word says I'm healed, so I am healed!

JULY 29

All Things Are Possible When You Believe

Jesus said unto him, If thou canst believe, all things are possible to him that believeth.

—Mark 9:23

Jesus made a powerful statement to the man who brought his son to Him for deliverance. He said, "All things are possible to him that believeth."

The reason Jesus could say that is shown in Hebrews 1:1-2: "God, who at sundry times and in divers manners spake in time past unto the fathers by the prophets, hath in these last days spoken unto us by his Son, whom he hath appointed heir of ALL things...." How many is all? All is all! Jesus has been made heir of all things.

Then Romans 8:16-17 says, "The Spirit itself beareth witness with our spirit, that we are the children of God: and if children, then heirs; heirs of God, and joint-heirs with Christ...." Many times we in the Church world have shouted about this promise, but most of us have never gone back to find out what it means.

If you are a joint heir with someone, then whatever he inherits also belongs to you. Well, what did Jesus inherit? God appointed Him heir of all things.

Jesus said in Mark 10:27, "For with God all things are possible." Well, that's great for God, but what about us? Jesus cleared up that question as well when He said, "All things are possible to him that believeth." Why are all things possible to the person who believes? Because we are joint heirs with Jesus, the heir of all things!

So whatever God has, whatever He is and whatever He can do is available to us as we learn to believe God and tap our faith into His grace and His ability.

If we in the Church world would just get ahold of that, it would absolutely change our lives. All things are possible to us when we believe!

Confession:

With God, all things are possible. He is greater than any sickness, any disease, any difficulty, any lack. He's greater than all, and He lives in me—so all things are possible to me because I believe!

God forbid: yea, let God be true, but every man a liar.... —Romans 3:4

Let God Be True in Your Life

Paul was saying to the Romans, "You have to choose what you're going to believe." Every person in this world has to decide what is going to be true in his life.

Notice, Paul *didn't* say, "God is true." He said, *"Let* God be true." *You* is the understood subject of the sentence. That means *you* are to let God be true in your life. Are you going to let God be true, or are you going to let the problem be true?

The Bible says, "By Jesus' stripes you were healed." (Isa. 53:5; 1 Peter 2:24.) A lot of people say, "I know that's what the Bible says, but I know what I feel like." Well, they've chosen to let their symptoms be truth and God a liar. They've chosen to let the problems be truth and God a liar. They are living on the negative side of life, always focusing on their problems instead of God's Word.

You can't focus on the problem and go over in victory, and you can't focus on the answer and go under in defeat! So what are you watching? What are you focusing your attention on?

We have to let God be true, switch over to the realm of faith and declare, "Who cares what it looks like? Who cares what it feels like? The Bible says I'm healed!"

You may know God's Word is true, but Paul says in this Scripture that you have to choose what is going to be truth in *your* life. Are you going to believe the symptoms and the circumstances, or are you going to believe God?

Confession:

God's Word is true, and I choose to let His Word be truth in my life. I steadfastly focus on God's Word, and I receive what God says is mine.

JULY 31

Step out of the Boat by Faith

And in the fourth watch of the night Jesus went unto them, walking on the sea.

And Peter answered him and said, Lord, if it be thou, bid me come unto thee on the water.

And he said, Come. And when Peter was come down out of the ship, he walked on the water, to go to Jesus. —Matthew 14:25,28,29

In this passage, the disciples were out on the Sea of Galilee, fighting to keep afloat in a storm. Suddenly, Jesus came walking across the sea toward their boat! Jesus had been spending time with His Father, and He'd gotten so caught up in the glory that He didn't even need a boat!

Peter saw Jesus and called, "Lord, if that's You, I want to come out there!" Jesus called back, "Come on out!"

I like Peter; he was a pioneer. He didn't want to walk the same road everyone else traveled. He wanted to plow a new one!

Peter stepped out of the boat and began to walk on the water toward Jesus. Now, it wasn't the water that held Peter up. Just go try it sometime, and see if water will hold *you* up! No, it wasn't the water—it was *Jesus' word* that kept Peter on top of the water.

Jesus had said to him, "Come." And every time Peter put his foot down to take another step on the water, he landed on that word. So Peter first heard and believed what Jesus said. Then Peter acted on what He'd said, keeping his eyes on Jesus all the while.

Also, did you notice that no one followed Peter out of the boat? No, the other disciples were probably all standing back, thinking, *If it works for Peter, maybe I'll try it.* That's the attitude that causes people to run into problems. They say, "Well, so-and-so got healed. I believe I'll try that." Then they wonder why it doesn't work for them.

We aren't healed because someone else was healed. We can't live continually off someone else's faith. We're healed because the Bible says, "By Jesus' stripes you were healed." (Isa. 53:5, 1 Peter 2:24.) Just like Peter, we have to take a step of faith out on the Word and believe God for the miracle we need!

Confession:

When the One who made the water tells me I can walk on it, I can.
The One who made my body tells me it's healed, so it's healed.
The Word of God is the unsinkable foundation I walk on!

And in the fourth watch of the night Jesus went unto them, walking on the sea.

And Peter answered him and said, Lord if it be thou, bid me come unto thee on the water.

And he said, Come. And when Peter was come down out of the ship, he walked on the water, to go to Jesus.

But when he saw the wind boisterous, he was afraid; and beginning to sink, he cried, saying, Lord, save me. —Matthew 14:25,28-30

AUGUST 1

Keep Your Eyes on Jesus

Peter stepped out of the boat and walked on the water. But then Peter made a mistake. He was hearing, believing and acting right, but then "he *saw* the wind boisterous." He took his eyes off Jesus and started watching the strong wind blowing on the stormy sea.

At that moment, fear entered in, faith stopped and Peter started to sink. It was as though he was thinking, *I can't walk on water when the wind is blowing, especially when the waves are big!* He must have forgotten who had made it possible for him to walk on the water when it had been *smooth!*

When we're believing God, we need to hear God's Word, believe God's Word, say God's Word and act on God's Word. But we also need to keep our eyes *off* the problem and *on* Jesus, who *is* God's Word. No matter what stormy circumstances we face, Jesus is the answer to our every need.

Confession:

I keep my eyes on Jesus, not looking at the circumstances or impossibilities that surround me. I choose to believe His Word, and my faith holds me up!

AUGUST 2

"Fear Not"

And when Peter was come down out of the ship, he walked on the water, to go to Jesus.

But when he saw the wind boisterous, he was afraid.... —Matthew 14:29,30

See if this scenario sounds familiar: You're in the midst of a trial, but you're believing right, talking right and acting right. Then circumstances pull your eyes off Jesus and onto the problem. Suddenly, your faith is replaced with fear, and you begin to lose ground.

That's what happened to Peter. When he stepped out of the boat and began walking on the water, he was believing right, hearing right and acting right. But the minute Peter took his eyes off Jesus and looked back on the problem, his faith stopped working. His eyes started looking in the wrong direction, and fear entered in.

People deal with many types of fears—fears of accidents, of diseases of death and so forth. I used to be afraid of everything. But then I got a revelation of Psalm 91. If I didn't know Psalm 91 worked today, I would never get on a plane. But Janet and I travel all the time. We fly across the ocean several times a year, and I never have a problem. And I never will, because He's given His angels charge over me to keep me in all my ways. (Ps. 91:11.)

Sometimes Christians make the mistake of just rebuking the fear without replacing it with anything. Jesus said, "Fear not; only believe." (Mark 5:36.) In other words, He was saying, "If you want to believe God, you have to let your belief drive out the fear."

You see, you can't operate in fear and faith at the same time in the same situation. Now, some people say, "I'm believing God, but I'm a little afraid." But that's impossible. They're either operating in faith or fear, but not both of them at the same time. When fear enters in, faith goes out.

How do you strengthen your belief and get rid of fear? Belief comes by hearing God's Word. As you build your belief in God's Word in a situation, the power in that Word will drive out the fear and enable you to keep your eyes where they belong—on Jesus.

Confession:

*God loves me so much. He saved me, heals me, guides me, protects me.
He said, "I will never leave you, nor forsake you." So I boldly say,
"The Lord is my helper, and I will not fear!" (Heb. 13:5,6.)*

And immediately Jesus stretched forth his hand, and caught him, and said unto him, O thou of little faith, wherefore didst thou doubt? And when they were come into the ship, the wind ceased. —Matthew 14:31,32

AUGUST 3

Don't Get Under Condemnation

Peter was actually walking on the water. But when he got his eyes off the answer and onto the problem, he began to sink. However, notice that Jesus didn't just walk over, slap him and say, "Swim back to the boat!"

That's the impression a lot of people have of God. They think, *I missed it; God is going to get me now.* They come under condemnation because they've had a faith failure.

But God doesn't want you to feel condemned when you miss it and get out of faith. He's not condemning you. His hand is always reaching out to pull you back up on top of the situation!

Jesus didn't put Peter under condemnation. He just asked him, "Why did you doubt?" Then Jesus caught hold of Peter's hand and helped him stand up on top of the water again. And I don't believe Jesus just pulled Peter along back to the boat. I think they walked back together and had a good discussion about faith on the way!

Confession:

Even when I miss God's best, He doesn't condemn me. He picks me up and helps me on my way. There is no condemnation for me, because I'm in Christ Jesus and I walk after the Spirit of God.

AUGUST 4

Great Faith– Little Faith

And when Peter was come down out of the ship, he walked on the water, to go to Jesus.

But when he saw the wind boisterous, he was afraid; and beginning to sink, he cried, saying, Lord, save me.

And immediately Jesus stretched forth his hand, and caught him, and said unto him, O thou of little faith, wherefore didst thou doubt?

–Matthew 14:29-31

Peter was walking on the water. He had a miracle going. He had stepped out in faith on the strength of Jesus' word. But then Peter got his eyes off the answer and onto the problem and began to sink. Jesus caught him and said, "O thou of little faith."

Do you know what "little faith" is? It is keeping your eye on the problem instead of on the answer. Weak faith says, "I know what God says, but, man, look at the problem!" Great faith says, "I don't care what it looks like—look at what *God* says." The difference between great faith and weak faith is found in *what you dwell on—the problem or the answer.*

One example of great faith can be found in Romans 4:19: "And being not weak in faith, [Abraham] considered not his own body now dead, when he was about an hundred years old, neither yet the deadness of Sarah's womb."

Now, just take the two *nots* out of that Scripture, and you'll see an example of weak faith: "Being weak in faith, he considered his own body now dead." Weak faith considers the body; strong faith considers what God says. Weak faith watches the problem; strong faith watches the answer.

Abraham looked at his body, which was 100 years old. He looked at his wife, Sarah, who was 90 years old and barren. But then he said, "Who cares? I've got God's Word on it." Abraham was *fully* persuaded that what God had promised, He was able to perform.

That's the mark of great faith. And you obtain that measure of faith by keeping your eyes on God's Word instead of on your problem.

Confession:

I will not keep my eyes on the symptoms in my body or the circumstances that surround me. I choose to look at the Word of God. I believe the Word and walk in victory in every situation!

They that observe lying vanities forsake their
own mercy. —*Jonah 2:8*

Don't Observe "Lying Vanities"

Jonah had a whale of a problem. God told him to go to Nineveh and preach, but he said, "I won't do it." He got into a boat to run away from the Lord. But then a storm arose, threatening to sink the boat. Jonah knew he was the cause of the storm, so he told the crew to throw him overboard. As soon as he hit the water, a great fish swallowed him! (Jonah 1:1-17.)

At that point, Jonah realized he'd missed it. (Most people would by then!) But he also realized it wasn't too late to set things straight. So Jonah prayed and repented before God. Then he made this powerful statement: "They that observe lying vanities forsake their own mercy."

Every one of us needs God's mercy. Hebrews 4:16 says, "Let us therefore come boldly unto the throne of grace, that we may obtain mercy, and find grace to help in time of need." Whatever we need—forgiveness, healing, deliverance, wisdom— is available to every one of us by God's mercy.

But Jonah said, "If you observe lying vanities, you're going to forsake your own mercy." You see, anything contrary to God's Word is a lying vanity. Jonah was saying, "I can sit here in this whale and dwell on my predicament, or I can close my eyes and think about the divine mercy that belongs to me. I can either observe the problem, or I can observe the answer. But if I observe the problem, I'm going to forsake my own mercy."

A lot of us have been watching the symptoms, the pain and the bad reports. Then we wonder why God's mercy doesn't show up! We forsake our own mercy when we choose to observe lying vanities.

Jonah made the right choice in the belly of that whale. He decided, *I've repented. I don't know how God is going to get me to Nineveh, but I believe it's done!* Jonah observed his answer instead of the problem, so it wasn't long before he was out of the fish's belly and safe on dry land. God's mercy came through in his time of need.

Confession:

I won't keep my eyes on the symptoms or pain and
forsake the mercy available to me. I choose to observe
God's Word and receive His benefits of healing and health today!

AUGUST 6

Abraham, the Father of Our Faith

God talked with [Abraham], saying, As for me, behold, my covenant is with thee, and thou shalt be a father of many nations. Neither shall thy name any more be called Abram, but thy name shall be Abraham; for a father of many nations have I made thee. —Genesis 17:3-5

R omans 4:16 calls Abraham our father of faith. God made a covenant with Abraham, saying, "I have made you the father of many nations." He didn't say, "I *will* make you." He said, "I *have* made you."

You see, God always calls those things that be not as though they were. (Rom. 4:17.) He talks about what doesn't exist as though it already existed. That's why it's all right for us to do the same. We're not lying; we're just following God's example.

God told Abraham, "I have made you the father of many nations." Remember, He was talking to a 100-year-old man and his 90-year-old wife! Abraham and Sarah were past the age for having children. Medically speaking, it was impossible.

Abraham could have said, "Now, God, I appreciate Your enthusiasm, but we're a little old to have a baby. Why don't You talk to the nice young couple down the street who already have four kids?"

But Abraham didn't act that way. He had a deep awe and respect for Almighty God. In the natural, the situation looked hopeless, but Abraham believed what God said. That's the key. *Abraham had to believe what God said before he could become what God said.* "[Abraham] against hope believed in hope, that he might become the father of many nations, according to that which was spoken..." (v. 18).

When it comes to your faith walk, you're no different than the father of faith. You have to *believe* what God has said about you before you can *become* what God has called you.

Confession:

God says that by Jesus' stripes I am healed, and I believe His Word. So when symptoms come against me, I call those things that be not as though they were: I am healed!

And being not weak in faith, [Abraham] consid-
ered not his own body now dead, when he was
about an hundred years old, neither yet the
deadness of Sarah's womb. —Romans 4:19

Don't Deny the Problem

D id you notice that Abraham never denied the problem? He just didn't consider it. He never said, "No, I'm not 100 years old. I'm more like 20 or 25."

God doesn't want us to deny that the problem exists. He doesn't advocate lying or "mind over matter." He's just saying, "You can look at the problem, but don't consider it. Switch over and consider the Word. Don't deny that the problem is there; just observe the Word. Keep your eyes on the answer."

I once overheard someone say to another person, "Oh, you look sick! You look like you have a cold."

The other person replied, "No, I don't. I'm not sick."

The first person said, "Well, your nose is running."

"No, it isn't."

"But you sound sick."

"No, I'm *not* sick," the second person insisted. But everyone around him could see he *was* sick. This person thought he was in faith, but he was just denying the problem.

God doesn't want us to do that. He just wants us to say, "It doesn't matter what I look like, feel like or sound like. The only thing that matters is what God says. God tells me that by Jesus' stripes I was healed, and I've chosen to believe Him!"

So don't deny the problem or try to think it away. Just look at it and say, "Who cares? The answer is mine—I have God's Word on it!"

Confession:

I don't deny the problems that arise in my life. I just
believe God's Word, which is greater than any symptoms,
circumstances or problems. I am fully persuaded that what
God has promised, He is able to do. (Rom. 4:21.)

AUGUST 8

Fix Your Eyes on God's Word

Wherefore let him that thinketh he standeth take heed lest he fall. —1 Corinthians 10:12

The enemy will do anything in the world to get a believer's eyes off the answer and back on the problem. For instance, I've heard people say, "I believe I'm healed! I believe I'm healed!" But when their bodies have started to feel a little better, they've gotten their eyes off the Word and back over on their bodies. Then they say, "Oh, I know I'm getting better now because I *feel* better."

That sounds good, but if believers get their eyes off the Word for *any* reason, it could get them in trouble. If they say, "I know I'm healed because my body feels better," what will they do if their bodies feel worse the next day? More than likely, they'll fall back into doubt and unbelief.

We don't need any other reason to believe we're well except 1 Peter 2:24: "By Jesus' stripes, we *were* healed." If the enemy can keep us watching our symptoms— whether those symptoms are getting better *or* worse—he has control over us.

But as we keep our eyes on the Word, it doesn't matter what our bodies feel like. Ultimately, they will have to respond to that anointed Word!

Confession:

I'm not moved by what I see or feel. I'm moved only by the Word of God. I know I'm healed, simply because the Bible says that by Jesus' stripes, I was healed.

In those days was Hezekiah sick unto death. And Isaiah the prophet the son of Amoz came unto him, and said unto him, Thus saith the Lord, Set thine house in order: for thou shalt die, and not live.

Then Hezekiah turned his face toward the wall, and prayed unto the Lord.   –Isaiah 38:1,2

AUGUST 9

Turn Your Face to the Wall

Hezekiah was the king of Judah, and he was sick unto death. In other words, he suffered from a terminal illness. A lot of people are shaken when doctors tell them that they're not going to live. Imagine what it was like for Hezekiah when *God* gave him that message!

The prophet Isaiah came to the king and said, "Thus saith the Lord, Set thine house in order: for thou shalt die, and not live." It's important to understand that God wasn't judging the man. God was simply telling him that his disease was terminal. God gave Hezekiah a natural diagnosis: He was going to die and not live. Therefore, Hezekiah was supposed to set his house in order.

But the king decided he would rather live. The next verse says, "Then Hezekiah *turned his face toward the wall,* and prayed unto the Lord." Hezekiah not only prayed, but he turned his face to the wall. What does that mean? Well, the prophet Isaiah had just laid out King Hezekiah's situation before him. The king could see his symptoms, his pain and his dismal future. But in response, he just turned his face to the wall—away from all natural circumstances—and started talking to God.

Hezekiah decided not to watch the symptoms or the pain. He chose not to dwell on the bad report. Instead, he turned away from all of that and fixed his eyes, his attention, his words and his prayers on Almighty God.

Confession:

When symptoms attack my body, I turn my face to the wall and say, "Father, I thank You that Your Word is true." I don't deny the symptoms, but I don't dwell on them either. I look to Jesus and receive the healing He has provided for me.

AUGUST 10

Believing God Is Easy!

Have faith in God. For verily I say unto you, That whosoever shall say unto this mountain, Be thou removed, and be thou cast into the sea; and shall not doubt in his heart, but shall believe that those things which he saith shall come to pass; he shall have whatsoever he saith.

Therefore I say unto you, What things soever ye desire, when ye pray, believe that ye receive them, and ye shall have them.   *—Mark 11:22-24*

Jesus gives His disciples some good instruction on the subject of faith here. He starts out by saying, "Have faith in God." Then in verse 23, Jesus gives the two foundational principles: Believe in your heart and say with your mouth.

Verse 24 starts with the word *therefore,* which connects verse 24 with the previous two verses. That tells us Jesus is still teaching on the subject of having faith in God: "Therefore I say unto you, What things soever ye desire, when ye pray, believe that ye receive them, and ye shall have them."

I used to look at that verse and think, *Lord, why did You make it so hard to receive from You? Why do we have to believe? Why can't we just throw a prayer out in the atmosphere and see if You take it or leave it?* I tried that method for years, and it didn't work, because I wasn't praying the way He'd told me to pray.

"When ye pray, *believe."* But why did I have to believe? It all seemed so hard. Then one day I read that verse and realized, *Lord, that's not hard! It's the easiest thing in the world!*

You see, you've never prayed a prayer in your life without believing *something.* Believing is the easiest, most natural thing in the world. The question is, *what* do you believe?

And what does God want you to believe? "When ye pray, believe *that ye receive."* Believe that your request is granted unto you—and you *shall* have it!

Confession:

God says He is the God who heals me. I ask Him right now to heal me according to His Word, and I believe I receive my request!

Therefore I say unto you, What things soever ye desire, when ye pray, believe that ye receive them, and ye shall have them. —Mark 11:24

Believe That You Receive

I remember when I first got saved, I'd pray, "Oh Lord, I ask You to heal me in Jesus' name. I ask You for healing. Amen." Then when someone would ask, "Did you get anything?" I'd check and say, "Well, no, I don't believe so." And according to my faith it would be done unto me. I'd pray and then I'd believe I wouldn't get anything, so I wouldn't get anything. My faith worked all the time!

Jesus did *not* say, "When you pray, believe you don't receive anything, and you'll have it." It sounds funny, but a lot of us prayed that way for years. A lot of people still do. They pray and then check to see whether their bodies feel any better or whether the symptoms are gone. And if nothing is different, they don't believe they received anything.

That's not what Jesus said to do. If we want His results, we have to follow His instructions. He didn't say, "When you pray, believe you didn't receive anything." He said, "When you pray, *believe you receive.*"

Confession:

When I pray for healing, I don't check to see if symptoms are gone or if anything in my body has changed. I believe I receive when I pray, and God sees to it that my healing manifests.

AUGUST 12

The Present Tense of Faith

Therefore I say unto you, What things soever ye desire, when ye pray, believe that ye receive them, and ye shall have them." —Mark 11:24

Here's another way to pray and believe that sounds really spiritual but is wrong: "Oh Father, I ask You to heal me in Jesus' name. I ask You for results. Amen." Now, up to this point this person is doing fine.

But then when someone asks the person, "Well, did you get anything?" the person checks to see and says, "Well, I tell you one thing. I believe God *is going* to heal me."

That sounds really good because the person is saying, "I believe."

I've seen people do this. They're sincerely believing in their hearts, but they're sincerely wrong in the way they're believing.

I was talking recently with a friend, and he mentioned a person we both knew. He said, "Man, he didn't get his healing, and I know he was in faith. I know he was believing God."

"Really?" I asked.

"Yes, I heard him. He kept saying, 'You watch—God is going to heal me. I believe God is going to heal me.'"

But Jesus didn't say, "When you pray, believe you're going to get something, and you'll have it." No, faith always speaks in the present tense.

If we analyze that person's words a little, it becomes obvious what he's saying: "Well, I prayed. I don't feel any better; I don't sound any better; I don't look any better. Therefore, I don't believe I am better. But although I don't believe I've received a thing yet, you can bet I'll believe it when I feel better!"

A lot of us were caught up in that erroneous way of thinking at one time. We'd say, "You watch—I believe God is going to work a miracle for me someday. God will heal me when He's ready."

Jesus didn't say, "When you pray, believe you *didn't* get anything." Neither did He say, "When you pray, believe you're *going to* get something." He told us exactly how to pray in faith: "When you pray, *believe that you receive*"—present tense!

Confession:

*Healing belongs to me as a child of God.
I'm not going to be healed—I'm already healed
because I believe I receive my answer when I pray.*

Therefore I say unto you, What things soever ye desire, when ye pray, believe that ye receive them, and ye shall have them. —Mark 11:24

Two Points in Time

We're still talking about the prayer of faith—the kind of prayer that receives from God what legally belongs to you because of the death, burial and resurrection of Jesus. When you pray, believing you receive, you shall have what you pray for.

I always thought the prayer of faith and receiving from God involved just one point in time. I thought, *Well, you're supposed to pray and then look to see if anything happened. If it didn't, tough luck—try again later. See if you can catch God in a better mood.* That was the way my prayer life operated for a long time.

But this Scripture shows us that the prayer of faith includes two points in time. Jesus said, "When you pray, believe you receive your answer"—present tense. Then He said, "And you *shall* have it"—future tense.

When will you have it? After you believe you receive it. When do you believe you receive it? Before you have it.

"Well, I can't believe it then, because I don't have it." But you have to believe it *before* you have it. "But how can I believe I have it when I don't?" You believe you receive when you pray, and you *shall have* your answer. "Yes, but I don't have it." But you have to believe you receive *first.*

Some people get hung up on this key point. They put the cart before the horse. They want to pray and receive their answer before they believe they received it. But Jesus said, "When you pray, believe you receive, and you shall have what you pray for."

The first step is to pray and believe we receive the answer. Then we go through the period of time that the Bible calls "walking by faith and not by sight." (2 Cor. 5:7.) Then our second step is to actually see our answer come into full manifestation.

Confession:

When I need healing in my body, I ask God for it, believing I receive what He said is mine. Then I stand in faith until the healing manifests in my body. My Father is pleased when I believe and act on His Word.

AUGUST 14

First the Believing, Then the Having

Therefore I say unto you, What things soever ye desire, when ye pray, believe that ye receive them, and ye shall have them.   –Mark 11:24

We are to pray, believing we receive our answer; then the answer comes. But well-meaning Christians say, "Well, you know, I have trouble believing I have something until I feel it." These people say, "I'm not going to believe I'm healed until I feel better. I just can't believe I've received anything I can't see."

In case that thought has ever come to you, let me ask you this: Do you believe you have a brain? Have you ever seen your brain? That may seem like a strange question, but it proves a point. You have no proof that you have a brain. The anatomy book says it's there; a doctor may say it's there. But otherwise, you have no proof.

When you stop to think about it, about 80 percent of the things we believe are accepted as truth without feeling or seeing them. I know when I was going through school, I believed what I read in the history books. For instance, I wasn't around when George Washington was alive, but I believed the history book when it said he was our first president.

We need to attribute more credibility to God's Word than we do to history books. Sometimes we're willing to believe anything we read *except* the Bible; then we say, "Lord, give me a sign."

We have to believe we receive; *then* we will have. First comes the believing; then comes the having. When we operate in that kind of faith, we'll get so excited about believing for our answer that we will forget to check to see when it actually manifests!

Confession:

The blessings God has provided for me come to pass in my life. I believe I receive the healing I've asked of Him. Therefore, I shall see healing manifested in my body.

Therefore I say unto you, What things soever ye desire, when ye pray, believe that ye receive them, and ye shall have them. —Mark 11:24

Believe Without Seeing First

S ome people ask, "Is it scriptural to believe you receive before you see or feel anything?" Let's look at a Bible illustration to find the answer to that question.

Remember, Jesus told the Jews, "Tear this temple down, and I'll raise it in three days." (John 2:19.) He told the disciples over and over again, "I'm going, but I'll be back." But when He went to the Cross, the disciples thought He was dead and gone for good.

But then Jesus was resurrected, and He appeared to His disciples. Thomas, however, wasn't present when Jesus came. When Thomas showed up later, the others told him, "Thomas, we've seen the Lord!" Thomas replied, "Except I shall see in his hands the print of the nails, and put my finger into the print of the nails, and thrust my hand into his side, I will not believe" (John 20:25).

Thomas, who probably thought he was being spiritual, was saying, "You say you saw Jesus, but I'm not getting caught up in your imaginations. I'm not believing anything until I can see and touch Him."

A few days later, the disciples were all together, and Jesus apparently came walking in without opening the door. The first thing He did was walk over to Thomas and say, "Reach hither thy finger, and behold my hands; and reach hither thy hand, and thrust it into my side: and be not faithless, but believing" (John 20:27). Thomas had thought he was being really spiritual, but Jesus told him, "Quit being faithless; just believe."

Jesus continued to set His doubting disciple straight: "Thomas, because thou hast seen me, thou hast believed: blessed are they that have not seen, and yet have believed" (John 20:29).

Jesus said the blessed ones are those who believe without seeing first. I want to be on the blessed side of life; don't you?

Confession:

I'm blessed because I believe the Word of God. The moment I pray for my healing, I believe I receive my healing, and I know it is mine. But even before the manifestation comes, I'm blessed!

AUGUST 16

Move Up to the Next Faith Level

And there was a certain nobleman, whose son was sick at Capernaum. When he heard that Jesus was come out of Judea into Galilee, he went unto him, and besought him that he would come down, and heal his son: for he was at the point of death.

Then said Jesus unto him, Except ye see signs and wonders, ye will not believe. —John 4:46-48

Understand this situation. This man was a nobleman. He was a ruler; he was important. When he said, "Come to my house," people didn't question it; they just asked, "What time?" I'm sure no one argued with him; no one refused.

The nobleman had heard of Jesus, the miracle worker, the One who never turned anyone down. So the nobleman came to Jesus and said, "Come down to my house; my son is at the point of death. Come and heal him."

Jesus turned to him and said, "If you don't see signs and wonders, you won't believe." Jesus had instantly located this man's faith level.

Think back to Jairus, the ruler of the synagogue in Mark 5, who came to Jesus and said, "Come to my house. My little daughter is at the point of death. But if You lay hands on her, she will live and be healed." Jesus went with him, and the child was healed.

Why did Jesus go with one father and not with the other? I don't know, but He got results in both cases. Both fathers needed miracles for their children, so Jesus just followed the Holy Ghost.

The nobleman had faith to believe that if Jesus came to his house, his son would receive a miracle. But Jesus wanted more than just to heal this father's son. He wanted to grab the man by his faith and yank him up to a higher level. He wanted to teach him a lesson in faith and show him the power of His Word so his life would be changed forever.

Confession:

Jesus wants me well, but He also wants me to keep moving up to higher levels of faith. So I step out this day on His Word of healing and expect that Word to effect a healing and a cure in my physical body!

The nobleman saith unto him, Sir, come down ere my child die.

Jesus saith unto him, Go thy way; thy son liveth. And the man believed the word that Jesus had spoken unto him, and he went his way.

—John 4:49,50

Faith Comes Before the Physical Evidence

The nobleman said, "Jesus, if You come, my son will live; if You don't, he'll die. Work a special miracle. Move in a sovereign way."

Jesus replied, "Go your way, and believe what I say: Your son lives."

That put the nobleman in a difficult spot. He had traveled more than twenty miles to see Jesus. That was a long trip, even if he had the fastest chariot around! He didn't see or feel anything—no burning bush, no goose bumps, no gifts of the Spirit in manifestation. All he had to hold on to were the bare words of Jesus the master.

So the nobleman had to make the choice: *Should I stand here and argue with Jesus, or should I take Him at His Word?*

The man decided to turn around and head home. He simply stepped out, believing the word that was spoken. As he traveled back to his home, the devil probably tried to talk to his mind, saying, *How can you just accept Jesus' words? Your son is in bad shape! Don't you have any feelings? Jesus isn't coming back with you!*

The nobleman demonstrated true faith. He traveled home, believing his son was well, with nothing but the Word of God to stand on. He probably traveled at least ten miles before he met his servants, who gave him the good news about his son: "Thy son liveth" (v. 51).

The nobleman had already believed for an entire day with no physical evidence that his son was getting better. Then he heard the good news about his son's healing and realized it had occurred at the same time that Jesus had said, "Go thy way; thy son liveth" (v. 50)!

This is a picture of faith toward God. The minute the nobleman believed the spoken Word and headed for home, acting as though it were true, his son began to amend.

Confession:

The Word says by Jesus' stripes I am healed. I believe that Word, not according to how I feel, but according to what God has said. I count the work done! My body will begin to amend from this very hour!

AUGUST 18

Amending "From That Hour"

And as he was now going down, his servants met him, and told him, saying, Thy son liveth.

Then inquired he of them the hour when he began to amend. And they said unto him, Yesterday at the seventh hour the fever left him. So the father knew that it was at the same hour, in the which Jesus said unto him, Thy son liveth: and himself believed, and his whole house.

—John 4:51-53

Jesus had told the nobleman, "Thy son liveth" (v. 50). The next day, the servants who met the nobleman on the road home said the same thing to him, word for word. When the man believed the Word Jesus spoke, his son was healed, and it changed his entire household.

God's Word is just as powerful as His physical presence. If we'll take Him at His Word, His Word will do anything He could do if He stood right here in the flesh. That's what God is trying to teach His Church right now.

Have faith in God's Word. You can believe what God says, no matter what the situation looks like, seems like, sounds like, tastes like or feels like. Just take God at His Word.

Notice that the nobleman inquired the hour his son *began* to amend. He understood that his son's healing had been gradual.

This is where a lot of people have trouble in receiving from God. Many times after people stand in healing lines and have hands laid on them for prayer, they go back to their seats, thinking, *Well, I don't feel any better; I don't believe I got a thing. I'll just have to try this again.* These people think all healings have to be instant.

Instant healings *are* available. But at the same time, it is just as scriptural to begin to amend "from that hour" as it is to be instantly healed. The truth is that more people gradually recover than instantly get healed. But all we should care about is that God is our healer, whether our healing is instantaneous or gradual—even if it takes a few minutes, hours or even days.

Confession:

The moment I ask for healing, my body begins to amend. The minute I take God at His Word, His power starts working on the problem and bringing the manifestation.

And as he entered into a certain village, there met him ten men that were lepers, which stood afar off: and they lifted up their voices, and said, Jesus, Master, have mercy on us.

And when he saw them, he said unto them, Go shew yourselves unto the priests. And it came to pass, that, as they went, they were cleansed.

—Luke 17:12-14

AUGUST 19

Healed as They Went

The ten lepers cried out, "Jesus, Master, have mercy on us." Apparently, they had heard of Jesus the healer, because they called Him "Master." And since faith comes by hearing, they came expecting something. They came in faith.

However, under the Levitical Law, lepers were to be stoned if they came within 100 paces of a healthy human being. So these ten lepers stood afar off and cried out to Jesus for help. Jesus instructed them to go show themselves to the priests. Verse 14 says, "And it came to pass, that, *as they went,* they were cleansed."

Did you notice that the lepers weren't cleansed until *after* they went? Many people don't get healed because they don't "went"! They sit around hoping they will somehow receive a miracle. Meanwhile, God wants them to believe they receive their healing and then go their way in faith.

That "went" part was the lepers' act of faith. When Jesus told them, "Go show yourselves to the priests," they immediately turned around and started on their way. They didn't feel anything; they didn't see anything. In the natural, their condition wasn't any better. But when they obeyed what Jesus had told them to do, they were healed.

Like the ten lepers, we have to take God at His Word, regardless of what we see or feel. We have to believe we have the answer and go our way in faith. Remember, those lepers were healed *as they went.* But they had to "went" before they were healed!

Confession:

Symptoms may seem to keep me "afar off" from victory, but I believe I receive God's provision of healing. And as I go my way, believing, God's healing power works wholeness and strength in my physical body!

AUGUST 20

Healing Is the Work of God

And as Jesus passed by, he saw a man which was blind from his birth. And his disciples asked him, saying, Master, who did sin, this man, or his parents, that he was born blind?

Jesus answered, Neither hath this man sinned, nor his parents: but that the works of God should be made manifest in him. I must work the works of him that sent me. —*John 9:1-4*

In Jesus' day, religious people thought that if someone was born with a sickness or disease, then either the parents had sinned before the child was born or the child had sinned while in the mother's womb. So the disciples asked Jesus, "Who sinned—the man or his parents?"

Now, Jesus' response in the *King James Version* is a little unclear: "Neither hath this man sinned, nor his parents: but that the works of God should be made manifest in him." It sounds as though God made this man blind just so Jesus could heal him and give God the glory.

But, remember, the New Testament was originally written in Greek, and there was no punctuation—no periods, no commas. All punctuation was later inserted by the Bible translators. Therefore, you could change a period or question mark without changing anything in the original manuscripts.

So let's look at this verse another way. "Neither hath this man sinned, nor his parents [period]." Jesus answered their question. "But that the works of God should be made manifest in him [comma], I must work the works of him that sent me."

When we change those two punctuation marks, which were not in the original manuscripts, it changes the whole meaning of Jesus' response to the disciples and takes all the blame off God. Suddenly the verse lines up with the context of the rest of Scripture.

Jesus didn't attribute the blindness to God. Healing is the work of God; sickness is the work of the enemy. Instead, Jesus said, "Now I'll work the works of Him who sent Me." Then He healed the man.

Confession:

Jesus never made anyone sick but healed all who came to Him in faith. I come to Him now in faith and receive God's work of healing in my body.

That it might be fulfilled which was spoken by Esaias the prophet, saying, Himself took our infirmities, and bare our sicknesses.

–Matthew 8:17

AUGUST 21

Jesus Bore Our Sickness

Jesus took our infirmities and bore our sicknesses. Some people have said to me, "Now, Brother, you must realize this verse is talking about a spiritual healing." But that erroneous way of thinking has put people in early graves. The infirmities and sicknesses God is talking about here aren't spiritual in nature. Just back up about four verses, and you'll see what Jesus did to fulfill that Old Testament Scripture.

A centurion had come to Jesus and said, "My servant is home sick of the palsy. Just speak the Word and my servant will be healed." (Matt. 8:8.) "And Jesus said unto the centurion, Go thy way; and as thou hast believed, so be it done unto thee. And his servant was healed in the selfsame hour" (v. 13). That's physical healing.

Then Jesus went to Peter's house, where Peter's mother-in-law lay sick with a fever. "And he touched her hand, and the fever left her: and she arose, and ministered unto them" (v. 15). That's physical healing.

Finally, verse 16 says, "When the even was come, they brought unto him many that were possessed with devils: and he cast out the spirits with his word, and healed all that were sick." That's physical healing.

Then, after all those physical healings, Matthew says, "That it might be fulfilled which was spoken by Esaias the prophet, saying, Himself took our infirmities, and bare our sicknesses." Jesus fulfilled this Scripture by physically healing people. That means Jesus bore our physical infirmities on the Cross so we could live healthy and whole all the days of our lives!

Confession:

In His death, burial and resurrection, Jesus paid for both my sins and sicknesses. I am free from sickness and pain, because He already bore them for me!

AUGUST 22

Let God Use You To Heal the Sick

And he said unto them, Go ye into all the world, and preach the gospel to every creature.

And these signs shall follow them that believe; In my name...they shall lay hands on the sick, and they shall recover. —Mark 16:15,17,18

Jesus listed several signs that are to follow those who believe in Him. One important sign is that "they shall lay hands on the sick, and they shall recover." This sign is not just for preachers. It's for all believers.

Some say, "Well, I don't know why God never uses *me* that way." I made the mistake of thinking that one time. I read that Scripture and thought, *Boy, I don't know why God never uses me to heal anyone. He never works through me through the laying on of hands to heal the sick.*

But then I got quiet for a minute down on the inside. (You know, if you'll get quiet, you'll receive some answers!) All of a sudden, I heard this: *How many people have you laid hands on recently?*

Well, that woke me up. I started laying hands on people, and guess what? They got healed!

If we'll just be obedient to the Word, it will work. We don't have to wonder why God never uses us. As we start laying hands on the sick, He will! It's up to us. It's our job. Healing the sick is part of the Gospel, and we're to take the Gospel into all the world!

Confession:

I'm a believer, so I expect signs to follow me according to the Word. When I lay hands on the sick, they are healed. God's Word works in me, for me and through me!

In the beginning was the Word, and the Word was with God, and the Word was God.

And the Word was made flesh, and dwelt among us.... —John 1:1,14

Tell the World, "God Wants You Well!"

Jesus Christ was the Word that became flesh and dwelt among us. During His earthly ministry, Jesus healed all who came to Him in faith. Now we have the written Word, and it's full of healing from one end to the other.

No wonder God said, "He sent *his word,* and healed them, and delivered them from their destructions" (Ps. 107:20). No wonder He said, "Attend to *my words;* incline thine ear unto *my sayings.* Let them not depart from thine eyes; keep them in the midst of thine heart. For they are life unto those that find them, and health to all their flesh" (Prov. 4:20-22).

If we take time to read and study the Word, the revelation knowledge that God wants us healthy and whole will become a part of us. We'll be able to step into a life of divine health. You see, we can only receive healing by faith when we know it's God's will to heal us, because faith is believing God's known will and acting like it's true. We have to know the Word says healing is ours.

Jesus, the Word made flesh, was sent to heal us. When we received Jesus as Savior, He also became our healer. Now, by inspiration of the Holy Ghost, we've been given the Word in written form. No matter how we look at the Word, we'll find healing from every angle, because in the beginning was the Word, and the Word was with God and the Word was God. Jesus is the Word, and Jesus is the healer!

Confession:

God's Word was sent to heal me. I attend to His Word and keep it before my eyes, and it becomes life to me. His Word becomes medicine to my flesh, and I am healed and made whole.

AUGUST 24

Under the Shadow of His Wings

But unto you that fear my name shall the Sun of righteousness arise with healing in his wings....
—Malachi 4:2

One day I was meditating on the Word, when suddenly Malachi 4:2 rose up in me: "But unto you that fear my name shall the Sun of righteousness arise with healing in his wings." Who is the "Sun of righteousness"? Jesus! When I read this, I thought, *Glory to God! He arose with healing in His wings!* Then I asked, "Lord, why is healing in His *wings,* and how do I get under those wings?"

I remembered Psalm 91:1-4 AMP:

He who dwells in the secret place of the Most High shall remain stable and fixed under the shadow of the Almighty [Whose power no foe can withstand]. I will say of the Lord, He is my Refuge and my Fortress, my God; on Him I lean and rely, and in Him I [confidently] trust!

For [then] He will deliver you from the snare of the fowler and from the deadly pestilence. [Then] He will cover you with His pinions, and under His wings shall you trust and find refuge.

You find refuge under God's wings when you say, "Thank God for Jesus! He's my refuge, my fortress, my healer and my Savior." Once you're under His wings, you'll find they're full of healing. All you have to do is reach up and pluck out a couple of those feathers; there are plenty to go around!

Jesus arose with healing in His wings. We can abide in His healing power and find refuge in the shelter of His wings. All we have to do is confess Jesus as our Lord and put ourselves under His protective covering. In that secret place of the Most High, we're surrounded by healing. We just have to reach out and grab ahold of it!

Confession:

Jesus is my Savior, my God, my healer, my refuge, my fortress.
He arose with healing in His wings, and I take refuge under those wings.
I put my trust in the Sun of righteousness and His healing power.

I beseech you therefore, brethren, by the mercies of God, that ye present your bodies a living sacrifice, holy, acceptable unto God, which is your reasonable service. —Romans 12:1

Present Your Body a Living Sacrifice

Paul tells us here to present our bodies as a living sacrifice to God. It's interesting to note what God says about sacrifices in Malachi 1:7-8,13.

Ye offer polluted bread upon mine altar; and ye say, Wherein have we polluted thee? In that ye say, The table of the Lord is contemptible. And if ye offer the blind for sacrifice, is it not evil? and if ye offer the lame and sick, is it not evil?...

...And ye brought that which was torn, and the lame, and the sick; thus ye brought an offering: should I accept this of your hand? saith the Lord.

God isn't saying He gets angry with us when we present our sick, broken, lame bodies as a sacrifice to Him. He's saying we need to line our bodies up with His Word and believe that Jesus took our infirmities and bore our sicknesses. Then we can present our bodies as a living sacrifice to Him, and He'll make them whole.

God wants your body presented as a living, *wholly acceptable* sacrifice, but only He can make it that way. He said in His Word that by Jesus' stripes, you were healed. Just begin to believe that in your heart, say it with your mouth and act like it's true. Then you can present your body as a living sacrifice, no matter what it looks like or feels like, and the power of God will make it whole!

Confession:

I present my body to the Lord as a living sacrifice, believing I am healed because Jesus took my sicknesses and carried my pains. The greater One inside me heals this body I offer, so that it is acceptable and pleasing to the Lord.

AUGUST 26

In Remembrance

The Lord Jesus the same night in which he was betrayed took bread: and when he had given thanks, he brake it, and said, Take, eat: this is my body, which is broken for you: this do in remembrance of me. After the same manner also he took the cup, when he had supped, saying, This cup is the new testament in my blood: this do ye, as oft as ye drink it, in remembrance of me. For as often as ye eat this bread, and drink this cup, ye do shew the Lord's death till he come.   —1 Corinthians 11:23-26

In Exodus 12, God told His people, who were living in bondage in Egypt, "Slay a spotless lamb and put its blood on the doorposts; then roast the lamb and eat it. But before you do, pack your bags, put your marching shoes on and get ready to travel, because after you partake of the lamb, you're coming out of this bondage."

As the Israelites ate the body of that Passover lamb, they *looked ahead* to the redemptive work that would be accomplished when Jesus Christ went to the Cross. Under the new covenant, we take Communion to *look back* and remember what Jesus did for us.

We once were trapped in the bondage of sickness, worry, fear, discouragement and depression. But the perfect Lamb shed His blood to redeem us from every yoke of bondage. Therefore, God's message to us is similar to what He said to the Israelites in Egypt. He says to us, "When you partake of the symbols of the body of the Lord Jesus Christ, put your marching shoes on and get ready to come out of bondage!"

Communion services should be some of the biggest healing rallies around. When we partake of Communion, we remember what Jesus Christ did for us. For instance, we partake of the bread in remembrance of Jesus' body, broken for our physical healing. Therefore, we should say, "Thank You, Jesus, that by Your shed blood on the Cross, my sins were washed away. By Your broken body, I've been healed. And by Your chastisement, I have peace of mind." (Isa. 53:5.)

Confession:

On the Cross, Jesus freed my spirit, soul and body from all bondage. Now I partake of Communion, believing I'm freed from sin and sickness because of His finished work.

Even when we were dead in sins, hath quickened us together with Christ, (by grace ye are saved;) and hath raised us up together, and made us sit together in heavenly places in Christ Jesus.

–Ephesians 2:5,6

AUGUST 27

Seated in Heavenly Places

We are seated in heavenly places in Christ Jesus. Ephesians 1:3 says, "Blessed be the God and Father of our Lord Jesus Christ, who hath blessed us with all spiritual blessings *in heavenly places in Christ.*" We're blessed to be a part of the body of Christ, because all things have been put under His feet. We may just be the skin on the bottom of the left foot; but sickness and disease are still beneath us, and we're walking on top of them!

No sickness or disease can exist in heavenly places, and that's where we are. That's the way God looks at us. When we beg or plead for healing, He doesn't know what we're talking about. He sees us seated with Him in heavenly places, with every satanic bondage beneath our feet!

Sickness and disease keep trying to crawl up on the body of Christ, and it's up to us to resist them. James 4:7 says, "Resist the devil, and he will flee from you." And Paul exhorts us never to give place to the devil. (Eph. 4:27.)

Jesus gave us all authority over the devil. He told His disciples, "All power is given unto me in heaven and in earth. Go ye therefore" (Matt. 28:18,19). He also said, "Behold, I give unto you power to tread on serpents and scorpions, and over all the power of the enemy: and nothing shall by any means hurt you" (Luke 10:19). Sickness and disease hurt when they attack, but Jesus said, *"Nothing* shall by any means hurt *you."*

We need to use our authority to keep the enemy from climbing back up on the body of Christ. Let's overcome sickness. Let's get rid of it! Jesus has already overcome the enemy. But it's up to us to stand in faith for our rights and refuse to let the devil rob us!

Confession:

I'm part of the body of Christ, so I'm seated with Jesus in heavenly places. Sickness is under my feet. Jesus has already destroyed the devil's works, so I walk in my Lord's victory!

AUGUST 28

I can do all things through Christ which strengtheneth me. —*Philippians 4:13*

Draw Strength From Jesus

Jesus Christ is our strength. I don't know about you, but every time I've had a disease or sickness try to attach itself to me, it hasn't given me strength; it's drawn strength *out of* me. But then I turn to the promises in God's Word. As I continually keep my eyes on Jesus and draw strength from Him, that sickness has to leave!

In the Old Testament, when the children of Israel were bitten by serpents, they had to look steadfastly at the brass serpent on the pole in order to be healed. (Num. 21:8,9.) That brass serpent was a type of Jesus Christ, because when Jesus hung on the Cross, He became sin for us. (2 Cor. 5:21.) And if we fix our gaze upon Jesus Christ and what He did for us on the Cross of Calvary, then we, too, can receive our healing.

But that means we must look at *Him* and not at the symptoms. The reason we've had such trouble getting rid of symptoms is that we've spent too much time looking at them. Second Corinthians 4:18 says, "We look not at the things which are seen, but at the things which are not seen: for the things which are seen are temporal; but the things which are not seen are eternal."

That which is seen is temporal, or subject to change. That which is not seen is eternal, or *not* subject to change. In other words, we could say, "For we look not at the symptoms but at the promises of God's Word, because the symptoms are subject to change according to the promises of God's Word!"

Confession:

I keep my eyes on Jesus, my strength. Circumstances, situations and symptoms must change, but the Word of God will never change. I constantly attend to His Word, and it is life to me and medicine to my flesh.

Submit yourselves therefore to God. Resist the devil, and he will flee from you. —James 4:7

Don't Accept the Devil's Package!

If the devil is trying to put symptoms on you, you have the authority to get rid of him!

The reason Christians have so much trouble getting rid of sickness and disease is that they accept the symptoms to begin with. A little, green-eyed monster comes knocking on their door to deliver the package, and they say, "Oh, let's see—watery eyes, runny nose, sore throat, headache. Yes, I do believe I'm getting the flu!" They take the package and then suddenly say, "Hey, wait a minute! I don't want this!" But once received, the package is difficult to give back.

So when sickness comes knocking on your door, remember not to accept the package! Say, "Let's see—watery eyes, runny nose, headache, sore throat. No, no, no, no! I'm not going to take that. Devil, I resist you in the name of Jesus! You won't put that on me! I've been redeemed from poverty, sickness and death. You won't give that to me. In the name of Jesus, you take your symptoms and get out of here!"

You have the authority to do that. So take your stand against the enemy. Refuse every package of symptoms he tries to deliver to your doorstep!

Confession:

*I rebuke sickness when it tries to come on me.
I exercise my faith when I first notice symptoms,
and those symptoms have to go, in Jesus' name!*

AUGUST 30

For God hath not given us the spirit of fear; but of power, and of love, and of a sound mind.

—2 Timothy 1:7

Fear Not— Only Believe

Do you know what happens when you fear something? Job tells you in Job 3:25: "For the thing which I greatly feared is come upon me...." Fear opens the door for the things you fear to enter your life.

Fear often opens the door to sickness in people's lives. It produces worry, and worry is what puts about 80 percent of the people who are in the hospital there. They say, "Oh, I'm afraid I'll catch the flu," or "I'm afraid I'm going to get cancer," or "I'm afraid I'll have an accident." They're continually confessing, "I'm afraid of this; I'm afraid of that."

The Bible says, "Fear not; only believe." (Luke 8:50.) You see, you can't fear and believe at the same time. Fear opens the door to the devil and gives him room to move. In fact, *fear is faith in the devil.* Faith in God receives the best God has for you. Fear, or faith in the devil, receives the worst the enemy can give you.

But fear can't just latch onto you. It has to present itself to you; then it's up to you whether you want to receive it or resist it.

So when fear hits you, realize that you have the ability to get rid of it. You can say, "Fear, I resist you in the name of Jesus! You'll have no part of me, and I'll have no part of you!"

It's your choice. If you're experiencing all kinds of fear in your life, don't worry about the fear. Start putting the Word down inside you. Build your faith in the Word, and the fears will disappear!

Confession:

Jesus said, "Fear not; only believe." So the choice is mine, and I choose to believe God's Word. I do not fear sickness, for God sent His Word to heal me. I am confident, for my God is with me.

Now faith is the substance of things hoped for, the evidence of things not seen.

—Hebrews 11:1

AUGUST 31

Know God's Will

It's important to know God's will regarding the healing you need, because faith only operates on God's known will.

For example, if I told you I had $1000 in my pocket, you wouldn't come running over to me to get it, because I never promised I'd give it to you. You'd realize I had the money, but that wouldn't necessarily mean it was for you.

But suppose I said to you, "I have $1000 in my pocket, and I want to give it to you. Just come and get it." At that point, you'd have my promise as a foundation for your faith. And undoubtedly you'd quickly take hold of my promise and come receive your money! Once you knew my will on the matter, you could operate in faith.

It's the same way with God. You can't operate in faith until you know what His will is in the matter. But as you go through His Word, you can find His will concerning anything you need, including healing. You can find out that Jesus took your infirmities and bore your sicknesses. You can discover that by Jesus' stripes, you are healed. You can know beyond a shadow of a doubt that *God wants you well.*

Confession:

I know absolutely and without a doubt God's will for me regarding healing. Jesus took my infirmities and bore my sicknesses because my Father wants me well!

SEPTEMBER 1

Faith Turns God Loose!

And, behold, there cometh one of the rulers of the synagogue, Jairus by name; and when he saw him, he fell at his feet, and besought him greatly, saying, My little daughter lieth at the point of death: I pray thee, come and lay thy hands on her, that she may be healed; and she shall live.

And Jesus went with him.... —Mark 5:22-24

Jesus started walking with Jairus toward his house. About that time, the woman with the issue of blood came up behind Him in the crowd and touched the hem of His garment. Jesus turned and asked, "Who touched Me?" The woman fell down before Jesus and told Him how she had been healed. (Mark 5:25-33.)

All this was going on while Jairus' daughter was at home at the point of death. When Jesus finished with the woman, they all started again toward Jairus' house. But just then someone came running from Jairus' home and told him, "It's too late. Don't trouble the Master; your daughter has died."

Jesus immediately turned to Jairus and made a profound statement: "Fear not; only believe." At that moment, He laid out a choice before Jairus, telling him, "You're either going to fear, or you're going to believe. If you keep operating in faith, your child will be healed. But if you step over into fear, you shut off My power."

You see, our words can open the door for the devil to attack us. Proverbs 6:2 says, "Thou art snared with the words of thy mouth, thou art taken with the words of thy mouth." Fear allows Satan to work in our lives. It often starts out with worry, which is an offspring of fear, and that turns the devil loose.

When Jairus first found Jesus, he had spoken words of faith: "Jesus, if You lay hands on her, she will be healed and live." Now Jesus was giving him a choice, and Jairus chose to believe. He didn't speak one word of doubt or fear, and his little girl was raised from the dead. His faith turned God loose to work in his daughter's life.

Confession:

I refuse to allow fear to operate in my life. I make the choice to walk in faith. I speak words of life and truth that open the door for God to make me healthy and whole!

And lest I should be exalted above measure through the abundance of the revelations, there was given to me a thorn in the flesh, the messenger of Satan to buffet me, lest I should be exalted above measure.

For this thing I besought the Lord thrice, that it might depart from me. And he said unto me, My grace is sufficient for thee: for my strength is made perfect in weakness.

Most gladly therefore will I rather glory in my infirmities, that the power of Christ may rest upon me. —2 *Corinthians 12:7-9*

SEPTEMBER 2

Paul's "Thorn"— Persecution

The subject of Paul's thorn is a common argument against healing. Many have taught that Paul's thorn was a sickness or disease in his body. But in context, you can see that Paul was talking about *persecutions:*

Of the Jews five times received I forty stripes save one. Thrice was I beaten with rods, once was I stoned, thrice I suffered shipwreck, a night and a day I have been in the deep.

In weariness and painfulness, in watchings often, in hunger and thirst, in fastings often, in cold and nakedness.

2 Corinthians 11:24-25,27

Every place Paul went, there was a spirit that stirred people up to persecute him. He was beaten, whipped, stoned and left for dead. He talked about being cold, hungry and thirsty, floating around in the sea and experiencing distresses of all kinds.

These were all persecutions in one form or another. But Paul never said anything to indicate his thorn in the flesh was even remotely connected to sickness and disease.

However, Paul did say the thorn was a messenger of Satan, not a messenger of God: "There was given to me a thorn in the flesh, the messenger of Satan to buffet me." So we see that Paul's thorn wasn't sickness, it wasn't disease and it wasn't from God.

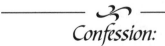

Confession:

Paul's thorn wasn't from God and neither are sickness and diseases that attack me. God gives me His grace, strength and ability to overcome the devil in every situation. I am the healed of the Lord!

SEPTEMBER 3

Paul's "Thorn in the Flesh"

And lest I should be exalted above measure through the abundance of the revelations, there was given to me a thorn in the flesh, the messenger of Satan to buffet me, lest I should be exalted above measure. —2 Corinthians 12:7

People have been telling me for years that Paul's "thorn in the flesh" was sickness. Some say it was an eye disease that God gave him to keep him humble. But that explanation twists the Scriptures.

How was Paul exalted beyond measure? He received visions and revelations from the Lord. God revealed to him great mysteries, which those who walked and talked with Jesus for three years didn't yet understand. Paul was also in the process of writing two-thirds of the New Testament, which we live by today.

Paul said, "There was given to me a thorn in the flesh, a messenger of Satan, to buffet me." Well, God wouldn't have sent a messenger of Satan to Paul. And God certainly wasn't going to exalt Paul by giving him visions and revelations just to make him sick and to keep him from being exalted!

The word *messenger* in the original Greek is the word "angelos." It refers to an angel or "one sent."[1] In this case, it refers to a demon spirit that Satan sent to harass Paul. Satan wanted to hinder Paul any way he could because he knew that those who read Paul's letters would follow his Holy Spirit-inspired instructions and walk in victory. So let's defeat Satan's purpose and start walking in God's victory today!

Confession:

God didn't send sickness to humble Paul, and He doesn't send sickness to humble me. I rebuke sickness and disease, for they have no part in God's plan or His will for me. I receive God's will of healing now.

For this thing I besought the Lord thrice, that it might depart from me. And he said unto me, My grace is sufficient for thee: for my strength is made perfect in weakness.

Most gladly therefore will I rather glory in my infirmities, that the power of Christ may rest upon me. —2 Corinthians 12:8,9

SEPTEMBER 4

His Grace Is Sufficient

Some people interpret this Scripture by saying, "Well, that means that after Paul prayed three times, God replied, *No, I want you to keep that "thorn." You need it. It will keep you humble and pious.*

No, that isn't what God meant! God said, "My grace is sufficient for thee."

What is God's grace? It's God's unmerited favor given to us in the form of His Word, His name, His kingdom, His Spirit, His healing, His power and His authority. God's grace is the source of the unmerited blessings He sent us through Jesus Christ. We didn't deserve any of those blessings, but Jesus made us righteous so we *could* deserve them. That's the measure of God's grace, and He told Paul, "My grace is sufficient for thee."

One aspect of God's grace is the name of Jesus. Jesus delegated His authority, might and dominion to us through His name. Then He said in Mark 16:17, "In my name shall [believers] cast out devils."

Jesus was telling Paul, "Look, I've given you everything you need to get rid of that evil messenger. Now just take authority over it." He was *not* saying, "I want you to keep that thorn in the flesh, Paul. You need it to help you stay humble and pious."

No, God was actually telling Paul, "My grace is sufficient for you. Don't go after that messenger of Satan in your own strength—go in *My* strength. From the position of your own weakness, make use of My strength. Resist the devil in the name of Jesus, and he'll flee from you!"

Confession:

God's grace is sufficient for me in every area of my life.
He has given me the name of Jesus—the name that is
greater than any other power that can come against me.
Through faith in Jesus' name, I am healed and made strong!

SEPTEMBER 5

The End Result

Now a certain man was sick, named Lazarus, of Bethany, the town of Mary and her sister Martha.

Therefore his sisters sent unto him, saying, Lord, behold, he whom thou lovest is sick.

When Jesus heard that, he said, This sickness is not unto death, but for the glory of God, that the Son of God might be glorified thereby.

–John 11:1,3,4

Don't misunderstand Jesus' comment about Lazarus' sickness. He was *not* saying, "Lazarus' sickness isn't unto death; nevertheless, he's suffering with this sickness to bring God glory."

If we're not careful, we can get confused because we don't study the Word enough to rightly divide it. Jesus wasn't talking about the *problem;* He was talking about the end result. Jesus always talked about the *end result.* He was saying here, "The end result of this sickness will not be death but the glory of God."

Again in John 11:40, Jesus told Martha, "I told you if you'd believe, you'd see the glory of God." The sickness took Lazarus' life for awhile, but his life was given back to him when Jesus raised him from the dead. Thus, Lazarus' sickness wasn't for God's glory; it was his resurrection from the dead that brought God glory. That was the end result.

Confession:

God is glorified when I am healed and walking in health. The end result of my life will be to God's glory. I walk in health and run my race, and I will finish my course with joy!

And on the morrow, when they were come from Bethany, he was hungry: and seeing a fig tree afar off having leaves, he came, if haply he might find any thing thereon: and when he came to it, he found nothing but leaves; for the time of figs was not yet. And Jesus answered and said unto it, No man eat fruit of thee hereafter for ever. —Mark 11:12-14

SEPTEMBER 6

Speak the Word and Go Your Way

Jesus came to a fig tree looking for fruit, but there was no fruit on it. So He cursed the fig tree, saying, "No man eat fruit of thee hereafter for ever," and then He just walked away.

We can learn something on the subject of faith right here. Jesus spoke the Word and then went His way. Although the tree didn't change immediately, Jesus didn't wonder whether His words had worked. He just walked away in faith that what He said would come to pass.

Jesus and the disciples left for Jerusalem. When they came back the next day, his disciples said, "Master, the fig tree you cursed is withered away! It died from the roots!" (v. 21.)

Second Corinthians 5:7 says, "For we walk by faith, not by sight." You see, it didn't matter what Jesus *saw*. It was what He *believed* that made the difference.

That's the very basis of faith. Faith is walking by what God says instead of by what you see—because what God says will *change* what you see! Faith is placing your confidence in the *truth*.

Romans 3:4 says, "Yea, let God be true, but every man a liar...." In John 17:17, Jesus is praying for us and says, "Sanctify them through thy truth: thy word is truth." God's Word takes precedence above any of our experiences, beliefs, opinions or doctrines. The only real truth we will ever find in this world is the Word of God. We can believe that Word and speak it forth in faith, confident in the knowledge that our words *will* come to pass!

Confession:

God's Word is true. I act on His Word—believing it, receiving it and speaking it—and it changes my circumstances. I walk in agreement with God's Word, and I enjoy His very best.

SEPTEMBER 7

Have the Faith of God

And in the morning, as they passed by, they saw the fig tree dried up from the roots. And Peter calling to remembrance saith unto him, Master, behold, the fig tree which thou cursedst is withered away.

And Jesus answering saith unto them, Have faith in God. —Mark 11:20-22

Jesus was about to teach his disciples about faith. Personally, I can't think of a better subject in the Bible to get ahold of than the subject of faith. It touches every other area of life. It touches everything we do. Everything we do is supposed to be in faith, "for whatsoever is not of faith is sin" (Rom. 14:23).

Faith is the easiest thing in the world to understand. When faith is taught, little children usually understand it first; then they go teach the adults! Faith is so simple that most adults spend all their time trying to figure it out. They think, *It can't be that simple!*

But Jesus made things simple for us. When He taught, He talked about everyday things, such as fishing and farming. He made spiritual principles simple so everyone could understand them.

So Jesus starts out His teaching on faith by saying, "Have faith in God." God is the One who works the miracles. He's the One who heals our bodies. He's the One who purchased all things that pertain to life and godliness. Therefore, our faith is to be placed in Him. If we only have faith in ourselves, we're in trouble.

So, according to Mark 11:22, our faith is in God. But in some Bibles, margin notes for this verse say, "Have the faith *of* God." If we have the faith of God, we have the kind of faith God has.

Romans 12:3 says, "...God hath dealt to every man *the measure of faith.*" So Jesus is telling us, "Just operate in faith as God does. God gave faith to us; He planted it on the inside of us, and it will operate for us the same way it does for Him." We're God's children, and He gave us His very own faith.

Confession:

*Because I'm God's child, He has planted His faith in me.
Now I'm able to operate in faith just as He does. I have
a sure foundation because I have the faith of God.*

And Jesus answering saith unto them, Have faith in God. For verily I say unto you, That whosoever shall say unto this mountain, Be thou removed, and be thou cast into the sea; and shall not doubt in his heart, but shall believe that those things which he saith shall come to pass; he shall have whatsoever he saith.

—Mark 11:22,23

SEPTEMBER 8

You Have the Faith To Receive

Here the Lord Jesus gives us the two basic foundational principles of operating in faith: *believing in the heart* and *saying with the mouth*.

Have you ever thought that the believing part sounded hard? People say all the time, "Oh, it's so hard to believe. I just wish I could believe God."

One fellow replied to that comment, "Well, if you can't believe, you ought to get saved." Let me explain what he meant by that.

Ephesians 2:8 tells us how we get saved: "For by grace are ye saved *through faith;* and that not of yourselves: it is the gift of God." Then Romans 10:10 says, *"With the heart man believeth* unto righteousness; and with the mouth confession is made unto salvation."

So the simple fact that you are saved proves you have faith. You have already used your faith to believe God for the biggest miracle in existence—the new birth. When you were born again, God took out that heart of stone and put in a heart of flesh, giving you a brand-new spirit.

You used your faith to receive the gift of salvation. That proves you have the ability to believe God. Now it's just a matter of learning how to point your faith in another direction to receive God's other benefits and blessings!

Confession:

By God's grace, I believed and received salvation through Jesus Christ. Now I believe and receive healing just as easily as I received eternal life!

SEPTEMBER 9

Faith Is of the Heart

For verily I say unto you, That whosoever shall say unto this mountain, Be thou removed, and be thou cast into the sea; and shall not doubt in his heart, but shall believe that those things which he saith shall come to pass; he shall have whatsoever he saith. –Mark 11:23

L et's look at two major principles of faith in this verse: *believing in the heart* and *saying with the mouth.*

People often make mistakes in the believing side of faith. You see, real faith is of the *heart,* not the *head.* Romans 10:10 confirms this, saying, "For with the heart man believeth unto righteousness...." People need to realize they don't have enough strength in their heads to believe in something they can't yet see.

Now, it's important to understand that you can have faith in your heart while doubts are coming into your head. For instance, at times I find Scriptures in the Word that cover my needs. I pray the prayer of faith, believe I receive and take my stand on the Word. On the inside, I have peace and rest; I know I'm in faith. But at the same time, doubts hit my mind one after another: *What if it doesn't work? It's not going to work.*

When these types of doubts start coming into your mind, it's easy to think, *Well, I thought I believed, but I guess I didn't.* But just realize that those doubts aren't yours. When thoughts of doubt come, cast them down and get rid of them in the name of Jesus. Don't try to believe with your head, or your faith level will be up and down like a yo-yo.

Remember, it's with the *heart*—the spirit, the inner man—that man believes. So if your mind is giving you fits when you're trying to stand in faith, just shut your head off and follow what's in your spirit!

─── ✌ ───

Confession:

With my heart I believe. I don't lean to my own understanding or allow doubts to hinder me. I pray for healing, and despite what I feel, think or see, I know I'm healed according to God's Word.

For verily I say unto you, That whosoever shall say unto this mountain, Be thou removed, and be thou cast into the sea; and shall not doubt in his heart, but shall believe that those things which he saith shall come to pass; he shall have whatsoever he saith.   *–Mark 11:23*

The Power of Words

A number of years ago, I heard a minister teaching on the subject of faith, and he said something that got my attention. Once as he was meditating on Mark 11:23, the Spirit of God spoke to his spirit and asked, *Did you notice that in Mark 11:23, Jesus talked about* saying *three times as much as He talked about* believing?

The minister said, "Apparently, we need to hear about the subject of saying three times more than we need to hear about the subject of believing. And if we're having trouble in our faith walk, it is probably in the saying part three times as often as it is in the believing part."

You see, we are a direct result of our words. Our lives today are a direct result of what we've been saying up until now. And what we say today is what we will be tomorrow. So as someone once said, "If you don't like what you are, quit saying what you're saying."

This is not "mind over matter" or "mind science"; these are Bible truths. Hebrews 11:3 says, "Through faith we understand that *the worlds were framed by the word of God....*" How did God create the earth? *By His words.* "And God *said,* Let there be light: and there was light" (Gen. 1:3). "And God *said,* Let there be a firmament in the midst of the waters..." (Gen. 1:6), and there was a firmament. How did God cause these things to come to pass? *By speaking.*

Romans 1:17 says that the just shall live by faith. How do we operate in faith? We have to *believe* and *say.* What we believe and what we say ultimately determine who we will be and what we will have in life.

Confession:

The words I speak today create who I will be and what I will have tomorrow. Therefore, I speak words of truth, grace, healing and abundance and they become reality in my life!

SEPTEMBER 11

Change From the Inside Out

Man shall not live by bread alone, but by every word of God. —Luke 4:4

Man is a three-part being: He is a spirit; he has a soul; he lives in a body. The Bible says he has an inward man and an outward man. (2 Cor. 4:16.)

The outward man is just your "earth suit." It's the vessel you live in that keeps you here on this earth. The outward man, which includes the soul and the body, is the part of you that everyone else sees; and it is probably the source of most of the problems you deal with.

The Bible says, "Therefore if any man be in Christ, he is a new creature: old things are passed away; behold, all things are become new" (2 Cor. 5:17). Where are old things passed away? Inside your spirit! You have the same body and mind you had before you were saved. Your body has to be healed and strengthened, and your mind has to be renewed through God's Word. However, your inner man is a brand-new creation.

The inward man is the spirit man. The outward man is simply a reflection of the inward man. So if I'm having problems in one area of my outward life and I hammer away on those problems from the outside, then I'm wasting my time. I'd better go back and make some adjustments on the inward man. Then the change that occurs on the inside will reflect on the outside.

For instance, suppose I'm having trouble in the area of healing and health. What should I do? I should find out what the Bible says about healing and health and then feed my spirit a steady diet of that truth. I have to read it, meditate on it, think about it and say it until it gets planted deep in my spirit. Jesus talked about this process when He said, "Let these sayings sink down into your ears" (Luke 9:44).

So eat some "faith food" from the Word of God. When you get full of the Word on the inside, it will show up on the outside, bringing peace to your mind and health to your body!

Confession:

I attend to God's words, and they are life to me and medicine to all my flesh. God's Word works mightily in my spirit to bring health, strength and wholeness to my outward man.

A good man out of the good treasure of his heart bringeth forth that which is good; and an evil man out of the evil treasure of his heart bringeth forth that which is evil: for of the abundance of the heart his mouth speaketh.

–Luke 6:45

SEPTEMBER 12

Locate Your Faith

You can locate your faith by your own words. Your words are your faith speaking.

Now, it's good practice to consciously make a good confession about your circumstances. But if you want to find out where you really are in your faith walk—if you want to know why some things aren't going right in your life—then listen to yourself talking when the pressure is on. See what comes out of your mouth when you're not making a conscious effort to speak something good. In other words, see what comes out of the abundance of your heart. Then you'll know if you need to make some major adjustments.

It's like a bank account. The bank sends you a statement each month. If you want them to add more to the final balance, what do you do? Put more money in the bank, and the next statement will show the difference.

It's the same way spiritually. When you want something to show up in your outward man, deposit the treasures of God's Word in the inward man. Feed on the Word continually. Treat your inner man like a bank vault, and just keep putting deposits of God's gold in there. Once the Word is deposited in your inner man, you'll believe it. Then once you believe it, you'll find yourself saying it. And once you start saying it, your entire being will reflect the treasure of His Word inside!

***

Confession:

I fill my heart with God's words of healing. Then when the pressure is on, I don't speak the symptoms. I speak only God's Word of life and health, and the power in His Word heals my body!

SEPTEMBER 13

...for of the abundance of the heart his mouth speaketh.   *—Luke 6:45*

What Are You Believing?

You can sometimes find out why a person is struggling in faith just by listening to him for a few minutes. For instance, people have come up to me after being prayed for in a healing line and have said, "Well, I still have such-and-such in my body. I don't know why I can't get rid of it."

I want to say to them, "You just told me why you haven't gotten rid of your condition! You see, they're believing they can't get rid of it.

I've had other folks say, "I never get healed. When someone prays for me, I never receive anything." These people receive nothing because *nothing* is exactly what they're believing for!

When people come to receive prayer, they ought to be saying, "I've come to get rid of these symptoms."

"What do you have?"

"Well, I don't 'have' anything, but the devil is trying to put symptoms of sickness on me. I've come to get rid of them. You lay hands on me in the name of Jesus, and I'll receive my healing!"

Not only can we locate other people's faith by their words, but we can also discover what *we* really believe as we listen to our own words. When things aren't working right, we must listen to what we say.

Our words are important. If we can get our thinking, our believing and our speaking straightened out, our lives will get straightened out. It may not happen instantly, but it *will* come to pass!

Confession:

I change my thinking, my believing and my speaking by feeding on God's Word. As I think, believe and speak God's truth, His Word changes every area of my life!

Death and life are in the power of the tongue: and they that love it shall eat the fruit thereof.

–Proverbs 18:21

Choose Words of Life

Sometimes Christians take God's sovereignty a little too far. They think they're supposed to walk through life just "rolling with the punches," taking whatever comes. I did that for years. But I got punched most of the time and spent the rest of my time rolling!

No, we make the choice in life whether we walk in blessing or cursing. We're not puppets. God doesn't arbitrarily decide who gets His blessings and who doesn't. We aren't supposed to just walk around wondering what God has for us on this earth. God has already told us what He has for us. It's all written in the pages of the Bible.

Then He gives us the choice to either accept or reject His blessings. Deuteronomy 30:19 says, "I call heaven and earth to record this day against you, that I have set before you life and death, blessing and cursing: therefore *choose life,* that both thou and thy seed may live." The choice is ours.

But how do we choose between death or life, blessing or cursing? Proverbs 18:21 tells us: "Death and life are in the power of the tongue: and they that love it shall eat the fruit thereof." We make the choice between death or life by what we say.

Now, *I* didn't say that—God did! Our tongues point us in one direction or the other. They're like the rudders on ships. The direction we turn them is the direction our bodies, our lives and our very natures will go. That's why it's so important that we choose words of life!

Confession:

My future is affected by the words I speak today. Therefore, I choose to speak God's Word over my life, my circumstances and my body. I speak words of life in every situation, and a blessed, healthy future is the result!

SEPTEMBER 15

Control Your Mouth—Control Your Life

For we all often stumble and fall and offend in many things. And if anyone does not offend in speech [never says the wrong things], he is a fully developed character and a perfect man, able to control his whole body and to curb his entire nature.
                                                 —James 3:2 AMP

The truth is, we've all made mistakes. But in the last part of this verse, James says, "If you can control your mouth, you can control your body and your entire nature." That's a strong statement!

In verse 3 AMP, James gives us more information about the tongue: "If we set bits in the horses' mouths to make them obey us, we can turn their whole bodies about." Now, I'm not a horseman, but I know horses are too big to grab around the neck and pull around wherever you want. However, if you can put a bit in a horse's mouth, you can control the direction it goes.

James continues: "Likewise, look at the ships: though they are so great and are driven by rough winds, they are steered by a very small rudder wherever the impulse of the helmsman determines" (v. 4 AMP). Ships are big, and winds are strong. But when you control the rudder, you control where the ship goes.

Think about it this way: A horse wants to go a particular direction by its own inner will. A ship has no will, but outside forces, such as the wind and waves, try to drive it. So, putting a bit in a horse's mouth and directing a ship by its rudder are examples of controlling both inside desires and outside forces.

Apply this to your own life. The problem you face may come from within—a resistant will, the lusts of the flesh and so forth. Or outside forces, such as symptoms of sickness, may be coming against you. Either way, the principle holds true: As you control your mouth, you can control yourself—inside *and* out!

Confession:

By the words of my mouth, I control the direction of my life.
I speak only what God says about me and my circumstances,
so I'm headed straight toward victory!

Even so the tongue is a little member, and it can boast of great things. See how much wood or how great a forest a tiny spark can set ablaze.

—James 3:5 AMP

SEPTEMBER 16

Control Your Tongue With God's Word

James is saying that just as a spark can set a forest ablaze to destroy it or set a fire ablaze to keep us warm, we can use our tongues to destroy ourselves or to make ourselves victorious.

Our words will make us or break us. If we allow our tongues to speak words of complaining and doubt, they will defeat us every time. But when we line up our words with God's Word, our tongues will put us over every time—no matter what comes against us.

Sometimes Christians are the most negative people in the world. Many say things like, "I'm just an unworthy worm," or "Here I wander like a beggar through the heat and the cold."

We used to think we were being humble and spiritual when we talked like that. But what we thought was humility was really spiritual pride.

To be spiritual is to line up with God's Word. True humility is admitting that God knows more than we do. True humility says, "I don't feel worthy or righteous. But, Lord, if You said I'm the righteousness of God in Christ, then I must be. I'm going to humble myself to Your Word and believe what You said, no matter what I feel." (Rom. 3:22.)

James said we can use our tongues to light a warm fire or to set a forest ablaze. Personally, I prefer that my spark set a fire to warm me rather than to destroy the "forests" of God's blessings in my life. So I've made a decision: I'm lining up my words with the Word of God!

Confession:

I find out what God says and fill my mouth with His Word.
My words add healing, comfort and joy to my life.
God's Word is working mightily in me right now!

SEPTEMBER 17

Break out of Captivity With Your Words!

Thou art snared with the words of thy mouth, thou art taken with the words of thy mouth.

–Proverbs 6:2

The words of your mouth can snare you. Or, to paraphrase this verse, "Thou art *taken captive* with the words of thy mouth." Have you ever been in captivity? More than likely, your words put you there.

Job 42:10 bears this out when it explains why Job's ordeal ended: "And the Lord turned the captivity of Job, *when he prayed for his friends.*"

Job first got himself into trouble through fear: "For the thing which I greatly feared is come upon me, and that which I was afraid of is come unto me" (Job 3:25). Job was saying, "That which I greatly feared has come upon me. I didn't have any peace; I didn't have any rest. I thought my good fortune was too good to be true."

Many folks say that today. Everything is going well in their lives, but they still speak negative words: "Man, this can't last. This is too good to be true." Sometimes they talk themselves right out of the good things that are happening.

Don't make that mistake. When something good comes into your life, say, "Glory to God! I'm walking in abundant life. Thank God, I'll just keep right on going from glory to glory!"

Confession:

My life just keeps getting better and better. Blessings are overtaking me more and more. My needs are met; my body is healed. And the best is yet to come!

A man shall be satisfied with good by the fruit of his mouth: and the recompence of a man's hands shall be rendered unto him.

–Proverbs 12:14

SEPTEMBER 18

Be Satisfied With Good

"A man shall be satisfied with good by the fruit of his mouth." Or you could say it another way: "A man shall be satisfied with all kinds of good." But notice this verse *doesn't* say, "A man shall be satisfied with good *if* it's God's will or *if* God decides to smile upon him."

I don't know about you, but I like the promise in this Scripture. I want to be satisfied with good!

You have a choice between good and evil in life, and that choice is determined by the fruit of your mouth. In other Scriptures, God associates "good" with healing. (Acts 10:38; Luke 6:9.) So you could say, "A man shall be satisfied with *healing* by the fruit of his mouth."

I'm telling you, there is power in your words. Your mouth can get you over your circumstances and into the blessings of God! Proverbs 18:20 says, "A man's belly shall be satisfied with the fruit of his mouth; and with the increase of his lips shall he be filled." (I suggest that you read through Proverbs and see everything God says just in this one book about your words. After all, Proverbs is called the Book of Wisdom!)

Now look at Proverbs 15:4: "A wholesome tongue is a tree of life…. Adam had access to eat from the Tree of Life, and so do we—by making our tongues line up with God's Word!

Confession:

*I am satisfied with good by the fruit of my mouth.
I speak God's Word concerning healing, and those words
become life to me and produce healing, strength and
wholeness in my body. I believe I receive my healing now.*

SEPTEMBER 19

Our Words Preserve Us

...God, who quickeneth the dead, and calleth those things which be not as though they were.

–Romans 4:17

Words are important to God. This Scripture says that God uses words to call those things that are not as though they were. Some people say, "Well, that's fine for God, but we shouldn't be doing that." But the Bible says *our* words are important as well.

First, look at Proverbs 14:3: "In the mouth of the foolish is a rod of pride: but the lips of the wise shall preserve them." Notice it doesn't say the lips of the wise will *pickle them;* it says their lips will *preserve them!*

Then in 1 Thessalonians 5:23, Paul told the Thessalonian church how he prayed for them: "I pray God your whole spirit and soul and body be preserved blameless unto the coming of our Lord Jesus Christ."

Paul prayed that we'd be preserved blameless while we walk on this earth. But what preserves us from the enemy who wants to steal, kill and destroy us? Proverbs 14:3 gives us the answer: "the lips of the wise."

As our own mouths speak forth God's wisdom, our faith-filled words will preserve us from the enemy's strategies arrayed against us. That's why it's wise to follow God's example and *call those things that be not as though they were!*

Confession:

I speak God's purpose for my life into existence, calling those things that be not as though they were. In Jesus' name, I speak healing to my body and health and wholeness to all my flesh!

If thou hast done foolishly in lifting up thyself,
or if thou hast thought evil, lay thine hand
upon thy mouth. —*Proverbs 30:32*

SEPTEMBER 20

Refrain Your Lips From Evil

What does it mean to "think evil"? You are thinking evil when you dwell on any kind of thoughts that are contrary to God's Word.

What are you supposed to do if you are guilty of thinking evil? "Lay thine hand upon thy mouth." God is telling you, "If you've thought evil, that's one thing. But don't verbalize it, or you might get the evil you've been thinking! If you've done foolishly or thought evil, *lay your hand on your mouth."*

Proverbs 10:19 says, "In the multitude of words there wanteth not sin: but *he that refraineth his lips is wise."* Sometimes the wisest thing to do is to keep our mouths closed. James 1:19 says, "Wherefore, my beloved brethren, let every man be swift to hear, slow to speak, slow to wrath."

So refuse to dwell on evil thoughts of doubt, unbelief, complaint or worry. Don't let them come out of your mouth. Be slow to speak. Refrain your lips from doubtful and evil speaking. Put your hand on your mouth if you have to! Do whatever you have to do to make sure your words line up with the Word of God!

Confession:

I guard my words and keep them in line with God's Word.
The words of my mouth and the meditation of my heart are acceptable
in the sight of God, my strength and my redeemer! (Ps. 19:14.)

SEPTEMBER 21

The Tongue of the Wise

There is that speaketh like the piercings of a sword: but the tongue of the wise is health.

—Proverbs 12:18

Our words have a lot to do with our own physical healing and health. We have the ability to talk ourselves into all kinds of problems or to speak words of faith, which cause miracles to manifest.

Many times people get sick or don't receive their healing because they believe and speak according to the natural symptoms. These people may receive temporary relief when they're prayed for. But if they don't straighten out what their mouths are saying, they'll eventually find themselves back in the same unhealthy conditions.

These very same people who have talked themselves into sickness and disease often say, "I don't know why God put this on me. I don't know why He allowed this to happen."

But the Lord didn't have anything to do with it. You see, faith is a law, and we operate it with our words, either to our benefit or to our destruction. Proverbs 12:18 says, "The tongue of the wise is health." We could turn that around and say, "The tongue of the unwise is sickness"!

It's your choice. You can operate the law of faith by hooking up your mouth and heart with your symptoms and what the devil tells you. Or you can operate the same law of faith by lining up your mouth with God's Word and pointing it toward His blessings. Faith in God works by believing and saying what God says. So speak His words of healing, and receive the healing God has reserved just for you!

Confession:

I speak words of health to my body because the tongue of the wise is health. Disease cannot attach itself to me, because Jesus took my sicknesses and pains; He bore them for me, so I don't have to. I walk in excellent health.

Whoso keepeth his mouth and his tongue keepeth his soul from troubles.

–Proverbs 21:23

Keep Your Soul From Trouble

Many people have trouble in the area of the soul, which includes the mind, will and emotions. Some suffer from emotional hurts or from mental torment and are looking for help. But God has provided the answer they need in this Scripture: "Whoso keepeth his mouth and his tongue keepeth his soul from troubles."

We've all dealt with doubts and fears at one time or another. Fear often starts as a thought. As we dwell on that thought, it produces a feeling of fear. And if we continue to dwell on fearful thoughts, our feelings of fear may escalate into panic.

The devil likes to insert those kinds of thoughts in your mind. For instance, he may say, *I'm going to kill you. You won't live out your full life. You'll contract cancer and die.* Most of the time there isn't even any basis or symptom for what the enemy is saying to your mind. He doesn't care. He just wants you to dwell on his evil suggestions long enough for fear to take over.

I finally realized that those demonic thoughts come to our minds because the devil isn't big enough to pull off his schemes on his own. He has to get us to agree with him before he can operate in our lives.

So you have to cast down the enemy's thoughts as soon as they come. How do you stop his thoughts? Well, you can't think one thing when you are saying something else. So the minute a fearful thought comes about sickness or death, just start confessing, "Glory to God! He sent His Word and healed me. Thank God, I'm healed. It's so good to be well!"

What happens to the satanic thoughts? They stop. What happens to the fear? It leaves.

So control your mouth by speaking God's Word. If you catch those demonic suggestions while they're still thoughts, they won't produce fear in you. When you control your words, you can control your thought life, and that will keep your soul from trouble!

Confession:

I don't allow Satan's thoughts of fear and doubt to control me. I keep my soul from trouble by speaking God's Word. I will live a long, healthy life, and God will fulfill the number of my days!

SEPTEMBER 23

Speaking the Word Works!

The tongue of the wise is health.

–Proverbs 12:18

When I was a youth minister at a church in Colorado, we held a youth camp in the mountains a couple of times a year. One morning at the camp, I led a group of teenagers on a hike to the top of a small, nearby mountain. We ate lunch and had a little Bible study before we started back down.

On the way down, one of the girls stepped on a rock in a way that caused her ankle to roll and made her foot turn sideways. When I reached her, her ankle was already swollen. I didn't know whether she'd broken her foot or sprained it, but she couldn't stand on it.

We prayed for the girl, and some of her pain was relieved. Then another man and I began to take turns carrying her piggyback down the mountain. It wasn't easy. I was having enough difficulty walking down the hill by myself, much less carrying someone else!

As I carried the girl down the mountain, I started talking to her about the power of the tongue. I told her, "The Bible says, 'The tongue of the wise is health.' Also, Jesus said that if we say to our mountains 'Be removed and cast into the sea,' and don't doubt in our hearts, but believe that what we say shall come to pass, we will have whatever we say. But we have to *say* it." (Mark 11:23.)

So this girl and I started confessing, "Thank God, it's so good to be healed!" We praised and worshipped God together as I carried her down the mountain.

About a third of the way down, the girl said, "Put me down. Just help me walk a few minutes." The other man and I supported her between us as she hobbled on that foot for a few minutes. The whole time she kept saying, "Thank God, I believe I'm well. It's so good to be healed." Pretty soon, she pushed one of us away; then she started walking on her own.

It looked as if her foot was hurting. But the more she walked, the better it got. By the time she got to the bottom of the hill, she said, "See you later!" and ran all the way to the bus. The Word works!

Confession:

In times of pressure, I speak God's Word, and the circumstances have to change. Thank You, Father, for the power in Your Word to heal my body and make me whole!

And all things, whatsoever ye shall ask in prayer, believing, ye shall receive.

—Matthew 21:22

SEPTEMBER 24

Pray the Answer, Not the Problem

I was born again right in the middle of the Charismatic move. I visited a small full gospel church and was filled with the Holy Ghost. I had a lot of enthusiasm and excitement in those days, but I didn't know a lot about the Bible.

I prayed a lot; in fact, I was constantly praying at the church late at night and early in the morning. The pastor finally gave me my own key to the church! But I didn't know how to pray. Over and over, I prayed, "Oh, dear God, You see how bad my problems are." But if anything changed in my situation, it was always for the worse.

I had a plaque hanging in my home that said "Prayer Changes Things," but I was saved, filled and defeated. It seemed as if everything was going wrong. After a year and a half of this, I couldn't decide whether to throw that plaque away or just burn it!

I finally thought, *The answer has to be in the Bible someplace.* So I started searching the Scriptures. Matthew 21:22 is the verse that got my attention. Jesus said, "And all things, whatsoever ye shall ask in prayer, believing, ye shall receive."

I found a key in this verse that unlocked a door of understanding how to pray in faith. Suddenly I realized I'd been talking to God about the *problem* instead of the *answer.* And I sure didn't want to believe I received my problems—I already had them!

Another key to praying in faith is found in Isaiah 43:26: "Put me in remembrance: let us plead together: declare thou, that thou mayest be justified." God wants you to remind Him of what He's already said about your need. So pray God's answer according to His Word; then believe you receive it by faith. That's the true prayer of faith!

Confession:

Father, I put You in remembrance of Your Word. I thank You because You said that by Jesus' stripes, I was healed. I know You're faithful to make Your Word true in my life, so I believe I receive my healing!

SEPTEMBER 25

Choose To Believe God's Word

How then shall they call on him in whom they have not believed? and how shall they believe in him of whom they have not heard?

So then faith cometh by hearing, and hearing by the word of God. —Romans 10:14,17

Believing is a result of hearing. Once you hear the Word, you have the ability and the capacity to believe it, but you still have to choose *what* you will believe. I've seen people hear and hear and hear the Word. But then when the pressure was on, they believed their symptoms instead of what God says.

In John 20, the resurrected Jesus had already appeared to His disciples at a time when one disciple, Thomas, wasn't present. Before His death, Jesus had told His disciples over and over again that He would be raised from the dead. After He appeared to the other disciples, they all told Thomas, "We've seen the Lord!"

So Thomas had the capacity to believe in Jesus' resurrection because he'd already heard about it from Jesus and the other disciples. But Thomas made his choice. He said, "Except I shall see in his hand the print of the nails, and put my finger in the print of the nails, and thrust my hand into His side, *I will not believe*" (John 20:25).

Thomas wasn't alone in his unbelief. That's often where we get in trouble as well. We hear the Word but then choose to believe the natural circumstances. As a result, we don't receive the blessings God wants to give us.

Don't make that mistake. As soon as you hear the Word, just make the quality decision to believe what you hear. That's how you keep God's blessings flowing into your life!

Confession:

Faith comes by hearing the Word of God. I hear the Word, so I have the capacity to believe it, even when I face adverse circumstances or painful symptoms. I choose to believe the Bible and walk in the fullness of His blessings!

This book of the law shall not depart out of thy mouth; but thou shalt meditate therein day and night, that thou mayest observe to do according to all that is written therein: for then thou shalt make thy way prosperous, and then thou shalt have good success. —Joshua 1:8

SEPTEMBER 26

Be a Doer of the Word

If you want to walk in divine health, as God desires, you have to be a doer of the Word. For one thing, that means meditating on God's healing promises. As you do, you'll find His Word getting so big on the inside that you start acting like a healthy person!

God told Joshua the results he could expect for being diligent in His Word: "For then thou shalt make thy way prosperous, and then thou shalt have good success." Did you notice that it doesn't say, "For then *God* will make your way prosperous"? No, it says, "For *you* will make your way prosperous." I've also heard it put this way—"Then you will deal wisely in all the affairs of life."

God has made health and success available in every area of your life. Now He says, "I give you the wisdom and ability to deal wisely in all the affairs of life. But it's your choice whether or not you become a doer of My Word and actually receive what I've given you."

Confession:

I have planted God's Word in my heart, and that Word is life to me and health to all my flesh. Because I meditate on God's Word, I deal wisely in all the affairs of life.

SEPTEMBER 27

"Mutter" the Word

This book of the law shall not depart out of thy mouth; but thou shalt meditate therein day and night, that thou mayest observe to do according to all that is written therein: for then thou shalt make thy way prosperous, and then thou shalt have good success. —Joshua 1:8

The word *meditate* means "to read; to study; to think about; *to mutter.*"[1] We are to keep that Word coming out our mouths.

It's ironic when you stop to think about it. The enemy has propagated a theory in this world that people who talk to themselves are going crazy. But we Christians ought to be speaking the Word to ourselves all the time. We ought to be meditating on the Word of God continually—reading it, studying it, thinking about it, "chewing on it" and saying it to ourselves.

For instance, you can use the time when you're driving in your car to speak the Word aloud to yourself. You can say: "Thank God, He sent His Word and healed me. Jesus had compassion on the multitudes, and He healed them all. Jesus went about all the cities and villages, teaching and preaching and healing every sickness and every disease among the people. By His stripes I am healed!"

The world might think you're a little strange when they see you muttering to yourself. But that's okay. You know something they don't know—you're on the edge of a miracle!

Confession:

*I keep God's Word before me and meditate on it day and night.
His Word is seed planted in my heart, and it's working
mightily in me to produce a harvest of healing!*

We having the same spirit of faith, according
as it is written, I believed, and therefore have I
spoken; we also believe, and therefore speak.

−2 Corinthians 4:13

SEPTEMBER 28

The Same Measure of Faith

Paul starts out in this Scripture saying, *"We having...."* I like that. The great apostle Paul was talking to the Church, not just to apostles, prophets, evangelists, pastors and teachers. He was writing to the body of Christ.

Then Paul said, "We having *the same spirit of faith...."* We have the same spirit of faith that the apostle Paul had. He had a measure of the God-kind of faith, and we have the same measure and the same faith.

God didn't give Paul a greater dose of faith than He gave us. If He did, He'd be a respecter of persons, because the Bible says, "This is the victory that overcometh the world, even our faith" (1 John 5:4). If God gave Paul a greater dose of faith, Paul would have had a greater ability than we do to overcome the devil's attacks.

But no, God gave each and every one of us the same exact dose, or measure, of the God-kind of faith. (Rom. 12:3.) Now it's up to us what we do with that measure of faith.

You see, faith is like a muscle. Think back on a time when you physically exerted yourself, such as in yard work or exercise, and you found a muscle you hadn't used for awhile. Maybe it hurt for two or three days, having become weak from lack of use.

If you start using that forgotten muscle every day, it will actually grow in size and strength. However, if you let it lie dormant, then the next time you use it, you'll have to pump it up and get it working all over again.

So use your faith on a daily basis. Be in faith all the time. As you diligently exercise your faith muscles, your faith will grow strong enough to overcome any obstacle!

Confession:

I exercise my faith by believing God's promises of healing
and divine health. By the power in His Word, I'm free from
all sickness and disease. Praise God, it's good to be well!

SEPTEMBER 29

Exercise Your Faith

We having the same spirit of faith, according as it is written, I believed, and therefore have I spoken; we also believe, and therefore speak.

—2 Corinthians 4:13

Our capacity to operate in faith comes from hearing the Word of God. However, our faith doesn't grow because we hear. We can feed and feed and feed a muscle, but it only grows in strength as we *exercise* it.

Faith is the same way. All over the world, believers sit back in their church pews week after week, just hearing and hearing and hearing the Word. Then they can't figure out why their faith doesn't work for them. I could tell them why: They're not using their faith every day.

We should make sure our faith is working on something all the time. When one answer comes in, our faith should still be out working in four or five other areas of our lives. We have to keep our faith muscles flexed. Then when a new problem arises, we won't flinch and say, "Oh, Lord, what am I going to do?" We'll look it square in the face and say, "Thank God, my faith works in this situation! This is a great opportunity to give my faith some exercise!"

We don't like problems, and God doesn't send them. But we can take anything the devil throws against us and turn it around for our good. We can use our faith to push the problem away from us, as a weight lifter uses weights. Every time he pushes the weights away, he gains a little more strength.

So anytime a new problem comes along, learn to count it all joy. Just look at the problem as an opportunity to exercise your faith. God's Word will work to drive that problem away, and your faith will come out of the trial that much stronger!

Confession:

When symptoms come against me, I count it all joy because I know God's Word working in me is greater than any sickness or disease. The Word was sent to heal me, and it's working mightily in me right now!

We having the same spirit of faith, according as it is written, I believed, and therefore have I spoken; we also believe, and therefore speak.

–2 Corinthians 4:13

SEPTEMBER 30

The Connection Between Saying and Believing

I heard a minister say, "Anytime you see a *therefore* in the Bible, stop and see what it's *there for.*" In this verse, Paul uses the word *therefore* to combine the two parts of faith: "I *believed* and therefore have I *spoken;* we also *believe,* and therefore *speak.*"

If we're going to believe something, we also have to speak it. Believing alone doesn't make it come to pass. It has to be combined with saying what God's Word says.

Jesus said, "If you believe in your heart that what you say will come to pass, you'll have whatever you say." (Mark 11:23.) The truth is, we can spend a lot of time feeding on God's Word, but what we continually *say* is what we'll ultimately believe.

When I was growing up, I had a friend who was a chronic liar. He started out lying just to get himself out of trouble, but it eventually became a habit. He'd make up a whopper of a lie about some situation; then six months later, no one could convince him it hadn't happened that way. He'd said the lie so much that he actually believed it.

If that can be done with a lie, we should be able to do the same thing with the truth of God's Word. When we first start saying, "By Jesus' stripes I was healed," it can sound hollow. It's easy to think, *I know the Bible says that by His stripes I was healed, but I feel sick from head to toe.* But as we keep saying it and saying it, soon we'll believe it no matter what we feel like.

How do you come to that place of faith? By feeding on God's Word and speaking it with your mouth. Once you believe in your heart what God says, you can declare it with the added push of faith behind your words. Then get ready, for your answer *will* come to pass!

Confession:

God's Word is truth. As I continually speak His Word and believe it with my heart, His Word becomes truth in me. I believe God's truth, I declare God's truth and I receive His very best!

OCTOBER 1

Faith for Salvation— Faith for Healing

But the righteousness which is of faith speaketh on this wise, Say not in thine heart, Who shall ascend into heaven? (that is, to bring Christ down from above:) or, Who shall descend into the deep? (that is, to bring up Christ again from the dead.)

But what saith it? The word is nigh thee, even in thy mouth, and in thy heart: that is, the word of faith, which we preach; that if thou shalt confess with thy mouth the Lord Jesus, and shalt believe in thine heart that God hath raised him from the dead, thou shalt be saved. —Romans 10:6-9

This one passage of Scripture tells you not only how to be saved but how to be healed—by *speaking* in faith. Notice what Paul says in verse 6: "But the righteousness which is of faith *speaketh...*." Faith always speaks. What you say is your faith speaking. I don't mean just what you say once, but what you say over a period of time.

Then in verse 8, Paul asks, "But what saith it?" What does the righteousness which is of faith say? "The word is nigh thee, even in thy *mouth,* and in thy *heart.*" Faith has to be in both places.

Verse 9 goes on to say, "That if thou shalt confess with thy mouth...." You may say, "I don't believe in Bible confessions." If you don't, you have to throw out the whole book of Romans!

That if thou shalt confess with thy mouth the Lord Jesus [or that Jesus is Lord], **and shalt believe in thine heart that God hath raised him from the dead, thou shalt be saved.**

You may argue, "But that verse is talking about salvation." Yes, I know, but the same faith that got you saved will get you healed. You just have to take your faith and point it in a different direction. Remember, Jesus said, *"All* things are possible to him who believes!" (Mark 9:23.)

Confession:

God's Word in my heart and in my mouth says that the Lord Jesus is my healer! By faith I speak healing to my body; and according to my faith, it will be done unto me!

For with the heart man believeth unto righteousness; and with the mouth confession is made unto salvation. —Romans 10:10

Release Your Faith With Your Words

The apostle Paul is saying by the Spirit of God that with the heart you believe unto the reality of God's Word. In other words, when you get a revelation of God's Word in your heart, it becomes real to you. God's Word is alive, quick and powerful, and feeding on it causes Jesus and the things of God to become real and alive to you.

But there's something else in this verse to understand. Paul is also saying by the Holy Ghost that with the mouth, confession is made unto the manifestation, or experience, of God's Word.

When you believe the Word, it becomes *real*. When you say it, it *manifests*. If you say it without believing it, it isn't real to you. If you believe it without saying it, it isn't manifested for you. But when you believe *and* say the Word, it starts working in your life.

We like it when God's Word becomes real in our spirits. But there's something about having it actually manifest in our lives that makes it more enjoyable yet. It's great when our healing becomes real to our spirits, but when we're actually walking in good health, it feels good to "feel good"!

Do you want to experience the manifestation of God's promises in your life? Then continually speak His Word with your mouth. That's how you release your faith. You see, you can have a heart full of faith, but it won't do you any good unless you release it.

It's like having a bank account full of money. That money won't do you any good unless you spend it. In the same way, after you fill your heart with faith by feeding on the Word, you have to spend, or release, it by the words you speak. Fill and spend. That's how you keep your faith working for you!

Confession:

I feed on God's Word, and it becomes real to me. I speak forth God's Word, and it manifests in me! The Word inside me produces healing in my body as I release my faith and proclaim His goodness.

OCTOBER 3

Have the God-Kind of Faith

Through faith we understand that the worlds were framed by the word of God, so that things which are seen were not made of things which do appear. —Hebrews 11:3

In Mark 11:22, Jesus said to us, "Have faith in God," or "Have the God-kind of faith." What is the God-kind of faith? Hebrews 11:3 gives us a clue; it says God spoke the universe into existence by faith.

We know God created the worlds in six days and then rested on the seventh. But I don't believe He stepped out on the first day and said, "I'm going to speak the worlds into existence. I've never tried this before. I sure hope it works!" No, God knew He could do it. He was confident; He believed in His own power to create.

Isaiah 40:12 says that God measured out the heavens in the span of His hand and measured the waters in the hollow of His hand. God thoroughly believed He could speak the worlds into existence. He knew exactly what it would look like when He was through.

God could have stepped out on the first day and said, "Universe, *be!*" and everything would have come into existence. I believe He slowed it down and created the heavens and the earth a day at a time so we could see how the God-kind of faith works. (Maybe He had other reasons as well, but that's a good one!)

So God said, "Let there be light," and there was light. (Gen. 1:3.) Now, suppose God had gotten what He *believed* when He said that. The entire *universe* would have come into existence! But God didn't get what He believed; He got what He *said.* He *said,* "Let there be light," and there was light. Nothing more, nothing less. God believed He could create the entire universe, but what He *said* came into manifestation.

That's how the God-kind of faith works, and it works the same way for us. As we speak what we believe, our faith-filled words *will* come to pass!

Confession:

I proclaim from a believing heart that healing is mine through Jesus Christ! My words release faith in my heart, and my healing is manifested!

...even God, who quickeneth the dead, and calleth those things which be not as though they were. —Romans 4:17

OCTOBER 4

Call That Which Is Not as Though It Were!

We are to call those things which be not as though they were. As someone once said, "We don't want to get that mixed up. God didn't say to call those things which *are* as though they *were not.*"

In other words, God didn't say to deny the symptoms, the circumstances or the problems. We're not supposed to say, "No, I don't have any pain. No, there aren't symptoms in my body."

No, we are to call those things that *be not* as though they *were.* You might say, "Well, I don't feel healed. But thank God, the Bible says I am, so I believe I'm healed. I don't feel strong; but the Bible says I am, so I believe I'm strong."

Talk about healing as though it already existed in your body. Say, "It doesn't matter what my body feels like; by Jesus' stripes, I was healed. It doesn't matter what the problem is; no weapon formed against me shall prosper! [Isa. 54:17.] Since God is for me, no one can stand against me. [Rom. 8:31.] So I believe I receive my healing by faith!"

Confession:

I don't deny symptoms or circumstances; I just call forth God's promises to be manifested in my life. I call my mind strong and at peace. I call my body healthy and whole.

OCTOBER 5

Call Forth Your Miracle by Faith

(As it is written, I have made thee a father of many nations,) before him whom he believed, even God, who quickeneth the dead, and calleth those things which be not as though they were.

—Romans 4:17

Our faith has to speak if we're going to see results. God calls those things which be not as though they were. Abraham called those things which were not as though they were. Certainly, if our heavenly Father and the father of our faith operated in this kind of faith, we ought to do the same!

"Call those things which be not...." To *call,* you have to *say.* Speak out loud, *calling* those things which be not in your life as though they were.

Which of God's blessings is not in your life? Is healing not in your life? Then call it as though it were: "Everywhere I go, healing and health are overtaking me, causing my body to be strong, healthy and whole!"

Someone may ask, "Is that scriptural?" I like what Joel said: "Let the weak say, I am strong" (Joel 3:10). He didn't say, "Let the weak say I'm weak and unworthy. I'll never make it." No, the weak are supposed to say they are *strong!* So calling those things that be not as though they were is *very* scriptural!

And the weak aren't supposed to wait until they *feel* strong! If they did that, they would never feel it. No, let the weak say, "I am strong" while they still feel weak.

Why is that? Because with your mouth, confession is made unto the manifestation of God's Word in your life. (Rom. 10:10.) So continually call your body healed as though it already were. The time *will* come when you experience the manifestation of your miracle in your physical body.

Confession:

My Father has given me all things that pertain to life and godliness. Jesus took my sin and sickness and gave me His righteousness and health. Therefore, I call my body healed. I call my body strong. I call myself the blessed of the Lord!

Paul, a servant of God, and an apostle of Jesus Christ, according to the faith of God's elect, and the acknowledging of the truth which is after godliness; in hope of eternal life, which God, that cannot lie, promised before the world began.

—Titus 1:1,2

OCTOBER 6

Making a Statement of Fact

S omeone may say, "If I say I believe I'm healed when I still feel sick, that's a lie."

No, it isn't. Number one, it's calling those things which be not as though they were. (Rom. 4:17.) If that's lying, then God lies all the time; and He *can't* lie.

Number two, it's a statement of fact. If I say, "I believe I'm healed," all I'm doing is telling you what I believe. However, if I say, "No, I have no symptoms in my body," when I *do* have symptoms, that's a lie. Or if I say, "I have five $100 bills in my pocket," when I don't, that's a lie. But if I say, "I believe I'm healed by the stripes on Jesus' back," I'm making a statement of truth because I do believe it.

You can believe anything you want to believe. If you choose to believe what God says above what the symptoms are telling you, is that a lie? No, that's truth. When you say, "I believe I'm healed," you're making a statement of fact.

In His prayer to the Father, Jesus said, *"Thy word is truth"* (John 17:17). Then in Romans 3:4, Paul says, "Yea, *let God be true,* but every man a liar." And Hebrews 6:18 states that it is impossible for God to lie. So when you choose to believe what God says, you come in line with the highest form of truth in the universe—the Word of God, which has been exalted above His name! (Ps. 138:2.)

Confession:

I believe I'm healed. I believe God's healing power is working in my body now, driving out every symptom and making my body completely whole!

OCTOBER 7

Hook Up With What God Says

Let the words of my mouth, and the meditation of my heart, be acceptable in thy sight, O Lord, my strength, and my redeemer. —Psalm 19:14

When I first found out that you can have what you say, I just shut up for about three weeks. I thought, *If I get what I've been saying, I'm in trouble!* For instance, when I was in high school, I was a good driver. But, like everyone else in my family, I drove too fast. I remember just laughingly saying, "Boy, the way I drive, I'll never live to be thirty years old!"

I thought it was funny back then. When I found out what the Bible said, though, I adjusted what I said. I said, "The way I drive, I'll live to be 125." (Of course, I had to change a few driving habits too!)

We all need to stop and listen to ourselves speaking. So often we speak negative phrases over and over without thinking. But if we ever did stop to think about it, we'd realize, *Dear Lord, that's not what I want in my life!*

If we keep speaking the same negative things over and over, eventually we will believe what we're saying, and then we'll have it. For example, I've heard people say, "I'm afraid I'll have an accident. I'm just so afraid I'll have an accident." Then when they have an accident, they ask, "Why did God do this to me?"

But God didn't have a thing to do with it. Those people stepped into a spiritual law that works either positively or negatively: They believed it, they said it and they received it.

Let's use this spiritual law to our advantage and hook up with what God says!

Confession:

I listen to the words I speak. When I discover I'm speaking something contrary to the Word of God, I change it. I speak God's blessings of divine health into my life. In Jesus' name, I am healed. I am whole!

When she had heard of Jesus, came in the press behind, and touched his garment. For she said, If I may touch but his clothes, I shall be whole.

–Mark 5:27,28

OCTOBER 8

Speak the Word From Your Heart

How did this woman with the issue of blood get faith? "When she had *heard* of Jesus...." Faith comes by hearing. But did you notice how she started releasing her faith? "For she *said*...." I like what *The Amplified Bible* says: "For she *kept saying*, If I only touch His garments, I shall be restored to health." She *kept* saying those words that released her faith.

Someone may ask, "How long do you speak the Word over a situation?"

Speak it until it manifests.

But don't rely on just simple confession alone to do the job. Feed on God's Word at the same time. Take time to read and study the Word. Meditate on it; speak it to yourself.

Matthew 9:20-22 provides another account of the same healing. Verse 21 says, "For she said within herself...." I like it better yet to say it this way: "For she said *from* within herself...."

Many people just mimic the way others speak the Word. However, they do it out of their heads instead of their hearts. They grab some Scripture and start saying it without even concentrating on it. These people are just saying a lot of empty words.

That kind of confession accomplishes nothing. You have to put some heart belief behind your words. So plant the Word down in your spirit until its truth is alive and real to you. Speak it forth from the inside of you. Release the faith in your heart with the words of your mouth!

Confession:

I abide in Jesus, and His words abide in me. I make my request according to God's Word, and He answers me. I believe and speak God's Word; therefore, His healing power is released in me, and I am healed!

OCTOBER 9

The Simplicity of Faith

For the Word that God speaks is alive and full of power [making it active, operative, energizing, and effective]; it is sharper than any two-edged sword. —*Hebrews 4:12 AMP*

God operates in faith by believing and saying, and God gets exactly what He says. Everything God does, He does by speaking.

Did you ever notice that everything God does in the world today, He does by His Word on the lips of believers? That's how God carries out His plan on this earth.

How did you get saved? By believing in your heart and saying with your mouth. Then how are you going to get healed? By believing in your heart and saying with your mouth. How are you going to get your needs met? By believing in your heart and saying with your mouth. How does faith work? By believing in the heart and saying with the mouth.

Thank God, He made it easy for us. Faith is so simple. Faith is just taking God at His Word.

So feed on God's Word until you get it on the inside. Read it, study it, mutter it, meditate on it and think about it until it is lodged deep down in your spirit. Then declare God's promises with your mouth and watch God bring them to pass. James 2:20 says that faith without actions is dead. So act on your faith: Open your mouth and boldly declare, "Thank God, by Jesus' stripes I am healed!" It's that simple!

--- ✍ ---

Confession:

I believe with my heart and say with my mouth that God's Word is true in my life. His Word says I am healed by the stripes of Jesus. The power in that Word is working in me now, healing, strengthening and restoring me to health.

Who is this uncircumcised Philistine, that he should defy the armies of the living God?

—1 Samuel 17:26

OCTOBER 10

Slay Your Giant of Sickness by Faith

Believing and saying the Word of God is a spiritual law, just as gravity is a natural law. You can find the spiritual law of faith all through the Bible.

Remember David and Goliath? David was just a shepherd boy, working out in the fields with a sling and a handful of stones. But in 1 Samuel 17, he fought against Goliath, who was a warrior from his youth. Notice what David said: "I come to you in the name of the Lord of Hosts. This day He's going to deliver you into my hands!" (vv. 45,46.)

That might seem pretty cocky for a little guy (at least compared to Goliath!). But David wasn't cocky. He wasn't speaking in arrogance. He just knew he had a covenant with God.

There is a difference between acting in arrogance and walking in confidence in our covenant with God. The difference lies in whether our confidence is in ourselves or in God and His Word.

David spoke out of confidence in his God, asking, "Who does this ugly Philistine think he is, defying the armies of the living God?"

Notice what David's motives were. He didn't challenge Goliath for his own glory. He didn't say, "I'm going to make myself famous over this." He just didn't like people defying the armies of the living God. He was proclaiming, "We have a covenant—why don't we walk in it?"

So David boldly told Goliath, "I'm going to take your head off your shoulders today!" Goliath may have laughed, but he didn't laugh long. David sank one of those stones in his forehead; then he cut off Goliath's head with the giant's own sword.

What did David get? Exactly what he believed and said. It was the spiritual law of faith in operation.

Confession:

Sickness and pain are my Goliath. I face the giant and, in the name of Jesus, recite the terms of my covenant with God: "Jesus bore my sicknesses and carried my pains. By His stripes I'm healed!"

OCTOBER 11

What Do Your Words Carry?

The words of a wise man's mouth are gracious; but the lips of a fool will swallow up himself.

–Ecclesiastes 10:12

Our words create an atmosphere. Words are powerful "carriers"; they carry faith, or they carry unbelief. And whatever we fill our words with will directly affect our lives.

Sit down sometime and take a look at your life. You'll find things you do like. But if you look hard enough, you'll find some aspects of your life you don't like. Then ask yourself, "What have I been saying about those parts of my life that I don't like?"

If you don't like where you are in life, change your words. Quit saying what you're saying. Proverbs 18:21 says, "Death and life are in the power of the tongue...."

For instance, have you ever said, "I never get anything from God. I tried that faith stuff, but it didn't work for me"? If so, switch over to speaking words of faith: "I've been feeding on God's Word for years, and my faith is growing exceedingly. God's Word is seed planted in my heart, and it's working mightily in me!"

We are a direct result of what we've believed and said about ourselves in the past. So to make sure our future is different than our past or present, we often have to go back to the Bible and get our minds renewed and our thinking straightened out.

Once you get your thinking lined up with God's Word, it's amazing how easily your believing will line up right behind it. And after you get your believing straightened out, your mouth will straighten out! Out of the abundance of your heart, your mouth will begin to speak faith. (Matt. 12:34.)

You're in good shape when you have your thinking, believing and speaking all lined up with God's Word. You're ready for your faith-filled words to carry you straight into a future of health and abundance!

Confession:

My words are carriers of faith. They create the blessings I live in. As I speak God's Word, He renews my mind, heals my body and gives me strength. God's Word works for me!

Hear; for I will speak of excellent things; and the opening of my lips shall be right things. For my mouth shall speak truth.... —Proverbs 8:6,7

The Problem Is With Your Mouth

Several years ago, I went to a small campmeeting in another state. While I was there, the minister in charge asked me to preach at an evening service, and I agreed. However, I was new in the ministry, so I prayed, "Dear Lord, what am I going to do?"

At that point, I taught from manuscript sermons I had written down almost word for word. So I got out my notes and found a sermon I was comfortable with. I thought, *Here's a good message. I'll use this one.*

When I got to the service, I sat reviewing my notes. All of a sudden, I heard on the inside: *Your problem is not with your faith, and it's not with God; it's with your mouth.* When I heard that, I knew it was for someone else, not for me.

When I got up to teach, I looked at my notes. Suddenly they didn't make a bit of sense to me; I just went blank. So I said, "All right, Lord, You win. I'm just going to start off with what You said." So I began, "Your problem is not with your faith, and it's not with God; it's with your mouth," and I preached for about an hour.

To this day, I don't know what I said, but after the service a lady came up to me. She had driven from the other side of the state and could only stay for that one service. She said, "I'm in a life-and-death situation. I've been battling this physical condition for quite awhile, and I've tried to figure out why I haven't received my healing."

The woman continued, "At first, I thought maybe there was some reason God wasn't healing me. Then I thought, *No, the problem is my faith. I don't have any faith.*

"But now I know where the answer is," the woman said. "The problem is not with God, and it's not with my faith. The problem is with my mouth. Well, I'm changing what I'm saying. And you just watch—now I'll live and not die!"

Confession:

I feed on God's Word continually. My words line up with what He says. As I speak the Word, I hear myself say it and my faith rises to the level of my confession.

OCTOBER 13

Understanding Biblical Confessions

In those days came John the Baptist, preaching in the wilderness of Judaea, and saying, Repent ye: for the kingdom of heaven is at hand.

Then went out to him Jerusalem, and all Judea, and all the region round about Jordan, and were baptized of him in Jordan, confessing their sins.

—Matthew 3:1,2,5,6

People have gone to extremes with the subject of Bible confessions. Many misunderstand this subject because so much tradition and religious doctrine have been taught. But we shouldn't throw out the whole spiritual principle because of extremes. We just have to go back to the Word and find the truth.

You can find four basic types of confession in the Bible. Usually when the word *confession* is mentioned, people automatically think of confessing *sin*. This is the first type of confession, and it is discussed in Matthew 3:1-6.

This passage addresses John's baptism—the baptism of repentance and the confession of sins. However, we need to understand that this was before the death, burial and resurrection of Jesus. Under the old covenant, people couldn't be born again, because Jesus hadn't been to the Cross yet. So to be in right relationship with God, they had to confess their sins.

This type of confession is biblical. However, confessing each and every one of our sins to get in right relationship with God, to be born again, doesn't apply to us today, because we've changed covenants. Hebrews 8:6 tells us that we live under a new and better covenant established on better promises.

Paul tells us how to enter that new covenant: "If thou shalt confess with thy mouth the Lord Jesus, and shall believe in thine heart that God hath raised him from the dead, thou shalt be saved" (Rom. 10:9). Salvation comes by believing in our hearts and confessing with our mouths that Jesus is Lord and that God raised Him from the dead. This is the second type of biblical confession and the one that leads us into salvation under the new covenant.

Confession:

I confess that Jesus is my Savior and my healer.
He took my pain and sickness so I could have His health.
I walk in the healing covenant God has provided for me.

> *If thou shalt confess with thy mouth the Lord Jesus, and shalt believe in thine heart that God hath raised him from the dead, thou shalt be saved. For with the heart man believeth unto righteousness; and with the mouth confession is made unto salvation.* —Romans 10:9,10

Confessing Jesus as Lord

This Scripture gives us the second type of Bible confession. Paul talks about *confessing with our mouths,* so he's talking about a verbal, audible confession. What do we confess? We confess that Jesus is Lord. This is the kind of confession that leads to salvation.

Just after I got saved, I went with a particular college campus group to Daytona Beach to share Jesus with people at the beach. I used to tell people, "If you'll confess your sins, God will save you." But technically, that's not true. The new birth does not come as a result of confessing all your sins. (You couldn't remember them all anyway.)

Paul didn't say, "If you will confess with your mouth every mistake you ever made." No, he said, "If thou shalt confess with thy mouth the Lord Jesus [or that Jesus is Lord], and shalt believe in thine heart that God hath raised him from the dead, thou shalt be saved."

The Bible says, "Go ye into all the world, and preach the gospel to every creature" (Mark 16:15). Is the Gospel bad news? No, it's good news. A lot of times, we've given people bad news: "You old rotten sinner, if you don't get saved, you're going straight to hell." But what is the Good News? Look at 2 Corinthians 5:19: "God was in Christ, reconciling the world unto himself, not imputing their trespasses unto them...." Jesus, the Lamb of God, came and took the sin, iniquity, sickness and disease of the world upon Himself.

Your sins have been paid for; God isn't holding them against you. So, you see, the confession of salvation is not a negative confession—it's a positive one. It's not the confession of sin. It's the confession of Jesus as Lord.

Confession:

Jesus, I call upon Your name. I believe in my heart God raised You from the dead, and I confess You as Lord of my life. I receive You as my Lord, my Savior and my healer.

OCTOBER 15

Confession and Cleansing for the Believer

If we confess our sins, he is faithful and just to forgive us our sins, and to cleanse us from all unrighteousness.

My little children, these things write I unto you, that ye sin not. And if any man sin, we have an advocate with the Father, Jesus Christ the righteous.   *—1 John 1:9; 2:1*

This Scripture reveals the third type of Bible confession—the believer's confession of sin. Notice John said, "My little children," so he's talking to the Church. When we're born again, God looks at us through the blood of Jesus as though we never sinned in our lives. We're cleansed by the blood of Jesus and robed in white robes of righteousness. Old things are passed away; all things have become new. (2 Cor. 5:17.)

But what if we make a mistake after we're born again? What do we do then? God doesn't condone our sin, but He has made provision for it. He knows that as long as we're on this earth in the flesh, we'll have difficulty. The devil tries to push us in one direction, and the flesh tries to drag us into mistakes from another direction.

So God says, "These things write I unto you, that ye sin not." He's telling us not to sin. But if we do make a mistake, we have an Advocate, a legal representative, in heaven to go to the Father on our behalf. How do we make use of that Advocate? *"If we confess our sins,* he is faithful and just to forgive us our sins, and to cleanse us from all unrighteousness." If we do our part, God does His.

Does this verse say, "He's faithful and just to forgive our sins but will hold them against us the rest of our lives"? No, God won't remind us of our mistakes and shortcomings. When we confess our sins to Him, He cleanses us of *all* unrighteousness and makes us as pure as if we'd never sinned.

So this third type of confession involves the confession of sins, but it's not the way the world gets saved. (Remember, we are saved by confessing Jesus as Lord.) The confession of sins is the way the Church stays in fellowship with the Father.

Confession:

I seek to please God in all I do and say. But even when I miss the mark, He's made a way to cleanse me by the blood of His Son. I walk in righteousness, for I am in Christ Jesus and follow the leading of the Spirit of God.

Let us hold fast the profession of our faith without wavering; (for he is faithful that promised). —Hebrews 10:23

Hold Fast to Your Confession of Faith

The fourth type of confession is the confession of faith, or the confession of what we believe. This is an important type of Bible confession that many in the body of Christ have missed.

We are to "hold fast the profession of our faith." In the *King James Version,* the word *profession* is used. But the same Greek word *homologeo* is translated as "confession" elsewhere in the New Testament and means "to speak the same thing as; to agree with."[1] So the writer of Hebrews is actually saying, "Let us hold fast the *confession* of our faith without wavering, for He who promised is faithful."

We often focus on God's faithfulness—and God *is* faithful. He said, "I watch over My Word to perform it." (Jer. 1:12.) Whatever He has said, He will do because "God is not a man, that he should lie" (Num. 23:19).

God is faithful, but notice that He requires something out of us. He's faithful to perform His Word—*if* we believe and act on it. He told us we have a part to play. If we want His faithfulness to operate in our lives, we must hold fast the confession of our faith without wavering.

What does *the confession of faith* mean? Faith is first of all what you believe, adhere to or put your trust in. For instance, you put your trust in the truth that by Jesus' stripes, you were healed. Your body may feel sick, look sick and act sick, but your faith is pointed toward that unchangeable truth. So the Bible says, "Now hold fast to your confession of that truth without wavering."

If you want God's faithfulness to bring about your healing, then hold fast to your confession of God's healing promises. God says you are healed, so line up your mouth with what you believe, and say, "Thank God, I believe I'm healed!"

Confession:

I hold fast to my confession that Jesus is my healer.
He took my sicknesses and bore my pains. My God is faithful
to heal me because I am faithful to believe and act on His Word!

OCTOBER 17

Unwavering Faith

Let us hold fast the profession of our faith without wavering; (for he is faithful that promised).
—Hebrews 10:23

What does Paul mean when he tells us not to waver? Let's look at another Scripture that addresses this issue. James talks about not wavering as well:

If any of you lack wisdom, let him ask of God, that giveth to all men liberally, and upbraideth not; and it shall be given him. But let him *ask in faith, nothing wavering.* For he that wavereth is like a wave of the sea driven with the wind and tossed. For let not that man think that he shall receive any thing of the Lord.

James 1:5-7

James was talking about asking for wisdom, but he gave us a Bible truth that applies to every area of our lives. He said, "Ask, and it shall be given—*but....*" Then he gave a condition to the promise. We have to "ask in faith, nothing wavering."

How are you going to waver? Most wavering comes in what you say. *Nothing wavering* means you're not wavering in what you believe or in what you say.

You get to that place of unwavering faith by getting your heart full of the Word. You see, you talk about what is closest to your heart. So when your heart is full of the Word, you can't talk about anything else. Every time you open your mouth, God's Word comes out. That's how you hold fast to your confession of what God says.

Confession:

Jesus, the Word, was sent to heal me, so I won't waver by speaking doubts. Symptoms don't move me. I know in my heart I've already received my healing!

Let us hold fast the profession of our faith
without wavering; (for he is faithful that
promised).   *—Hebrews 10:23*

OCTOBER 18

Seek Healing, Not Sympathy

Notice that this verse talks about *holding fast* to your profession of faith. You know, if you have to hold fast to something, it usually means it's trying to get away from you. You'll find in life that one of the most difficult things to hold fast to is the confession of your faith.

Folks will say to you, "You look terrible. How do you feel? I know what you *believe,* but how do you *feel?*" It's so tempting to switch over into the natural realm and just spew it all out, telling people how bad you really feel, how bad it looks and how bad the doctor's report says it's going to get. Flesh just likes to get down and wallow in that mire of doubt and self-pity, looking for sympathy.

But I'd rather have healing than sympathy. Sympathy feels good for a few seconds, but healing feels good for a long time. I can hold fast to my symptoms and get sympathy. But I'd rather hold fast to my confession of faith and get results!

Confession:

Jesus was faithful to heal those who came to Him in faith, and
He's still the same today. I hold fast to my confession that
I am healed because faithful is He who has promised!

OCTOBER 19

Return God's Word Unto Him

For my thoughts are not your thoughts, neither are your ways my ways, saith the Lord. For as the heavens are higher than the earth, so are my ways higher than your ways, and my thoughts than your thoughts.

For as the rain cometh down, and the snow from heaven, and returneth not thither, but watereth the earth, and maketh it bring forth and bud, that it may give seed to the sower, and bread to the eater: So shall my word be that goeth forth out of my mouth: it shall not return unto me void....　　　　*–Isaiah 55:8-11*

God's ways aren't our ways. His ways and His thoughts are as far above us as the heavens are above the earth. But God put His higher ways and thoughts into His Word and then gave them to us. As we feed on that Word, our thoughts become like His thoughts and our ways like His ways. How does this process take place? Only through the Word.

Folks often say, "Well, I tried the Word, and it just didn't work." If the Word of God isn't working in your life, perhaps you aren't returning it to Him, because He said "[My Word] shall not return unto me void."

How do we return the Word to God? The only way is *with our mouths:* "Father, I thank You that no weapon formed against me shall prosper. Thank You for sending Your Word to heal me!"

God sent His Word to us "as the rain cometh down, and the snow from heaven." We are to take the seed of the Word that came down to us from heaven and plant it in our hearts. We cause that seed to grow and develop by feeding on the Word. Then we return it unto the Lord with the confession of our faith.

So find an area in your life where the Word isn't working. Fill your heart with God's promises pertaining to that need. Then return the Word to Him by holding fast to your confession of faith. As you do your part, God will make sure His Word will *not* return void!

Confession:

Father, I don't care what my body feels like–I'm returning Your Word to You. I thank You that Jesus took my sicknesses and bore my pains. You are the God who heals me!

So shall my word be that goeth forth out of my mouth: it shall not return unto me void, but it shall accomplish that which I please, and it shall prosper in the thing whereto I sent it. For ye shall go out with joy, and be led forth with peace.... —Isaiah 55:11,12

OCTOBER 20

Go Forth With Joy!

God is talking here about an abundant, blessed life. I don't know about you, but I like that! God plans for His people to "go out with joy, and be led forth with peace." This is a provision under the old covenant and we live under a new and better covenant established on better promises!

Folks say, "Well, that's just a blessing for the Jews." But the Bible says we are grafted in through the blood of Jesus.

...they which are of faith, the same are the children of Abraham.

Galatians 3:7

If ye be Christ's, then are ye Abraham's seed, and heirs according to the promise.

Galatians 3:29

Some folks say, "Well, we're redeemed from the Old Testament." No, we're just redeemed from the curse of the law. (Gal. 3:13.) We still have a right to all the old covenant blessings.

We have everything the Israelites had, except the curse. In addition, we have the new birth, the infilling of the Holy Ghost and the life, nature and ability of God on the inside of us.

But how do all those blessings operate in our lives? How will we be able to "go out with joy, and be led forth with peace?" (Isa. 55:12.) God says our joy and peace will be the results of His Word: "So shall my word be that goeth forth out of my mouth" (v. 11).

Never underestimate the power of God's Word. If you want the best God has, it will *always* come through His Word.

Confession:

I meditate on God's healing promises, and joy and peace come to me.
I know my Father's Word does not return to Him void. I speak
His Word, knowing it is accomplishing in me what He sent it to do.

OCTOBER 21

God's Insurance Policy

He that dwelleth in the secret place of the most High shall abide under the shadow of the Almighty. I will say of the Lord, He is my refuge and my fortress: my God; in him will I trust.

There shall no evil befall thee, neither shall any plague come nigh thy dwelling.

—Psalm 91:1,2,10

I thank God for insurance policies that are available for us to use while we're on this earth. But even more that that, I thank God for the divine insurance policy He gave us in Psalm 91. I have more confidence in that policy than in any earthly one.

Thank God for divine protection! Janet and I have seen it work many times in our own lives. For instance, we frequently travel overseas. All you have to do is ride in traffic for a few days in some of the countries we've visited, and you'll know your angels are watching over you! People drive differently in other countries. In some places, whoever has his bumper out ahead first has the right of way. I love it. Janet closes her eyes and prays while I drive! But God has always protected us because we have made the Lord our refuge and dwelled with Him.

Verse 1 says, "He that dwelleth in the secret place of the most High shall abide under the shadow of the Almighty." In other words, if we want to stay within the boundaries of God's divine protection, we must abide in that place of safety. We must stay in fellowship with God and walk closely with Him.

We have to appropriate the divine protection that belongs to us. How do we appropriate our Psalm 91 insurance policy? Verse 2 tells us: *"I will say* of the Lord, He is my refuge, and my fortress: my God; in him will I trust."

As you speak God's promises of protection and deliverance, His Word will not return unto Him void. No evil will befall you, and no plague shall come near your dwelling!

Confession:

Psalm 91 works for me! I abide under the shadow of the Almighty. My God is my refuge and my fortress. No plague shall ever come near my dwelling place, because I put my trust in Him.

Can two walk together, except they be agreed?

—Amos 3:3

Walk in Agreement With God

I like walking with God. I want to walk with Him. He's my heavenly Father.

Remember, Adam walked and talked with Him in the cool of the day. That's the fellowship the first Adam had with God, but he lost it through the Fall.

Well, the Bible calls Jesus the last Adam, the One who came to restore to us what the first Adam lost. So under the new covenant, we have the ability to walk and talk with God again. In fact, He said, "I will dwell in them, and walk in them; and I will be their God, and they shall be my people" (2 Cor. 6:16). He not only walks with us—He comes to dwell on the inside of us!

But when we're in disagreement with someone, it's hard to walk with that person in comfortable fellowship. It's the same way in our relationship with God.

Sometimes we unconsciously disagree with God and then wonder why He won't help us. We ask, "Why isn't God helping me? Why isn't He working for me? He knows how bad things are!"

Yes, God knows the situation. He knows what we have need of before we ask. (Matt. 6:8.) Nothing catches Him by surprise. He doesn't look down and exclaim in surprise, "Wow! When did that happen?"

It isn't that God refuses to help us if we disagree with Him. There's just very little He can do for us when we won't walk with Him. That's why Amos 3:3 says, "Can two walk together, except they be agreed?"

One particular meaning of the word *confess* is "to agree with."[1] In order to hold fast to the confession of your faith, you have to agree with God in every area of your life. The best way to develop that agreement is to get in His Word and find out what He says. Then make a choice to agree with His Word by believing it in your heart and saying it with your mouth.

Confession:

God says I'm healed, so I agree: By Jesus' stripes, I'm healed. God says I'm more than a conqueror, so I agree: By His Word and in Jesus' name, I conquer every symptom or circumstance that comes against me!

OCTOBER 23

Guard Your Words

But the angel said unto him, Fear not, Zacharias: for thy prayer is heard; and thy wife Elisabeth shall bear thee a son, and thou shalt call his name John.

And Zacharias said unto the angel, Whereby shall I know this? for I am an old man, and my wife well stricken in years. —Luke 1:13,18

Zacharias was a priest under the old covenant. He and his wife were old and had no children. One day Zacharias was fulfilling his duties in the temple when the angel Gabriel appeared to him. Gabriel told the man that his wife would bear a child named John.

But Zacharias asked, "How in the world am I going to believe this? This can't work; we're too old." In other words, he doubted the word of the Lord that Gabriel delivered to him.

Now, if someone doubts, at some point he will say what he doubts. So to keep Zacharias from speaking his doubts, Gabriel said, "And, behold, thou shalt be dumb, and not able to speak, until the day that these things shall be performed, because thou believest not my words, which shall be fulfilled in their season" (v. 20).

Zacharias' son, John the Baptist, came to prepare the way for the first coming of Jesus; he was a crucial part of God's plan. If Zacharias had begun to doubt and speak against that divine plan, he could have messed up the whole thing. So Zacharias was made dumb and was not able to speak until the plan was fulfilled. God wasn't punishing Zacharias; He was just protecting His divine plan.

Now, God may not strike you dumb, but at times He will tell you to put a guard on your own mouth. Your words can put you on the path of God's plan for you—or they can throw you into a plan of your own making that leads to defeat. So protect God's plan for your life: Guard your words!

Confession:

My words keep me in the midst of God's plan for my life. I understand what the will of the Lord is, and I speak only in faith over His plan. I can do all things through Christ Jesus who strengthens me. I will finish my course with joy!

And the angel came in unto her, and said, Hail, thou that art highly favoured, the Lord is with thee: blessed art thou among women.

And, behold, thou shalt conceive in thy womb, and bring forth a son, and shalt call his name Jesus. —Luke 1:28,31

"Be It Unto Me According to Thy Word"

When the angel appeared to Mary and told her she, a virgin, would have a son, she didn't say, "I don't believe this." She didn't say, "Give me a sign that this is really true." Although she believed the word of the Lord, she simply questioned how it could happen, saying, "How shall this be, seeing I know not a man?" (Luke 1:34). She was saying, "I don't know how it's going to happen; but you said it, so I believe it." Verse 38 says, "And Mary said, Behold the handmaid of the Lord; be it unto me according to thy word."

The angel Gabriel appeared to both Zacharias and Mary. He brought the same message to both—the promise of a child. To Zacharias it was difficult to believe, because he and his wife were old. To Mary it was impossible to believe, because she was a virgin.

But Zacharias doubted and said, "I don't know whether I can believe that." He had to have his mouth closed for months so he wouldn't disagree with God's plan.

On the other hand, Mary just said, "I believe it. I don't know how it will work, but be it unto me according to thy word." Verse 45 gives us the result of Mary's faith: "Blessed is she that believed: for there shall be a performance of those things which were told her from the Lord."

Our words make a difference. If Zacharias' words could have fouled up part of God's plan for the entire world, don't you think our words could foul up His plan for our own lives?

But notice what Mary's words accomplished. Instead of taking her *out* of the plan of God, her words put her *into* it! She said, "Be it unto me according to thy word." And she was blessed when she experienced the performance of that divine plan according to her faith.

Confession:

My words cause me to walk in God's plan. His Word in my heart and my mouth renews my mind, heals my body and fills my life with joy. Be it unto me according to Your Word, Lord!

OCTOBER 25

Tell Yourself How You Are!

Verily I say unto you, That whosoever shall say unto this mountain, Be thou removed, and be thou cast into the sea; and shall not doubt in his heart, but shall believe that those things which he saith shall come to pass; he shall have whatsoever he saith.

Therefore I say unto you, What things soever ye desire, when ye pray, believe that ye receive them, and ye shall have them. And when ye stand praying, forgive, if ye have ought against any: that your Father also which is in heaven may forgive you your trespasses. But if ye do not forgive, neither will your Father which is in heaven forgive your trespasses.　　　　　　　　　　　　　　　*–Mark 11:23-26*

In this passage, Jesus gives us the most complete, condensed instruction of faith found in the Bible. In verse 23, He gives the two basic principles of faith—believing in the heart and saying with the mouth. Then in verse 24, He shows us how to apply our faith in prayer. Finally, Jesus reveals the greatest hindrance to faith—unforgiveness. (vv. 25,26.)

Paul said we are to walk by faith and not by sight.

I remember hearing that Smith Wigglesworth once said, "I never get up in the morning and ask Smith how he is. I get up in the morning and *tell* him how he is."

You can do the same thing. Take yourself to the Word of God every morning and say, "This is how you are. You're more than a conqueror. This is the victory that overcomes the world—even your faith. [1 John 5:4.] By Jesus' stripes you were healed. [Isa. 53:5; 1 Peter 2:24.] You've been delivered from the power of darkness and translated into the kingdom of His Son! [Col. 1:13.]"

We must believe and say what God says. We have to feed on the Word of God until we not only know what God says, but we also believe it in our hearts. Then when a situation arises, we can just lean back, look the problem square in the face and say, "I don't care what you look like, seem like, sound like or feel like. I believe God!"

Confession:

Every day I tell myself how I am according to God's Word.
I am healed by the stripes of Jesus. I'm abundantly blessed.
I believe God, and it shall be even as He told me in His Word!

Now all these things happened unto them for ensamples: and they are written for our admonition, upon whom the ends of the world are come.

—1 Corinthians 10:11

Taking Our Promised Land

The things that happened to Israel happened as examples for us. Many are types and shadows we can learn from because they point to our new covenant in Christ.

God delivered Israel from the bondage of Egypt. He supernaturally parted the Red Sea, brought His people through on dry ground and then closed up the Red Sea on the Egyptian army. God "brought them forth also with silver and gold: and there was not one feeble person among their tribes" (Ps. 105:37).

When the Israelites came out of Egypt and walked across that Red Sea, they were free, happy, healthy, prosperous and delivered from their enemies.

That's what the new birth looks like. The minute we're born again, God looks at us and sees us free, happy, healthy, prosperous and delivered from our enemies. If we trust Him, we'll ultimately walk in that kind of life. Of course, problems will come along, but the Bible says, "This is the victory that overcometh the world, even our faith" (1 John 5:4).

God prepared the Promised Land for Abraham's descendants. That land belonged to them. The Promised Land isn't a type of heaven; it's a type of the abundant Christian life on earth. (The Promised Land couldn't be a type of heaven, because there were giants in Canaan to overcome.)

God told them, "The land I give you flows with milk and honey. Giants live there, but don't be concerned about them. I'll drive them out from before you. You just go possess what I've given you!"

We're in a similar position. Our victory has already been given to us. The devil has already been defeated. Sickness and disease have already been conquered. Now we just have to exercise our rights and privileges in Christ and take what already belongs to us!

Confession:

God wants me free, healthy and delivered from my enemies. That's my promised land! In Jesus' name, I drive out all symptoms of sickness and take the health that is mine!

OCTOBER 27

Enter Your Promised Land Through Faith

And Moses sent them to spy out the land of Canaan, and said unto them, Get you up this way southward, and go up into the mountain: and see the land, what it is.... –Numbers 13:17,18

God told the Israelites that the land He had given them was a land flowing with milk and honey, so the twelve spies went in and checked it out for forty days. When they returned, they brought back one cluster of grapes that took two of them to carry. Those were pretty good grapes!

The Israelites had been out in the desert, getting their water from a rock and living on manna from heaven that sustained them but didn't have much taste. Now God said they were ready to move in and possess the Promised Land, a land flowing with milk and honey. However, Israel didn't go in; they stayed back in the desert.

You'll find that in the church world today. Some folks are satisfied to stay out in the "desert," getting a little water out of a rock and bit of manna from heaven each morning. They could move over into the promised land and enjoy an abundance of blessings, but they're satisfied where they are. "Don't push healing on me," they say. "I'm not interested. I'm happy as I am."

You see, the choice is ours. God doesn't force anything on anyone. I don't know about you, but I have a burning desire on the inside to move over into my promised land—into the best God has for me.

The Bible says the Israelites "could not enter in because of unbelief" (Heb. 3:19). The same is true for us. What determines whether we move into the abundance of our promised land or barely get along out in the desert is the extent to which we believe God. No wonder God says, "Without faith, you can't please Me"!

Confession:

I want God's best in my life. Healing is part of the abundant life He provided through Jesus. I enter my promised land by faith in His Word. I believe I'm strong, healed and able to possess my inheritance!

And they told him, and said, We came unto the land whither thou sentest us, and surely it floweth with milk and honey; and this is the fruit of it. Nevertheless the people be strong that dwell in the land, and the cities are walled, and very great: and moreover we saw the children of Anak there. —Numbers 13:27,28

OCTOBER 28

Nevertheless— Believe God!

Faith is a law that operates by believing and saying. Just like the natural law of gravity, this spiritual law works for everyone. If we jump off a platform, the law of gravity says we will hit the floor. And according to the law of faith, what we believe and say is what we will get.

The ten spies came back and told Moses and the people, "We entered the land where you sent us, and it does flow with milk and honey. This huge cluster of grapes is the fruit of it."

Now, if the spies had just stopped there, they would have been in good shape. But they said, "Nevertheless..." Then verse 32 says, "They brought up an evil report of the land...." (Notice that God associates an evil report with disagreeing with His Word!)

You know, that word *nevertheless* gets a lot of people in trouble, because it's a sign of their unbelief. "Yes, Lord, we know what Your Word says; nevertheless..."

But I like the way Peter used the word *nevertheless.* One morning after he had come in from a bad night of fishing, Jesus showed up and told him, "Launch out into the deep, and let down your nets for a draught" (Luke 5:4).

Peter replied, "Master, we have toiled all the night, and have taken nothing: nevertheless at thy word I will let down the net" (v. 5). As Peter obeyed Jesus, he and the other fishermen caught so many fish in their nets that their boats almost sank!

The ten spies said, "Oh, yeah, we know what the Lord said. Nevertheless, this is what we *saw."* Now, if we're going to use the word *nevertheless,* let's use it the way Peter did: "Natural circumstances and the devil say this; nevertheless, I believe God's Word!"

Confession:

Giants of symptoms and evil circumstances may stand against me in my promised land. Nevertheless, through the power in God's Word and Jesus' name, I am an overcomer!

OCTOBER 29

The Spirit of Faith

Surely they shall not see the land which I sware unto their fathers, neither shall any of them that provoked me see it: but my servant Caleb, because he had another spirit with him, and hath followed me fully, him will I bring into the land whereinto he went; and his seed shall possess it. —*Numbers 14:23,24*

God gave the children of Israel His Word. He told them about the Promised Land and said, "I've given it to you." When the twelve spies went to check it out, they discovered it was a land flowing with milk and honey, exactly as He'd said.

But when the spies came back out, three million and ten of the people said, "We can't possess that land." Only two—Joshua and Caleb—stood up and said, "Yes, we can. If God said it, we can do it!"

It's what Joshua and Caleb believed and said that made the difference. If you continue reading in the Old Testament, you'll find that the children of Israel had to wander in the wilderness for forty years. During those forty years, that entire unbelieving generation, including the ten spies, all died in the wilderness. But forty years later, Joshua and Caleb led the next generation of Israelites into the Promised Land.

But did you notice they all got what they *believed* and *said?* If that spiritual law worked under the old covenant, it will work under the new.

God said, "But my servant Caleb, because he had another spirit with him, and hath followed me fully...." What did God mean by "another spirit"? Caleb had the same spirit of faith that Paul talked about in 2 Corinthians 4:13: "We having the same spirit of faith, according as it is written, I believed, and therefore have I spoken; we also believe, and therefore speak."

We are a direct result of what we've been believing and saying about ourselves up until this present moment. Let's not give an evil report or rebel against the Word of the Lord. Let's hook up with God, agree with His Word and walk in the blessings He has provided!

Confession:

Lord, I agree with You. I believe, and therefore I say that You sent Your Word and healed me. You have delivered me from destruction. I'm healed according to Your Word, which works mightily in me now!

In the mouth of two or three witnesses shall
every word be established. —2 Corinthians 13:1

What Kind of Witness Will You Be?

There are two different witnesses talking to us in every situation.

First, there's the witness of the problem. The problem is speaking loud and clear, whether it's pain, symptoms, bad reports, depression, oppression or fear. This witness says, "Man, you're sick! You're not going to make it. You're defeated. You've failed. You're never going to recover."

On the other side is the witness of God's Word. This witness says, "By Jesus' stripes, you were healed. [Isa. 53:5; 1 Peter 2:24.] Thanks be unto God who always gives you the victory through the Lord Jesus Christ. [2 Cor. 2:14.] This is the victory that overcomes the world, even your faith. [1 John 5:4.]" On one side is the witness of the problem; on the other side is the witness of the answer.

But notice, it takes two witnesses for any of those words to stand. The word *establish* means "to cause to stand."[1] So God said, "In the mouth of two or three witnesses, let every word be established, or be made to stand."

The devil is on one side, and God is on the other; and one of these witnesses will be established in your life. The one who prevails will be the one with the majority, because nothing can be established without two witnesses.

Now, one more witness stands in the middle—*you*. The side you line up with becomes the side with the majority vote. If you line up with the problem, it becomes established in your life, and there's very little God can do about it. You've made your choice.

However, you can also choose to line up with what *God* has to say. You can establish God's Word and make it stand in your life.

How do you line up with one side or the other? Paul tells us: "In the *mouth* of two or three witnesses shall every word be established." The witness you believe and *verbally* agree with is the witness that becomes established in your life.

—— ✎ ——

Confession:

God's Word is truth to me. With my mouth,
I establish the Word in my life. God sent His Word and
healed me. I believe I am healed according to His Word!

OCTOBER 31

Choose To Receive by the Hand of Faith

I call heaven and earth to record this day against you, that I have set before you life and death, blessing and cursing: therefore choose life, that both thou and thy seed may live.

—Deuteronomy 30:19

As Christians living in these fleshly bodies, too often we agree with every problem that comes along: "Oh, I'm sick. I'm broke. I'm defeated. I'm discouraged. I'm depressed. Nothing ever goes right for me." Some of us constantly talk the blues, believe the blues and get the blues; then we wonder why God doesn't help us!

You know, if it were up to God, we'd never have a problem. The Bible says He has already given us all things that pertain to life and godliness. (2 Peter 1:3.) He has already redeemed us from sickness, disease, poverty, lack, failure and fear.

But notice, God left the matter in our hands. In Deuteronomy 30:19, He said, "I have set before you life and death, blessing and cursing: therefore choose life." It's our choice. God doesn't force anything on us. God already provided His best for us when He purchased everything we'd ever need that pertains to life and godliness, made it available and then said, "If you want it, you can have it—just come and take it by faith."

Faith is the hand that receives from God. When we choose to reach out and take hold of God's blessings by faith, we become overcomers in this world, walking in the fullness of His blessings!

Confession:

I choose to take hold of God's blessings by faith. I'm not moved by what I see or feel. I'm only moved by what I believe. He said I am healed; therefore, I agree and say, "I am healed."

Let your conversation be without covetousness; and be content with such things as ye have: for he hath said, I will never leave thee, nor forsake thee. So that we may boldly say, The Lord is my helper, and I will not fear what man shall do unto me. —Hebrews 13:5,6

Boldly Proclaim God's Truth!

Notice those two phrases "he hath said" and "that we may boldly say." As Christians, we ought to take what God has said about us and boldly say it. If He said, "By Jesus' stripes, you were healed," then we ought to boldly say, "By Jesus' stripes, I am healed." If He said, "I've delivered you from your fears," then we ought to boldly say, "Thank God, I've been delivered from fear! He has not given me the spirit of fear, but of power, love and a sound mind." (2 Tim. 1:7.)

We need to go through the Scriptures, find out what God said and then boldly say it with our mouths. Not timidly—boldly!

Now, we don't have to speak it out in front of everyone. Some won't believe or understand. But we can get before God and boldly plead our case according to His Word. We should let the devil hear, too, because there's not a thing he can do about it!

Some might say, "But I don't feel like it." But you never will feel like it until you start saying it.

So when the devil tries to remind you of mistakes you've made, you can boldly say, "Therefore if any man is in Christ, he's a new creature. Glory to God, I'm a new creature in Christ! Old things have passed away. All things have become new!" (2 Cor. 5:17.)

Or when the devil says, *You're just an old, unworthy thing, a miserable creature,* you can say, "He who knew no sin was made to be sin for me so I could be made the righteousness of God in Him. [2 Cor. 5:21.] I've been given the free gift of righteousness. I reign as a king in life. Glory to God!" He *hath said,* so that you may *boldly say* the truth and then watch the enemy flee!

Confession:

I boldly say the Lord is my strength and my helper. No plague shall come near my dwelling. No weapon formed against me shall prosper. Jesus Himself took my infirmities and bore my sickness, so I am healed!

NOVEMBER 2

Jesus, Our Advocate

Wherefore, holy brethren, partakers of the heavenly calling, consider the Apostle and High Priest of our profession, Christ Jesus.

—Hebrews 3:1

The word *profession* in the original Greek language is the same as the word used for *confession.* Jesus is the apostle and High Priest of our confession. First John 2:1 says, "If any man sin, we have an advocate with the Father, Jesus Christ the righteous." Jesus is our Mediator, our legal representative, our attorney.

We can better understand Jesus' role if we think of it in terms of a big court case. God is the judge. He makes the final decisions. Over in the far corner is the prosecutor—the devil, accuser of the brethren. (Rev. 12:10.)

But thank God, in our corner we have a legal adviser—Jesus! He shed His blood to redeem us, and now He's the apostle and High Priest of our confession.

Think about this scenario. The devil whispers to your mind, *I'm going to put sickness and disease on you.* Meanwhile, your Advocate is saying to you, "All right, give Me something to work with." But, instead, you agree with your accuser: "Oh, I'm so sick. Everything goes wrong for me. I hurt from head to toe. I'm sick, and I'm probably getting sicker."

Jesus looks at the Father and says, "I haven't got a thing to work with."

Now let's go back to the moment the devil whispers in your mind, *I'm going to put sickness and disease on you.* Suppose Jesus, the apostle and High Priest of your confession, checks with you and finds you boldly saying: "Thank God, by Jesus' stripes I was healed! [Isa. 53.5; 1 Peter 2:24.] Jesus took my infirmities and bore my sicknesses. [Matt. 8:17.] I'm redeemed from sickness, poverty and spiritual death. This is the victory that overcomes the world, even my faith. [1 John 5:4.] Glory to God!"

That's what Jesus has been waiting to hear. Now He turns to the judge and says, "Father, be it unto Your child according to his faith!"

Confession:

The Lord is my refuge and my fortress; in Him do I put my trust. God is the strength of my life. He heals me from the top of my head to the soles of my feet!

As the bird by wandering, as the swallow by flying, so the curse causeless shall not come.

–Proverbs 26:2

Redeemed From the "Curse Causeless"

Sometimes people get sick and think, *There must be some deep, dark, hidden sin in my life I don't even know about that's caused this curse to come on me.* But this Scripture indicates that some problems in our lives are "causeless." They are simply attacks from the enemy. So if you don't know about a deep, dark, hidden sin in your life, it's probably not there.

I was recently with a fellow in Europe who was upset because a physical ailment had come on one of his relatives. He told me, "We've gone all through her childhood, turning over every rock to see if she had any bitterness in her past that might have caused this condition. We found out she got angry at her mother one time when she was a little girl."

This man was viewing his relative's sickness from a psychological perspective. Now, sometimes bitterness *can* cause illnesses. But we need to be careful about getting into the realm of psychology. Although psychology can sometimes help locate the source of a problem, it doesn't have the ability to *free* us from it.

We don't need to go digging past the time we were born again. At that moment, we became new creatures, and our old man died. Any problems we had before that are gone.

Thank God, we've been redeemed from the "curse causeless" and every evil work of the enemy!

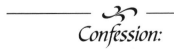

Confession:

I'm a new creature in Christ Jesus. When I was born again, my past was wiped away. In Christ, I am made righteous. Therefore, I come boldly to the throne of grace to obtain mercy and find grace to help in time of need!

NOVEMBER 4

"God's Word Works for Me!"

The secret things belong unto the Lord our God: but those things which are revealed belong unto us and to our children for ever....

–Deuteronomy 29:29

Sometimes God won't tell us why a particular individual didn't get his or her healing. For instance, one time Janet and I were at a certain church and someone asked us to pray with a man in the hospital who was very ill. When we went to visit the man, he was lying in his bed, saying everything right: "By Jesus' stripes I'm healed. [Isa. 53:5; 1 Peter 2:24.] Himself took my infirmities and bore my sicknesses. [Matt. 8:17.] I won't die, but I'll live and declare the works of the Lord. [Ps. 118:17.]"

We prayed for the man; but when we walked out of the hospital, we looked at each other. We both knew in our spirits he was going home to be with the Lord. We sensed that the man was talking right because if he didn't, his family would be angry at him but that in his heart he'd seen a glimpse of heaven and wanted to go home. He was tired of fighting.

In just a short time, the man went home to be with the Lord.

Some said of this man's death, "Well, all this faith stuff doesn't work. He was believing God." Yes, but he was believing God *to go home.*

So don't base your faith walk on what happens in another person's life. You can't let someone else's experience with faith affect you, because you never know what is in that person's heart. Don't look at another person's situation and say, "Well, if it didn't work for him, it sure will never work for me." Get your eyes back on the Lord and say, "Well, I don't know why it didn't work for that person, but I know one person it will always work for—me!"

Confession:

The Bible says God sent His Word and healed me, and I'm not letting go of that. My faith is not based on the experience of others but on the Word of God.

It is appointed unto men once to die, but after this the judgment.   *–Hebrews 9:27*

You Can Finish Your Course

Some people think that there's an appointed time to die and when that time comes for a person, he dies. But that's wrong thinking, and it leaves the door open to the devil.

Notice that this verse doesn't say there is an appointed time to die. It says it is appointed unto man to die *once.* I heard someone say, "It's appointed unto man once to die, but we don't have to let the devil set the appointment!"

The apostle Paul said in Philippians 1:23-24, "For I am in a strait betwixt two, having a desire to depart, and to be with Christ; which is far better: nevertheless to abide in the flesh is more needful for you." In other words, Paul was saying, "I haven't decided yet whether to go or stay." He was writing from prison, and they were ready to take his head off. Yet Paul was saying he hadn't decided whether to go or stay—as though he had a choice!

Paul *did* have a choice. Later in his writings, he said, "For I am now ready to be offered, and the time of my departure is at hand. I have fought a good fight, I have finished my course, I have kept the faith" (2 Tim. 4:6,7). He left when he was good and ready, and that wasn't until he'd finished his course.

You should desire to do the same thing. Dare to believe God for a long, satisfying life. Determine in your heart that you won't leave this earth until you can say with confidence, "I have finished my course!"

Confession:

My God is a healing God. I live to declare the works of the Lord.
I'll live out my full time on this earth. I'll fight the good fight
of faith, and I'll finish my course with joy!

NOVEMBER 6

Faith in God's Word Prolongs Life

My son, forget not my law; but let thine heart keep my commandments: for length of days, and long life, and peace, shall they add to thee.

–Proverbs 3:1,2

Someone might say, "Well, what is our full length of time on this earth?" Perhaps it's one age for one person and another age for another person. If God were making the appointment, we'd know that from the Bible.

But look at what Ephesians 6:1-3 says:

Children, obey your parents in the Lord: for this is right. Honour thy father and mother; (which is the first commandment with promise;) that it may be well with thee, and *thou mayest live long on the earth.*

In other words, the Bible tells children, "There's something *you* can do that will cause you to have a long life."

The book of Proverbs also talks about increasing the length of our lives:

The fear of the Lord is the beginning of wisdom: and the knowledge of the holy is understanding. For by me thy days shall be multiplied, and the years of thy life shall be increased.

Proverbs 9:10,11

The fear of the Lord prolongeth days: but the years of the wicked shall be shortened.

Proverbs 10:27

There are many other Scriptures that say, "If you do this, you'll live long on the earth," or "If you do that, you'll cut your life short on this earth." But the Bible *doesn't* say, "There's an appointed time, and when your time comes, you're going." No, God gives us all kinds of things we can do to prolong our lives. He puts it more in our hands than in His own.

Confession:

The life I find in God's Word drives sickness and disease far from me. My days are multiplied, and the years of my life are increased as I fear and reverence the Lord.

And if thou wilt walk in my ways, to keep my statutes and my commandments, as thy father David did walk, then I will lengthen thy days.

—1 Kings 3:14

NOVEMBER 7

Believe God for Length of Days

I knew a man who was only thirty-nine years old when he went home to be with Jesus. He had been sick for awhile. People had prayed and done everything they could, but he never got healed.

Later, this man's brother was talking to someone and said, "You know, it's the strangest thing. When my brother and I were younger, we spent a lot of time together. Every now and then, he'd get really serious and say, 'I'll never live to be forty.'"

The man didn't have any particular reason for believing that, but he kept thinking and planning for an early death. Just a matter of weeks before this man turned forty, he went home to be with the Lord. He could have had thirty, forty or fifty more years on this earth and done a particular work for God. He could have fulfilled God's will for his life.

Now, I don't mean to criticize people who go home early, and I don't want to make it sound as if they didn't have faith. But we need to keep our thinking right. The Bible says believers can enjoy abundant blessings in this life. We don't have to go home sick.

And the good news is that whether a Christian gets healed or goes home to be with the Lord, he can't be defeated. If he gets healed, he's going to go tell everyone about it. If he dies and goes home, he'll be with Jesus. Either way, he wins!

We have an eternity to spend in heaven, but we might as well accomplish all we can down here. Let's get the job done first. Let's finish what God has for us to do and then go home!

Confession:

I obey God's commandments with my whole heart. Therefore, long life and peace are added unto me. If Jesus doesn't come to take me and His Church home first, I'll live on earth until I'm satisfied!

NOVEMBER 8

Live Out Your Full Life on Earth

With long life will I satisfy him, and shew him my salvation. —*Psalm 91:16*

God wants you to live out your full life on the earth. But if you don't, He won't be mad at you.

We should never criticize anyone for going home early. For instance, Janet and I had a friend who was extremely ill and couldn't seem to get his healing. He was too young to go, but he saw a glimpse of the other side and told his family, "I'm not staying. I just can't stay anymore."

Sometimes people get a glimpse of the other side, and you can't hold them back. When we say it's not the will of God for people to go home early, we're not being critical of those who have. We're just saying to those who are still here, "Let's press on and stay as long as we can!"

Don't ever feel sorry for someone who has gone to heaven. Don't try to figure out why he didn't get his healing. Faith is a matter of the heart, and the only One who can look into the heart is God.

Someone may say, "Well, I knew so-and-so. He was believing God, and it didn't work."

No, that isn't right. It may have looked as if that person was believing God, but God doesn't fail. Sometimes people just don't make contact with their answers.

Don't try to figure it all out. Rejoice with those who have made it to the other side, and keep the Word working for yourself in this life!

Confession:

My God shows me His salvation. He preserves my life. He heals my body. I make contact with the promises of God, and His Word works mightily in me. I'll be satisfied with a long, fruitful life for His glory!

For we walk by faith, not by sight.

–2 Corinthians 5:7

NOVEMBER 9

Believe the Word, Not the Symptoms

I once heard about a lady who was a member of a particular church and had a big, visible, cancerous growth on her face. Apparently she made a point of contact, praying and believing she received her healing. But there was no change in her appearance.

Later at a testimony service, this woman stood and said, "I want to thank God for healing me." She sat down, and people started looking at her funny. The next Sunday, she stood and said, "I want to thank God for healing me." This went on for several weeks.

Some people got upset about it, and one person said to her, "Everyone can see you're not healed. You're causing confusion. You can't keep standing up telling people you're healed."

She went home that day and stood in front of the mirror. Then she prayed, "Now, Father, in Jesus' name, I know I'm healed by the stripes of Jesus. I know what the Bible says, and I know I believe it. I'd sure appreciate it, though, if You'd get rid of these ugly symptoms." All of a sudden, while the woman was still standing in front of the mirror, that big cancer just fell off and hit the floor! She looked in the mirror. The area where the growth had been a moment before was now covered in fresh baby skin!

When we make a point of contact with God, believing we receive our answer, we may not immediately look different. But we don't have to look different—we just have to believe what the Bible says and then say what we believe!

Confession:

*Thank God, I'm healed! I know in my heart that when I prayed,
my Father heard me and gave me the petition I asked for.
I believe I have received my healing.*

NOVEMBER 10

Switch Over to the Realm of Faith

We having the same spirit of faith, according as it is written, I believed, and therefore have I spoken; we also believe, and therefore speak.

–2 Corinthians 4:13

Perhaps you need a miracle and have been waiting for God to manifest Himself through the gifts of the Spirit. The trouble is that He hasn't done it. So what do you do now?

Do what the Bible says you're supposed to do. Switch over to the realm of faith. Believe God, and *draw* that power out of Him.

You see, Jesus ministered to people in two different ways when He walked on this earth. At times He walked up to individuals and sovereignly performed miracles that required no faith on their part. Other times people crawled up behind Jesus in a crowd and pulled power out of Him when He didn't even know they were there. (Matt. 14:36.) Their faith released the power of God.

Jesus still ministers both ways. In His sovereignty, He sometimes works miracles as *He* wills. But our faith in His Word will work *every* time at our will.

So don't wait for a miracle to happen—*make* one happen with your faith in God's Word!

Someone once said to me, "Oh, you make God sound like a heavenly butler." No, I don't make God sound like anything. I just tell you what He already said to you in His Word.

Besides that, there's a big difference between a heavenly butler and a heavenly Father. You tell a butler what to do. But with your heavenly Father, you find out what He has already done for you through His love and then you take hold of it by faith!

Confession:

My God always makes His healing power available to me. Therefore, I draw on God's power for my healing and appropriate what I need from Him by faith.

If ye abide in me, and my words abide in you, ye shall ask what ye will, and it shall be done unto you.   *—John 15:7*

"Ask, and It Shall Be Done Unto You"

Jesus said to His disciples, "If you abide in Me, and My words abide in you, My words abiding in you will produce faith. Then you'll ask whatever *you* will, and it will be done unto you." I didn't say that—Jesus did!

Now, Jesus did put limits on that promise. He didn't give us *carte blanche;* He wasn't saying, "Ask for anything you want, period." No, Jesus said, *"If* you abide in Me and My words abide in you...."

You see, if His Word is abiding in you and you're walking with Him, you won't be able to ask in faith for anything that's unscriptural; you'll only ask for things that line up with the Word. That's God's checks-and-balances system.

What Jesus *is* saying in this verse is that *you can have a miracle at your own discretion.* You don't have to sit back and wait to see whether it's God's own good time. He said, "If you abide in Me and My words abide in you, ask whatever *you* will, and it shall be done for you!" You have Jesus' word on it—you can initiate a miracle anytime you want!

Confession:

I abide in Jesus, and His Word abides in me. Therefore, I ask whatever I will, and it is done unto me. Healing is in God's Word. When symptoms try to come, I ask for healing, and it's given to me. I am healed!

NOVEMBER 12

The Power in Prayer

Is any sick among you? let him call for the elders of the church; and let them pray over him, anointing him with oil in the name of the Lord: and the prayer of faith shall save the sick, and the Lord shall raise him up; and if he have committed sins, they shall be forgiven him. Confess your faults one to another, and pray one for another, that ye may be healed....

—James 5:14-16

Who is the "ye" in the phrase "that ye may be healed"? "Ye" is the body of Christ. Each of us in the body of Christ is to pray for one another so that those in the Church may be healed.

We Christians will begin to be healthier when we start praying for one another. We need to understand that we have great power in prayer. James 5:16 AMP puts it this way: "The earnest (heartfelt, continued) prayer of a righteous man makes tremendous power available [dynamic in its working]."

Now, we're not going to be able to help others receive their healing in every situation. The Holy Ghost will let us know when we can help and when we can't make any progress. In some situations, people stay afflicted because they let someone else do all their praying for them. That's why James 5:13 says, "Is any among you afflicted? let *him* pray."

But in other situations, praying for each other *can* make the difference. You see, there are people in the Church and in the world today who will never be healed unless someone goes to the Father in prayer for them. Why? Some people have never even heard about divine healing. Isaiah 5:13 says, "Therefore my people are gone into captivity, because they have no knowledge...." Others can't receive divine healing because they've never been taught *how* to receive from God. These people need someone to go to the throne of God in prayer for them.

You can be that someone! Your earnest, heartfelt and continued prayers for another can make tremendous power available to heal, deliver and set free!

Confession:

I pray effectually and fervently for others so they can receive their healing. As I pray, tremendous power is made available to effect a healing and a cure in others and in me!

When the even was come, they brought unto him many that were possessed with devils: and he cast out the spirits with his word, and healed all that were sick. —Matthew 8:16

Coming to Jesus for Others

This verse says "they" started bringing people to Jesus. Let's talk about how prayer relates to this Scripture. You'll find cases again and again in the Bible where people were healed because someone went to Jesus on their behalf.

For instance, did you ever notice in Matthew 8 that the centurion's servant who needed healing stayed home? This servant had palsy, or what we'd call paralysis, but he was healed because someone went to Jesus on his behalf. In a sense, the centurion was an intercessor because he went to Jesus on behalf of someone in need. (vv. 5-13.)

In Matthew 15, the woman from Canaan came to Jesus on behalf of her daughter, who was grievously vexed with a devil. This girl was healed because of her mother's faith. (vv. 22-28.)

In John 4, the nobleman traveled approximately twenty-five miles from Capernaum to Cana of Galilee to reach Jesus. The nobleman said, "My son is at home at the point of death. Come and heal him." Jesus said, "Go your way; your son is all right." The man went his way believing the word Jesus had spoken. And because he had gone to Jesus on his son's behalf, his boy was healed. (vv. 47-53.)

Years ago, when someone in a church was sick, it was a common occurrence for the church to rally around and pray twenty-four hours a day until that person was healed. It wasn't something they organized; it was Holy Ghost-inspired. We need to continue in this practice today because "the earnest (heartfelt, continued) prayer of a righteous man makes tremendous power available [dynamic in its working]" (James 5:16 AMP).

Confession:

It's God's will that all be healed. Today I can bring people before God's throne in prayer so Jesus can work His healing power in their lives. Healing belongs to them and to me because we serve a good God!

NOVEMBER 14

Persistence in Prayer

One of [Jesus'] disciples said unto him, Lord, teach us to pray, as John also taught his disciples.

—Luke 11:1

Apparently the disciples were impressed by Jesus' prayer life because He got results. So they asked Him to teach them how to pray. Jesus first taught the Lord's Prayer. Then He shared another key to prayer:

And he said unto them, Which of you shall have a friend, and shall go unto him at midnight, and say unto him, Friend, lend me three loaves; for a friend of mine in his journey is come to me, and I have nothing to set before him?

Luke 11:5,6

What is bread? Well, when the woman of Canaan in Matthew 15 asked for healing for her daughter, Jesus called *healing* the children's bread. (v. 26.) So in this parable, when the man asked for three loaves of bread, he could have been asking for healing for his friend.

And he from within shall answer and say, Trouble me not: the door is now shut, and my children are with me in bed; I cannot rise and give thee. I say unto you, Though he will not rise and give him, because he is his friend, yet *because of his importunity,* he will rise and give him as many as he needeth.

Luke 11:7,8

Jesus said the man finally gave the bread to the petitioner because of his importunity. One meaning of that word *importunity* is "persistence." *The Amplified Bible* says, "because of his shameless *persistence and insistence....*"

Do you know someone with a need who can't seem to make contact with God for himself? You can go into the presence of God on his behalf. God will hear your persistent prayers and provide your friend with exactly what he needs—the children's bread of healing.

Confession:

I boldly go to my Father on behalf of another, and my Father gives me what I ask for in faith. I am persistent to ask and to believe God will answer because healing is the children's bread.

Confess your faults one to another, and pray one for another, that ye may be healed. The effectual fervent prayer of a righteous man availeth much. —James 5:16

Helping Others Make Contact With God

Have you ever been in a situation where you knew what the Word said, you knew how to believe God, you were keeping your words in line with the Bible—and still you were getting nowhere fast?

Those are the times when you need to get before God and say, "God, I'm missing it. *You* never miss it, because You can't change. Let me know where I'm missing it, and I'll make the adjustment."

But sometimes people get into situations where, for one reason or another, they just can't seem to make that contact with their answer. In many of these cases, other believers can go before God's throne on their behalf and help them make a connection in the Spirit.

For example, years ago the daughter of a friend of ours became very ill. Although her friends and family were doing all they knew to do, she continually grew worse. She wasn't making contact with her healing.

Another friend of ours came home from work one day and told his wife that he sensed a strong urge to pray for this young lady. The couple prayed about five hours before the unction to pray lifted off them. They knew they had the answer.

This couple found out later that the very evening they prayed for the sick young woman, she suddenly started getting better, until soon she was perfectly normal.

We don't know why the young woman was having trouble making contact with her answer for herself. But God supernaturally moved on another believer to pray and "make tremendous power available" on her behalf.

----------------- ❧ -----------------

Confession:

I am faithful to pray fervently for others, and God's power is made available for their healing. When I don't know how to pray as I should, the Holy Spirit helps me pray, making intercession with groanings that cannot be uttered. (Rom. 8:26.)

NOVEMBER 16

Do the Works of Jesus

Believest thou not that I am in the Father, and the Father in me? the words that I speak unto you I speak not of myself: but the Father that dwelleth in me, he doeth the works.

–John 14:10

Jesus said, "I'm not healing people. The Father inside Me is the One doing the works. He's healing them through Me." He also said, "The Son can do nothing of himself, but what he seeth the Father do: for what things soever he doeth, these also doeth the Son likewise" (John 5:19).

Anytime God can get inside a human body, He'll start doing the same works He did through Jesus. That's why in John 14:12, Jesus said, "Verily, verily, I say unto you, He that believeth on me, the works that I do shall he do also; and greater works than these shall he do; because I go unto my Father." Jesus was saying, "I'll go to the Father, and God will come live inside *you.*"

The entire plan of God is to dwell inside of us: "Know ye not that ye are the temple of the living God, and that the Spirit of God dwelleth in you?" (1 Cor. 3:16). We are the temple of the Holy Spirit. That's why the believer's ministry is so powerful.

If you're a believer, God already lives inside you. Now it's up to you to release His power residing within you through faith. As you do, He will start doing the same works through you that He did through Jesus!

Confession:

I am the temple of the living God; the Spirit of God dwells in me. Jesus said that as I believe on Him, I am able to do the works He did—and even greater works—because my Father does the work through me.

But if the Spirit of him that raised up Jesus from the dead dwell in you, he that raised up Christ from the dead shall also quicken your mortal bodies by his Spirit that dwelleth in you.

–Romans 8:11

NOVEMBER 17

The Holy Spirit–God's Powerhouse

I've heard people say, "Well, miracles don't happen anymore. God doesn't heal people anymore." Those people sure don't get that idea out of the Bible. No one could prove that by God's Word. Those people may be speaking their own opinions, experiences or ideas, but they can't give Scripture to back up that statement.

Who is the healer? Jesus is the healer! He's the One who purchased and provided healing for us. And who is the powerhouse who manifests healing in our physical bodies? This Scripture says the Spirit who raised Jesus from the dead quickens our mortal bodies. So the Holy Spirit is the One who has the power to manifest what Jesus purchased and provided for us.

The Holy Ghost operated in a measure in the four Gospels. First, He operated through Jesus. Then Jesus gave power to the twelve disciples and seventy others. (Luke 10:1,17.) So during Jesus' earthly ministry, about eighty-three people had the power of God on them to heal people at one time or another.

Today, the Holy Ghost is the One doing the mighty works of God through those who yield to Him. But the Holy Ghost didn't even come into the fullness of His ministry until the Day of Pentecost, when He was poured out on all flesh.

So to those who say that God doesn't perform miracles today, I ask this question: How could healings and miracles have stopped at the very time the One who manifests those healings and miracles came into the fullness of His ministry?

The truth is, healings and miracles have *not* stopped. The Holy Spirit was poured out on all flesh almost 2000 years ago, and He's *still* moving over all the earth like a mighty wind!

─────── ✂ ───────

Confession:

When Jesus ascended to the right hand of the Father, He sent the Holy Spirit to dwell within me and upon me. The Holy Spirit's power manifests the healing Jesus purchased and provided for me. His healing power is working in me right now!

NOVEMBER 18

Was It Profitable That Jesus Went Away?

Nevertheless I tell you the truth; It is expedient for you that I go away: for if I go not away, the Comforter will not come unto you; but if I depart, I will send him unto you. —John 16:7

Jesus is the healer, but the Holy Ghost is the means by which Jesus manifests healing to us.

Jesus said in John 16:7 that it was *expedient,* or *profitable,* for us that He should go away. How could it be profitable for us if it would mean we'd have to live below what He provided for us? It couldn't. That's why Jesus said, "I will pray the Father, and he shall give you another Comforter, that he may abide with you for ever" (John 14:16).

Jesus was saying, in essence, "There's only one of Me. But if I go, I'll pour out the Holy Ghost. He will come into anyone who accepts Me as Lord and Savior, and that same power will dwell in him."

Jesus was also saying, "I'm not taking away healing when I go away. When I send the Holy Ghost, My healing power in the earth will be multiplied many times over!"

Regardless of what some people say, healing didn't stop when Jesus ascended to heaven. It hasn't dwindled down to nothing. On the contrary, it has been multiplied hundreds of thousands of times over! Just ask the countless people living on this earth today who have been healed by God's power!

Confession:

*The greater One dwells within me and infills me with His power.
Healing is mine because the Spirit who breathed life back into
Jesus' body also quickens life to my mortal body!*

But the Comforter, which is the Holy Ghost, whom the Father will send in my name, he shall teach you all things, and bring all things to your remembrance, whatsoever I have said unto you. —John 14:26

NOVEMBER 19

The Holy Spirit, Our Teacher

Does God use sickness to teach us? This Scripture says that the Comforter will teach us all things. How much is "all things"? *All* means *all!* Well, if the Holy Spirit teaches us all things, how much does God reserve for us to learn through sickness and disease?

According to this verse, *nothing* is left for us to learn through sickness and disease. You'll never find one place in the Bible where sickness is the teacher of the Church. It's always the Holy Ghost who guides and teaches.

"Well, yes," someone might say, "but God sometimes teaches us through sickness and disease too." No, He doesn't. How could He teach through sickness and disease when He doesn't have any sickness or disease to give?

Second Timothy 3:16-17 shows us how the Holy Spirit uses the Word of God to teach us:

All scripture is given by inspiration of God, and is profitable for doctrine, for reproof, for correction, for instruction in righteousness: That the man of God may be perfect, thoroughly furnished unto all good works.

So the Holy Ghost is our teacher, and God's Word is our perfecter, correcter and instructor. The Spirit of God and the Word of God operate together in our lives to help us grow spiritually.

If we don't take advantage of the Holy Spirit and the Word, we leave the door open for the devil to have access to our lives. And the devil isn't trying to *teach* us when he attacks with sickness and disease—he's trying to *kill* us!

So draw on the ministry of the Word and the teacher within. Don't look for lessons to be learned from sickness and pain. Let the Holy Spirit take you higher in God while you enjoy His divine health!

Confession:

I don't look to sickness and disease to teach me anything. I treat them as enemies and cast them out of my body in Jesus' name! The Holy Ghost and the Word teach me everything I need to know to walk victoriously in life.

NOVEMBER 20

Tap Into God's Higher Ways

For my thoughts are not your thoughts, neither are your ways my ways, saith the Lord. For as the heavens are higher than the earth, so are my ways higher than your ways, and my thoughts than your thoughts. —Isaiah 55:8,9

I f the point God is making here ended in verse 9, we might as well just throw in the towel and quit because God's ways and thoughts are so far above ours. But don't quit! Look at what God goes on to say: "So shall my word be that goeth forth out of my mouth: it shall not return unto me void, but it shall accomplish that which I please, and it shall prosper in the thing whereto I sent it" (v. 11).

How can His Word prosper if we can't reach the height of His thoughts and ways? God says, "Since you won't find My thoughts or My ways on your own, I had holy men of old write them down as they were moved upon by the Holy Ghost. I've given you sixty-six books of My ways and My thoughts. These books include My old ways and thoughts, as well as My new ways and thoughts. The new ones are even better than the old, so make sure you live by the new."

You see, God is always the same, but He enacted two covenants, or contracts. Don't go back and try to live under the contract He gave to people who were lost. They were living under the old covenant—spiritually dead and separated from God. Their sinful, old nature was covered, not cleansed.

Today we are new creatures in Christ. We aren't just forgiven; our sins are washed away, and we're made new. We're alive, redeemed, liberated, delivered, healed and set free!

You can leave the lower, carnal ways of the flesh. Just keep feeding on God's Word. Let it renew your mind and bring life to your mortal body. As you do, God promises that His Word *will* accomplish the purpose for which He sent it—that is to help you walk in His higher ways of freedom, abundance and divine health!

Confession:

God sent His Word to heal me. He heals my body and renews my mind so I can think His thoughts and follow His ways. God's Word prospers in me!

He made known his ways unto Moses, his acts unto the children of Israel. —Psalm 103:7

NOVEMBER 21

Walk in God's Ways

God has two sides. His *acts* are the miraculous deeds He performs, but His *ways* are the road that takes you to the miracles.

Most believers have been satisfied for years to go to church and see God perform a few supernatural acts. Then they return home saying, "I've been blessed."

But we can go a step beyond that. Not only can we see His acts, but we can also learn His ways. Once we learn His ways, we'll find the pathway that takes us into the realm of continuous acts.

Everything God does on the earth, He does through the Holy Ghost. Think of it in terms of electricity. A power plant has plenty of electricity, but that power has to be moved from the power plant to electrical outlets so people can access it. That takes a conductor.

Well, God has plenty of power, and He wants to manifest the benefits of salvation in our lives. So He makes His divine power available to us through the blood of Jesus. I once heard salvation defined as the sum total of all the blessings bestowed on man by God in Christ, through the Holy Ghost. Jesus purchased our salvation and God sends forth the blessings, but the Holy Ghost is the conductor.

That's why it's important for us to know more about the Spirit of God. He delivers salvation to our spirits and healing to our bodies. He is the teacher of the Church, the One who declares, discloses and transmits to us what the Father has. He leads us into all truth and shows us things to come.

Psalm 103:7 says that God made His ways known to Moses. As the leader of God's holy nation, Moses in particular had to know God's ways.

But I'm convinced that we Holy Ghost-filled believers ought to know the ways of the Spirit of God as well. We're not supposed to just sit back and watch God move. He wants us to know His ways so we can be right in the middle of what He's doing on this earth!

Confession:

God is making His ways known to me.
I walk in the ways of God, and the Holy Ghost
delivers the healing Jesus purchased for me.

NOVEMBER 22

The Two Flows of Anointing

How God anointed Jesus of Nazareth with the Holy Ghost and with power: who went about doing good, and healing all that were oppressed of the devil; for God was with him. –Acts 10:38

We can learn God's ways as we watch the ministry of Jesus. It appears that two major flows of anointing operated in Jesus' ministry, and these same flows are still on the body of Christ today.

One flow is like lightning. It just hits every now and then; we don't know when, where or how. These "bolts of lightning" are manifestations of the Holy Ghost as *He* wills. The other flow of anointing is like electricity. It flows freely when activated by faith.

I was reading the *The Companion Bible,* in which a man named Bullinger wrote most of the notes. Bullinger said, "There are fifty-two times in the New Testament where the term 'Holy Ghost' should literally be translated not 'the *Person* of the Holy Ghost,' but 'the *manifestations* of the Holy Ghost.'"[1]

Acts 10:38 is one of those verses in which, technically, "Holy Ghost" should be translated as "the manifestations of the Holy Ghost." So it should say, "God anointed Jesus of Nazareth with *the manifestations of the Holy Ghost* and with power."

At times, Jesus would walk into a city or village and approach a specific individual. Then He'd operate in the gifts of the Spirit, delivering a miracle with no faith required on the recipient's part at all. These were manifestations of God's sovereign side.

But a majority of the time, Jesus would go into a city or village and begin teaching and preaching. His focus in ministry was to put God's Word into people to develop their faith. Then they'd touch Him or He'd touch them, and healing power would flow out of Him.

Jesus was anointed with power, and faith would draw that power out. The power would flow like electricity after the people had heard the Word. That's how about 70 percent of the people healed under Jesus' ministry received their healing.

Jesus hasn't changed since the days He walked on this earth. His healing virtue is available to flow out to *you* as you come to Him expecting your miracle and touch Him with the hand of faith!

Confession:

I come to Jesus to hear His Word and believe it, and I receive everything I need. His healing power flows to me and through me because I ask in faith.

For he whom God hath sent speaketh the words of God: for God giveth not the Spirit by measure unto him. The Father loveth the Son, and hath given all things into his hand.

—John 3:34,35

NOVEMBER 23

The Spirit Without Measure

We've been talking about learning the ways of God's Spirit—how He works, how He moves. Of course, the best way to understand God's ways is to look at Jesus. Jesus was God manifested in the flesh, but He laid aside His omniscience, His omnipresence, His omnipotence and glory to become a man.

Jesus had been with the Father from the beginning, but He put Himself in this little box called a human body, in which He could only know what God showed Him, He could only be in one place at a time and He could only do what God did in Him and through Him. He paid a huge price just in leaving heaven and coming down to earth.

The more we know about the price Jesus paid for us, the more we will love and appreciate Him. He left the rightful dignity and privileges He had enjoyed with the Father and was born on this earth as a baby. He grew to be a man, never working a miracle until He was thirty years old, after the Holy Ghost had come upon Him.

The Bible says, "God giveth not the Spirit by measure unto him." In plain English, that means God gave Jesus the anointing without limitations. Jesus didn't have one strong point, because He had *all* strong points. But when Jesus left this earth and went to the Father's right hand, He distributed the anointing that was on His earthly body throughout His new body of believers.

Individually, no other person will ever walk in the anointing without measure. Human beings were not designed for that capacity. But the body of Christ as a whole has the anointing without measure. So whatever manifestations of God's power we saw in Jesus' ministry, we should see operating through the body of Christ today as believers learn more about the ways of God.

Confession:

I'm a child of God, and I'm learning to follow the ways of my Father. He wants me to be healthy and whole. Healing is mine. It's bought and paid for by the blood of His Son, and I receive it by faith.

NOVEMBER 24

Our Family Is Cheering Us On!

And it came to pass, that, as he was praying in a certain place, when he ceased, one of his disciples said unto him, Lord, teach us to pray, as John also taught his disciples. And he said unto them, When ye pray, say, Our Father which art in heaven, Hallowed be thy name. Thy kingdom come. Thy will be done, as in heaven, so in earth.

—Luke 11:1,2

Jesus' disciples asked Him to teach them to pray. One part of the prayer Jesus taught them said, "Thy will be done, as in heaven, so in earth." You see, God doesn't have one will for His children in heaven and one will for His children down here on earth.

Many of us have always thought that the early Church and later Church are two separate churches. No, there's just *the* Church.

Then we've thought there are two different families of God: the family already in heaven and the family still on the earth. No, it's just one family.

Paul wrote to the Ephesians and said, "For this cause I bow my knees unto the Father of our Lord Jesus Christ, *of whom the whole family in heaven and earth is named"* (Eph. 3:14,15). Our family members in heaven are just as real as we are. They're leaning over the balcony of heaven, cheering us on, saying, "Go for it! Get with it, folks!"

All those great faith men and women in Hebrews 11 are watching, along with our relatives, friends and loved ones who have gone on before us. They're all cheering us on, encouraging us to overcome every obstacle in our spiritual race. That ought to make us excited!

Confession:

I want God's will to be done on earth, just as it is done in heaven. I know heaven has no sickness, so sickness must leave my body now in Jesus' name! God's healing power is continually at work in me to drive out sickness and make my body whole again.

And he said unto them, When ye pray, say,
Our Father which art in heaven, Hallowed be
thy name. Thy kingdom come. Thy will be done,
as in heaven, so in earth. —Luke 11:2

NOVEMBER 25

One Will on Heaven and on Earth

Is it ever God's will for His children here on earth to be sick? Well, God doesn't have one will for those who have gone on to the other side and another will for His family on earth. God's will for His children is God's will for *all* His children. He's no respecter of persons. He doesn't play favorites.

You don't plan to be sick when you get to heaven, do you? (If you do, stay away from my mansion!) No, there's no sickness in heaven. Besides, sickness wouldn't be able to touch you even if it were there. It couldn't attach itself to you, because you'll have a changed, glorified body, just like the body Jesus had when He was raised from the dead and walked through walls. No, you're not going to be sick when you get up there.

"Thy will be done, as in heaven, so in earth." Whatever God's will is for you up in heaven is His will for you down here. I plan to walk in God's wisdom while I'm on this earth, because I know I will walk in His wisdom in heaven. I plan to enjoy divine protection down here, because I know I will enjoy it up there. And I plan to be healthy in this life, because I know I will be healthy in the next. If God doesn't want us to be sick in heaven, He certainly doesn't want us to be sick here on earth.

Sickness is in the world, and it does attack. It even has the bold audacity to attack Christians. Can you imagine? But, thank God, we don't have to take it. We don't have to put up with it. We can rise up in the name of Jesus, and our faith in God's Word will run it off. Why? Because healing belongs to us!

Confession:

God's will for me is that I walk in perfect health. So when sickness tries
to attack me, I don't wonder whether or not it's from God. It isn't, and
I don't put up with it. I command sickness to leave in Jesus' name!

NOVEMBER 26

Take Care of the Temple

Wherefore take unto you the whole armour of God, that ye may be able to withstand in the evil day, and having done all, to stand.

–Ephesians 6:13

Over the next few days let's cover some reasons we sometimes fail to receive our healing. We may need to make some adjustments so God is free to give us what we ask for.

On one trip to Europe, Janet and I flew all night, arrived the next morning, took a short nap and started services that night. We held two services the next day. The following day we flew to another country and started services that night. Then we flew to another country and held services there.

I don't know how many services we held in all on that trip. The anointing we operate under in a service quickens our bodies and gives us an extra dose of strength. It takes a few hours to wind down, and by then the next meeting has begun. We can go on like that for weeks!

But during the trip some symptoms came on my body that concerned me. I prayed and believed I received my healing. I rebuked the symptoms, but they didn't leave. So I thought, *I'll do what Ephesians 6:13 says to do: "Having done all, to stand."*

But I had misinterpreted that verse. You see, I was trying to stand without having done *all* to stand.

Janet and I had arranged a short time off during this trip. We checked in to a little guest house, and I lay down for a two-hour nap. When I woke up, I went back to bed and slept twelve more hours. I was up for an hour and then took another nap. Then I went back to bed and slept another twelve hours! When I woke up, I said to Janet, "I think I've found what's been wrong with me!"

I was making the same mistake a man named Epaphroditus did. Paul said Epaphroditus almost worked himself to death in the ministry, but God had mercy on him. (Phil. 2:25-30.)

We live in physical bodies that are not redeemed yet, and we have to take care of them. Through that experience, I learned to treat my body rightly so I can walk in divine health and finish my course!

Confession:

*I do all I know to do to keep my body healthy, and
I stand in faith on God's promise of health.
I treat my body right; and, therefore, I walk in divine health.*

...that ye may be able to withstand in the evil day, and having done all, to stand.

–Ephesians 6:13

Take Care of Your Temple

Sometimes the reason we're experiencing difficulty getting rid of sickness in our bodies is that we've left a door open someplace. Either we're doing something wrong, or we're not doing something right. This isn't a hard-and-fast rule, because the devil will still try to attack when we're doing everything right. But sometimes we will find we left a door open.

For instance, I was a youth minister in Colorado for about thirteen months. I lived in a couple's home, and the wife was an amazing cook. I gained about twenty-five pounds.

But then life got very busy. I had an opportunity to minister in two different schools, and I was on a flat run all the time. For a couple of months, I ate a lot of very unhealthy junk food. All of a sudden, my stomach started giving me trouble.

Now, I'm not a nervous, high-strung person. But when I tried to eat, I'd almost get sick to my stomach. My stomach just burned all the time. I had unknowingly opened the door for the devil to bring me stomach problems.

I prayed, "Lord, I'm sorry. My body is the temple of the Holy Ghost, and I've been misusing it. Lord, I repent." Then I believed I received my healing and got healed instantly.

So don't mistreat your body and leave a door open for the devil to bring in sickness and disease. Eat right and get adequate rest and exercise. Never forget— you are the custodian of the Holy Spirit's dwelling place!

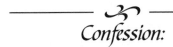

Confession:

My body is the temple of the Holy Ghost. I am the one responsible for taking care of it. So I purpose to eat the proper diet, get plenty of exercise and rest and allow my body to function according to God's design.

NOVEMBER 28

Be a Person of Your Word

Wherein God, willing more abundantly to shew unto the heirs of promise the immutability of his counsel, confirmed it by an oath: That by two immutable things, in which it was impossible for God to lie, we might have a strong consolation, who have fled for refuge to lay hold upon the hope set before us. —Hebrews 6:17,18

Hebrews 6:18 says it is impossible for God to lie. He doesn't have the capacity to be dishonest or to fail to keep His Word. God and His Word cannot be separated.

As God's children, we should also be people of our word. Now, sometimes a situation arises that makes it impossible to keep our word to someone, even though our intentions are good. With the exception of these extreme cases, we need to be people of our word.

If we can't believe in our own word, our faith will never work, because faith is believing that what we say will come to pass. Our faith has nothing to stand on when our word is no good. We never know what to believe.

As humans, we often have to choose whether we're going to tell the truth or "fudge" just a little bit. The flesh wants to rise up and say whatever it takes to keep us out of trouble. But compromising the truth even in little ways will short-circuit our faith.

In 1 Corinthians 9:27, Paul said, "I keep under my body, and bring it into subjection...." Well, if the apostle Paul had to keep his body under, we certainly do too! As long as we have human bodies, we'll have to keep them under the control of our spirits so we can be people of our word.

Confession:

I watch my words carefully and speak only the truth. Therefore, I can expect to walk in God's best. God's Word is truth, and as I speak His words, His truth is produced in me!

*But now hath he obtained a more excellent
ministry, by how much also he is the mediator
of a better covenant, which was established
upon better promises.* —Hebrew 8:6

NOVEMBER 29

Live a Long, Healthy Life

Wrong thinking can open the door to the devil. For instance, one time Janet and I were in another country talking to an older gentleman who had been on the mission field for many years. He had built church after church. Although this minister looked as if he could have worked another twenty years on the mission field, his denomination had recently called him back home.

This older gentleman said to me, "Young man, you believe God wants to heal people, don't you?"

"Yes, sir," I replied. "I believe His highest is to heal people."

"But if God wants everyone healed, how in the world is anyone ever supposed to die?" this minister asked. You see, someone had planted wrong thinking in his head.

That just hurt my heart. I thought, *Here's a man who has given his life to serve God on the mission field. Now that he's come back home, he's waiting to get sick so he can go home to be with the Lord!*

So I told the man, "Sir, I don't mean to be disrespectful, but I believe we ought to have it at least as good under the new covenant as God's people did under the old covenant. Back then, men of faith who served God lived long, healthy lives. They'd come to the end of their lives, call in their families, lay hands on them and bless them all, draw up their feet in the bed, say good-bye and take off for heaven. [Gen. 49:33.] Under a new and better covenant established on better promises, should we have any less than the godly men of old did?"

This elder minister needed the same revelation you and I need if we want to live out the full number of our days: We do not have to be sick to die. We can go to our heavenly home in perfect health!

Confession:

*The Word says God will satisfy me with long life and show me
His salvation. I will live a healthy, long and useful life for my God.
And when I'm satisfied, I'll go home to be with Him in perfect health!*

NOVEMBER 30

How Does God Perfect the Saints?

And he gave some, apostles; and some, prophets; and some, evangelists; and some, pastors and teachers; for the perfecting of the saints, for the work of the ministry, for the edifying of the body of Christ.   *—Ephesians 4:11,12*

Some people say, "I believe God wants to use sickness to perfect us." If that has been God's method of perfecting the Church, He has failed miserably. If sickness were supposed to be the perfecter, the maturer, the correcter and the teacher of the Church, then every Christian ought to be thoroughly furnished unto all good works. If that were God's plan, then He missed it big time!

Some people might say, "Yeah, but sickness ought to make you more pious." But sickness doesn't bring out the piety in people; it brings out their worst. If you've ever been sick, you know that. Sickness makes you mean, ornery and cantankerous. You either want a lot of attention, or you want everyone to leave you alone.

The idea of God's using sickness for our benefit is simply wrong thinking. God doesn't want us sick. It's not part of His plan for us. He never planned for sickness to perfect us, correct us or make us more pious.

God gave us the Word of God to correct and instruct us. He sent the Spirit of God to live inside us to teach, lead and guide us. And if we go a step further, Ephesians 4:11 says that He gave apostles, prophets, evangelists, pastors and teachers for the perfecting of the saints.

So the maturing of the saints doesn't come through sickness and disease. God designed it to come through the Word, the Holy Ghost and the ministry gifts.

Confession:

My God wants me well! He sent the Holy Ghost, the Word and the ministry gifts to instruct me in His ways. I receive those gifts and become a mature saint walking in His best for me!

Take my yoke upon you, and learn of me; for I am meek and lowly in heart: and ye shall find rest unto your souls. —Matthew 11:29

DECEMBER 1

Sickness Is Not Your Teacher

How do we learn about the things of God? By spending time in prayer and fellowship with the Holy Ghost and in study of God's Word.

I hear people say all the time, "I learned so much from being sick." I admit people have learned things while they were sick, but they didn't learn *because* they were sick. They learned because they fed on the Word of God and prayed. It may have been the first time they took time to do that in a long time. That's why a lot of folks mistakenly relate sickness to learning—they never took the time to study and pray until they got sick!

We'd be a lot better off if we learned to feed on the Word and pray when we're not sick. We'd learn just as much, and it would be a lot less painful!

Someone once said to me, "Yeah, but I know God made me sick and wanted me in the hospital, because I witnessed to someone while I was there."

But God is intelligent, and so are we. I believe that as we wait before God in prayer, He can drop something in our hearts about going to witness to someone in the hospital while we're well. Too often we rationalize everything, trying to figure it out in our heads. Let's just stick with the truth found in the Bible and accept God's promise of health and healing every day!

Confession:

God sent the Holy Ghost to be my teacher. The Holy Spirit shows me in the Word that Jesus took my sins and my sicknesses. I'm so glad I can learn of Him while I walk in His blessing of health!

DECEMBER 2

For I am the Lord, I change not.

–Malachi 3:6

Be Willing To Change

Lillian B. Yeomans was a medical doctor who lived many years ago. She was raised from her deathbed by the power of God, and she turned in her medical license and started practicing medicine with the Great Physician. Dr. Yeomans made a statement to the effect that if she were praying or believing God for something that belongs to us in the Word, if she didn't see something start changing in three days, *she* started changing. She had amazing results.

If something belongs to us, God has already paid for it. He has redeemed us, delivered us, healed us and set us free. God has already done His part. So when we see the answer to our need in the Scriptures, we latch on to God's promise with the hand of faith and say, "Father, You said it; I believe it, and I receive it!"

But if time passes and our answer hasn't manifested, something may have to change. Perhaps sin or disobedience is keeping us from receiving from God.

So often we say, "I'm going to keep standing. I'll keep doing what I'm doing until God does something." In other words, "I'll keep doing what I'm doing until *God* changes." Then we sit and do nothing, waiting for God to change.

That won't work. You have to accept that God can't change, Jesus can't change, the Holy Ghost can't change and the Word can't change. But if you're going to see results, *something* has to change. The only one left is *you.*

I'm not trying to put condemnation on you; I'm just showing you how you can get yourself into a position to receive. You can say, "I'll take the responsibility. Maybe I need to change." That will put you in motion. And as the Lord reveals the changes you need to make and you make them, you'll receive the results you desire!

Confession:

According to the Word, healing is mine. Jesus bought and paid for it with His own precious blood. God's Word produces healing in my life. I'll change when I need to, and I'll receive the results I desire!

Yet it pleased the Lord to bruise him; he hath put him to grief: when thou shalt make his soul an offering for sin, he shall see his seed, he shall prolong his days, and the pleasure of the Lord shall prosper in his hand. —Isaiah 53:10

DECEMBER 3

Jesus Was Bruised for Us

"Yet it pleased the Lord to bruise him."

How could it please the Father to bruise Jesus? I'll tell you how. It pleased the Father for Jesus to be bruised because it provided healing and health for His people. Jesus would die, descend into hell and be resurrected in three days with a new, glorified body free of all sickness and pain. From that day forward, God's people wouldn't have to suffer sickness, pain or disease.

Jesus was made sick, that we might be made well. He went down to hell so you and I could live eternally with Him. He left heaven so you and I could be welcome there. He left the throne room of God so we could go there in His name anytime we wanted.

And I tell you what—Jesus is alive and well and doing fine today! He's not hurting anymore. He took all the benefits of redemption, wrapped them up, put a bow and ribbon on the package, wrote our names on it and said, "Here—pick these up anytime you need them."

Jesus was bruised so you and I wouldn't have to be. The price has been paid. Healing and health belong to us!

Confession:

Healing belongs to me! Jesus' body was broken so I could walk in divine health. God was pleased to accomplish His redemption plan, and He's pleased when I walk in that plan by faith.

DECEMBER 4

Jesus Paid the Price

Yet it pleased the Lord to bruise him; he hath put him to grief: when thou shalt make his soul an offering for sin, he shall see his seed, he shall prolong his days, and the pleasure of the Lord shall prosper in his hand. —Isaiah 53:10

Several years ago, I heard that one of my relatives was very sick. Her husband said that the doctors couldn't figure out what was wrong. She'd been in for surgery two or three times, and there was nothing more they could do. Some kind of sickness had spread throughout her entire body, but they didn't know exactly what it was, and they couldn't get rid of it. They weren't even sure she would live.

After prayer, she went in for surgery one more time. But when they opened her up, they couldn't find a trace of any sickness in her body except in her appendix. They removed her appendix, and she's been healthy ever since.

As I pondered her situation, I thought, *That's a good picture of what God did for us! Just as it pleased Him to get the appendix that was full of sickness and disease out of my relative's body, it pleased Him to send Jesus to pay the price for our sickness and disease!*

You see, sickness and disease were destined to destroy the entire body of Christ. But God took all that sickness and disease and condensed it into Jesus' body. God removed the sickness and disease, but He had to let it fall on Jesus so the body of Christ could be free from it.

That's why it pleased God to bruise Jesus. Thank God for His love! In a moment of time, all the sickness and disease of mankind was centered in one Man. Jesus was willing to pay the price to destroy those works of the enemy. He paid the price for you and me to walk in health today.

Confession:

God so loved the world that He gave Jesus. Jesus so loved me that He willingly paid the price to set me free from sickness and disease. Praise God, I am free!

And it came to pass on a certain day, as he was teaching, that there were Pharisees and doctors of the law sitting by, which were come out of every town of Galilee, and Judaea, and Jerusalem: and the power of the Lord was present to heal them. —Luke 5:17

DECEMBER 5

Be Careful How You Hear

God's power was present, but none of the Pharisees and doctors of the law were healed. They weren't there to receive; they were just looking for a reason to accuse Jesus.

But what about the woman with the issue of blood? She heard of Jesus, pressed through a crowd, touched His garment and was healed. "And Jesus, immediately knowing in himself that *virtue* had gone out of him...said unto her, Daughter, thy faith hath made thee whole" (Mark 5:30,34). The same virtue, or power, was available to everyone in the multitude thronging Jesus, but only this woman was healed.

Now look at Luke 6:17-19. In this account, a great multitude of people "came to hear him, and to be healed of all their diseases.... And the whole multitude sought to touch him: for there went *virtue* out of him, and healed them all" (vv. 17,19). This time the entire multitude was healed.

All three of these accounts talk about the power, or virtue, Jesus was anointed with. He never ran out of that anointing. He never said, "Well, folks, I've healed too many people today; I just don't have any more anointing." No, John 3:34 says Jesus had the Holy Ghost *without measure.*

But these three stories each had a different result. The difference was in the *hearing.* In Luke 5, the Pharisees and doctors of the law *wouldn't* hear, so no one was healed. In Mark 5, the woman had heard of Jesus and came to Him believing, so she received her healing. And the multitude in Luke 6 all "came to hear him, and to be healed," and they *were!*

It's a constant pattern in Jesus' ministry: Those who heard and then acted in faith always received what they desired from the Lord.

Confession:

*What I hear and how I hear determine what I have in my life.
I choose to hear God's Word, and my faith increases
daily to receive all that He says is mine!*

DECEMBER 6

When God's Compassion Flows

As [Jesus] went out of Jericho with his disciples and a great number of people, blind Bartimaeus, the son of Timaeus, sat by the highway side begging. And when he heard that it was Jesus of Nazareth, he began to cry out, and say, Jesus, thou son of David, have mercy on me. And many charged him that he should hold his peace: but he cried the more a great deal, Thou son of David, have mercy on me.

And Jesus answered and said unto him, What wilt thou that I should do unto thee?

The blind man said unto him, Lord, that I might receive my sight.

And Jesus said unto him, Go thy way; thy faith hath made thee whole. And immediately he received his sight, and followed Jesus in the way. —Mark 10:46-48,51,52

Blind Bartimaeus cried out, "Thou son of David, have mercy on me!" In the Scriptures, *mercy* and *compassion* are used interchangeably. Bartimaeus wouldn't stop; he just kept crying out: "Have mercy on me! Have compassion on me!" And that divine compassion started to flow.

Jesus turned and asked, "What do you want?"

Bartimaeus replied, "That I might receive my sight." And he did!

When God's compassion flows, miracles happen. Jesus had compassion on the multitudes, and He healed them all. (Matt. 14:14.)

Sympathy feels sorry for people. But God's compassion causes His love to flow to meet needs or produce miracles in people's lives.

We have that same divine love shed abroad in our hearts. It's time we let that sweet love of Jesus flow forth to a sick and dying world. People are looking for love and compassion. When compassion begins to flow through us, God's power flows. And when God's power flows, miracles happen!

———— ✌ ————

Confession:

God's love and compassion flowed through Jesus to heal a blind beggar. His love hasn't changed; it flows to me and through me to others to heal, bless and deliver!

*For thou, Lord, art good, and ready to forgive;
and plenteous in mercy unto all them that call
upon thee.* —Psalm 86:5

Call on God's Mercy

When Bartimaeus called on the mercy of God in Mark 10:46-52, Jesus said, "What wilt thou that I should do unto thee?" (v. 51). In other words, Jesus asked, "What do you want Me to do for you?"

Bartimaeus touched the heart of God when he called on His mercy. During Jesus' ministry, many people called on God's mercy. When they did, blind eyes were opened, deaf ears could hear, the oppressed were set free from evil spirits and the sick were healed of sicknesses and diseases.

What good does it do us to know that fact? Well, Psalm 86:5 says that God is plenteous in mercy unto *all* those who call upon Him. His mercy endures forever, and He doesn't turn away anyone who calls upon Him. So just as people called on His mercy 2000 years ago, we can call on His mercy today and have the same results.

There's a time to rise up and operate in our own faith for our healing and other needs. But there are also times when we just need to get down to business and say, "Lord, have mercy on me. Because Your mercy endures forever and You give to all who ask, have mercy on me."

God's mercy is ready to manifest in your life as health, freedom, strength, liberty, wisdom and everything else you need. When you touch God's heart by calling on His mercy, He will manifest His mercy to you—spirit, soul and body.

Confession:

*My God is the Father of mercies and the God of all comfort.
He is plenteous in mercy to me because I call upon Him.
His mercies are new to me every morning!*

DECEMBER 8

Following the Holy Ghost

How God anointed Jesus of Nazareth with the Holy Ghost and with power: who went about doing good, and healing all that were oppressed of the devil; for God was with him.

–Acts 10:38

God anointed Jesus with the gifts and manifestations of the Holy Ghost. The gifts of the Spirit were working through Jesus when He walked through the crowd at the pool of Bethesda and asked a man, "Is it your will to be healed?" The man said, "I have no man..." But Jesus said, "Get up and walk anyway," and the man was instantly healed. (John 5:1-15.)

Many times Jesus just walked into a situation and delivered a miracle. In Mark 7:32-35, a deaf man with a speech impediment was healed. In Mark 8:22-26, a blind man at Bethsaida was healed. God sent Jesus to those individuals with the gifts of the Spirit in operation. But Jesus couldn't turn those gifts on and off at will. If He could have, He would have healed everyone in the place every time.

After studying the ministry of Jesus, I'm convinced that He was just following the leading of the Holy Ghost. Whenever He came to a new place, He checked in His spirit and asked, "Is there something You want Me to do sovereignly, Father?"

You see, God may not want to manifest Himself through the gifts of the Spirit in each case. If He did, people might begin leaning on the manifestations more than they lean on His Word.

So Jesus must have had His "spiritual antenna" up all the time, checking inside to see how the Holy Ghost wanted Him to minister healing. And we should be doing the same thing.

You may say, "But that was Jesus." Yes, but Jesus laid aside His mighty power and glory to live and minister as a man anointed by God. That means the strength of His ministry was in obeying the Holy Ghost and preaching the Word.

Well, if that method worked for Jesus, it will work for us! He's the same Holy Ghost who leads, guides and heals today, and He is dwelling in us!

Confession:

I follow the Holy Spirit's leading just as Jesus did. The Holy Spirit guides me each step of the way, telling me what to do to minister healing to others or to receive my own healing.

And being not weak in faith, he considered not his own body now dead, when he was about an hundred years old, neither yet the deadness of Sarah's womb: He staggered not at the promise of God through unbelief; but was strong in faith, giving glory to God.   –Romans 4:19,20

DECEMBER 9

Don't Consider the Circumstances

How could Abraham "stagger not" at the promise of God? A 90-year-old woman and a 100-year-old man having a child? That was a big promise! How could he *not* stagger? I mean, today many stagger at "by Jesus' stripes, you were healed"!

"Being not weak in faith, he considered not his own body." The word *considered* in the original Greek means "to observe" or "to perceive."[1] So you could say it this way: "And being not weak in faith, he *observed* not his own body now dead, when he was about 100 years old."

Abraham didn't sit there and perceive how his body felt. He didn't dwell on how old his body was. He didn't say, "Oh, Lord, I'm 100 years old, and Sarah is 90. It's just not going to work."

Abraham didn't observe his own body or the deadness of Sarah's womb. He was dwelling on the answer instead of the problem. That's why he could "stagger not" at the promise of God. And as Abraham filled his heart with the goodness and faithfulness of Almighty God, he became fully persuaded that what God had promised, He was also able to perform.

Confession:

*Being not weak in faith, I consider not my own situation or circumstances.
I consider not my own body or any symptoms of sickness.
I am strong in faith, knowing that what God has promised,
He is also able to perform in my life!*

DECEMBER 10

Keep Your Eyes on the Answer

Then on the third day Abraham lifted up his eyes, and saw the place afar off. And Abraham said unto his young men, Abide ye here with the ass; and I and the lad will go yonder and worship, and come again to you.

—Genesis 22:4,5

If you always have your eyes on the answer and consider only what God said, you'll overcome in the end, regardless of your situation. A good example of this principle is the story of Abraham.

Abraham's miracle child, Isaac, was born to him and Sarah because they "staggered not" at God's promise. But Isaac wasn't the fulfillment of the promise; he was just the *means* to the fulfillment of the promise. God didn't say, "I'll give you a son." He said, "I have made you the father of many nations. Your seed shall be numbered as the sands of the sea and the stars of the sky." (Gen. 17:4; 22:17.)

But in Genesis 22, God told Abraham to offer Isaac as a burnt offering to Him. Abraham would have been in trouble if he'd been walking around saying, "I know I'm the father of many nations because I have a son." If he had been thinking that way, he would have responded, "Lord, I can't do that. Isaac has to live, or I can't be the father of many nations."

But Abraham was absolutely convinced God's promise had to come to pass. He believed that if he sacrificed his son, God would have to raise him from the dead to fulfill that promise. (Heb. 11:17-19.) So Abraham told the servants, "I and the lad will go yonder and worship, and come again to you." He was saying, "Both of us will go up, and both of us will come back." And both of them did!

Don't take your eyes off the answer—off Jesus and the Word—for anything, whether good or bad. Even when your body is feeling better, don't dwell on that. Keep your eyes fixed on God's promises. Say, "I know I'm healed, not because I feel good, but because the Bible says, 'By Jesus stripes, I was healed.'"

Always keep your attention fixed on the eternal promises of God, not on the temporal circumstances of this world. Be fully persuaded that what God promised you *will* see come to pass!

Confession:

Whether my body feels good or bad, I keep my attention focused on God's healing promises. Situations and circumstances must change, but the Word will never change!

Verily, verily, I say unto you, He that believeth on me, the works that I do shall he do also; and greater works than these shall he do; because I go unto my Father. —John 14:12

Finishing What Jesus Began

Jesus says we are to do even greater works than the works He did while He walked on the earth. How can we do the greater works? Jesus explained how: "The Father that dwelleth in me, he doeth the works" (v. 10).

The greater One living in Jesus did the works. Jesus always made that clear, saying, "Everything I do is My Father's will. My meat is to do My Father's will. I do what I see My Father doing."

Then Jesus said, "I'm going to leave, but I'm going to send the Holy Spirit, the Comforter, and He'll live within you. Then it won't just be Me doing the works of the Father all alone. Thousands of believers will preach the Gospel and lay hands on the sick all over the world. My people will do even greater works because I'm going to be with My Father."

In Acts 1:1, Luke talks about "all that Jesus began both to do and teach." Jesus began to love and forgive people, to teach people and to lay hands on the sick and see them recover. But He couldn't do the job all alone, so He sent His Spirit to empower you and me to carry on His work. He has never stopped the ministry He began; He's continuing through His Church today. It's up to us to get the job done!

Confession:

I am an ambassador for Christ. I help continue the work Jesus began: teaching people, loving people, laying hands on the sick and seeing them recover. But it is my Father dwelling in me by the Holy Ghost who does the work!

DECEMBER 12

Get in the Life Raft of Deliverance!

[The Father] has delivered and drawn us to Himself out of the control and the dominion of darkness and has transferred us into the kingdom of the Son of His love.

–Colossians 1:13 AMP

We've been delivered from the power of darkness and translated into the kingdom of His dear Son. The kingdom of darkness is the kingdom of Satan. When we were delivered from the kingdom of darkness, we were delivered from the rule and authority of that king and everything that is a part of his evil kingdom.

That means we've been delivered from spiritual death, sickness, disease, bad habits, oppression and poverty. We've been delivered! We don't have to wait for God to do it; it has already been done. We just need to receive and walk in our deliverance.

If I were out in the middle of a lake drowning and my father threw me a big inner tube to hang on to, I'd grab hold of it! I wouldn't say, "Well, I just don't know if I can take that. You know, I'm the one who fell in the lake, and I probably deserve to be out here. I'd better just see if I can make it through." If I said that, my father would probably get a little perturbed at me!

I can't imagine what God must think when we do the same thing spiritually. He has delivered us from the power of darkness and translated us into the kingdom of His Son. Yet we sit around nursing our symptoms and say, "Well, I don't know if God wants me healed. He may want me to learn something from this sickness."

No, He's thrown us a life raft! He wants us to climb out of that sickness and disease and just float on in to safety and health!

Confession:

I've been delivered from the dominion of darkness! I'm under Jesus' authority now. I don't have to be sick anymore. Healing and health are mine! I walk in freedom, safety and health because I'm in God's kingdom!

To the end he may stablish your hearts unblameable in holiness before God, even our Father, at the coming of our Lord Jesus Christ with all his saints. —1 Thessalonians 3:13

DECEMBER 13

He's Returning for a Healthy Bride!

Jesus Christ, our soon-coming King, is coming back for a bride.

Well, how many grooms want to come back for a bride who is sick and emaciated? How many grooms say, "Well, Honey, I hope you're good and sick now so I can take you to the altar"?

No, Jesus wants a healthy bride. He is coming soon as the King of kings and Lord of lords, and He plans to return for a bride who is without spot or blemish. (Eph. 5:27.) That means in part that He wants to come back for a bride who is walking in health. That's His will!

So receive the healing Jesus purchased for you on the Cross. Walk in the divine health that belongs to you as part of the Church, the bride of Christ. Make sure you're preparing for the Bridegroom's return!

Confession:

I am a part of the Church, the bride of Christ. The Bridegroom has clothed me with the garments of salvation, and I walk in all that salvation includes: health, wholeness, deliverance and safety!

DECEMBER 14

Sanctifying Your Food

For every creature of God is good, and nothing to be refused, if it be received with thanksgiving: for it is sanctified by the word of God and prayer.
—1 Timothy 4:4,5

This Scripture tells us that when our food is sanctified by the Word and prayer we can eat anything without harm if we partake of it with thanksgiving.

After eating some food back in the bush country, I can tell you from personal experience that this verse is true! I didn't know what we were eating, and I decided it was better not to ask! Janet and I just ate the unfamiliar food in faith and didn't suffer any kind of ill effects from it.

We haven't experienced any problems from eating unknown foods in other countries. We've always walked in divine health. Why? Because every time we sit down to a meal, we say, "Thank You, Father, that this food is sanctified by Your Word and prayer." The food can't harm us then. We also frequently travel on the road. When I think of some of the restaurants we've eaten at along the way, I'm glad that particular prayer has worked there too!

The only way you could experience a stomach problem after that kind of prayer is by opening the door to the enemy through fear or worry. The solution to that problem is found further on in 2 Timothy 1:7: "For God hath not given us the spirit of fear; but of power, and of love, and of a sound mind." That's a good verse for preventing stomach problems!

If people would continually confess, "Thank God, He has not given me a spirit of fear, but of power and love and a sound mind," they'd stop getting sick. Fear is always the key that opens the door to the enemy. And when it comes to the food we eat, we never have to fear, because God has given us a way to eat safely in faith!

Confession:

When I pray over my food, it's sanctified by God's Word and prayer. I've been redeemed from the curse of the law. That includes every sickness and disease known to man. The Word creates life within me. I walk in health!

My speech and my preaching was not with enticing words of man's wisdom, but in demonstration of the Spirit and of power: that your faith should not stand in the wisdom of men, but in the power of God.   —1 Corinthians 2:4,5

DECEMBER 15

Light the Fuse of Faith

The power of God can be defined as the ability to act supernaturally and miraculously. According to this verse, our faith is to stand in the strength of God's divine power to remove every yoke of bondage from our lives.

But is there anything *we* can do to cause the power of God to manifest?

Power is released through faith. Faith is the fuse that releases the explosive force residing in God's power. Confession lights the fuse. You can put the fuse in, but it does no good unless you light it.

So confess the Word, and light the fuse of faith! Release God's power to perform miracles in your life!

Confession:

Speaking from a believing heart releases God's power on my behalf. I say to my mountain of difficulty, pain or sickness: "Be removed and cast into the sea!" I don't doubt in my heart but believe that what I say shall come to pass. And according to the Word, I have what I say!

DECEMBER 16

Gain Possession of God's Word

My son, attend to my words; incline thine ear unto my sayings. Let them not depart from thine eyes; keep them in the midst of thine heart. For they are life unto those that find them, and health to all their flesh. —Proverbs 4:20-22

God is telling us here how to find healing, health and abundant life. But these benefits we read about don't work for everyone. God's promises are conditional. What's the condition? He said His words and sayings are life *to those who find them.*

I used to think when God said, "unto those that find them," He meant unto those who look up three or four Scriptures in a concordance and read them a few times and maybe even make some notes. But you won't qualify as one who has grasped the Word just by reading a few verses a few times and making lists of Scriptures.

To find doesn't mean just to locate. Quite awhile ago, I did a study to discover what the word *find* really meant. I learned that it meant everything *but* locate! *To find* means "to attain or acquire, to get a hold upon, to have, to take hold on."[1]

God is telling you to do more than just locate Scriptures. He said His words are life to those who attain or take hold of them. He wants you to stick with His Word until His Word sticks with you!

Jesus desired the same thing for His disciples. In Luke 9:44, He instructed them, "Let these sayings sink down into your ears...."

The Word of God begins to work for you when it becomes rooted and grounded in your heart. So gain possession of the Word in your heart, and watch the Word come to pass in your life!

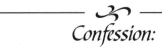

Confession:

As I obtain, take hold of and gain possession of God's Word, it becomes life to me. I believe God's promises with all my heart, and they come to pass in my life!

Let these sayings sink down into your ears.

–Luke 9:44

DECEMBER 17

Believe God With Your Heart

In today's civilized societies, we've spent a great deal of time educating our minds far beyond our spirits. So when we start reading the Bible, our minds often say, "I've got this already! I don't need to study anymore!" Unfortunately, that usually means we've grabbed hold of the Word with our minds and not with our hearts.

The only way to believe God's Word with the heart is to spend time feeding on it. You have to get the Word rooted deep in your heart so that its truth becomes more real than the doubts in your mind.

A lot of mental assenters haven't done that. They aren't believing anything, because they don't know *what* to believe. They've never taken the time to plant the Word in their hearts.

You can't believe God with your mind, because your mind always tells you about all kinds of problems. And you certainly can't believe God with your body, because it tells you how bad you feel or how much pain you have. If you try believing God with your mind or your body, your spiritual walk will be up and down like a yo-yo.

But when God's Word takes root in your heart, you can be strong and believe the Word in the face of big obstacles. Some of the greatest faith victories come when you are believing God with your heart while doubts are being fired at your mind and symptoms are being fired at your body like machine-gun bullets. So plant God's Word in your heart, believe it and act upon it, and win your victory today!

Confession:

I need the Word of God. It's life to me and medicine to my flesh.
God's Word was sent to heal me, so I plant it in my heart and
let it grow there. I believe and act upon it, and it works in my life!

DECEMBER 18

Follow God's Instructions

And be not conformed to this world: but be ye transformed by the renewing of your mind, that ye may prove what is that good, and acceptable, and perfect, will of God. —Romans 12:2

In order for the Word to work successfully, we must be sure we're following God's instructions. Many times people are deceived because they only attempt to stand on the Word and believe God for their healing. I remember some of my own early experiences. I attempted to stand on the Word. But when I first endeavored to believe for God to heal me of the flu, the sickness didn't go away for about seven days.

All that time, I knew if I were to let the sickness run its own course, it would also take about seven days. This frustrated me, until one day I realized I'd been doing something wrong. I'd been standing on the right Scriptures. I had them all located and memorized, but the Scriptures weren't planted on the inside of me. I had some head knowledge, but my heart hadn't grasped what the Word was really saying.

What's the solution to "head knowledge faith"? Read the Word, study the Word, meditate on the Word and confess the Word—and keep on doing it! It takes time and work to believe what God says in the face of obstacles.

It's so important to make sure the Word goes from the mental realm to your heart! As a matter of fact, the difference between victory and defeat in the Christian life is the eighteen inches between your head and your heart. Do you just mentally agree with the Word, or is the Word planted in your heart? The answer to that question determines whether or not the Word will work for you.

As long as we live in this world, problems are going to come. That's all the more reason to do what God said: "Go to the Word." Grasp it, believe it and then watch the Word go into action. God watches over His Word to perform it! (Jer. 1:12.)

Confession:

I renew my mind with the Word and think God's thoughts. His Word is planted and rooted deep inside my heart. No matter what obstacle I face, I believe God's Word is true, and it changes my life!

This book of the law shall not depart out of thy mouth; but thou shalt meditate therein day and night, that thou mayest observe to do all that is written therein.... —Joshua 1:8

DECEMBER 19

Pain Doesn't Change God's Word

Sometimes people ask me, "How can I believe I'm healed? I still have pain in my body." But it doesn't matter whether or not there is pain in your body. Pain doesn't change the promise of God.

Let me ask you this: Does the pain in your body affect the fact that Jesus is coming again? No. Regardless of the symptoms or circumstances we deal with in life, we are always "waiting for the coming of our Lord Jesus Christ" (1 Cor. 1:7).

Well, if your pain doesn't affect one of God's promises, then it doesn't affect another of His promises. If it doesn't affect God's promise of Jesus' soon return, it doesn't affect the fact that by His stripes you were healed (1 Peter 2:24).

You see, as we start believing God's Word, it will begin working the change we desire in our symptoms, our circumstances and our problems.

How do we develop our faith in the Word? We feed on it! That means we read it, study it, think about it, meditate on it and mutter it to ourselves. Soon our hearts will be so full of the Word that our faith in God's promises will drive every remnant of pain and sickness away!

Confession:

Even when my body is in pain, the Word of God is still true. And as I walk by faith, its healing power manifests in my life!

DECEMBER 20

God Isn't Our "Heavenly Butler"

For therein is the righteousness of God revealed from faith to faith: as it is written, The just shall live by faith. —Romans 1:17

Someone once said to me, "You faith people make God sound like a heavenly butler."

I replied, "Let me ask you something. Suppose you meet someone on this earth who has unlimited means. As he gets to know you, this wealthy person decides he likes you, so he goes out and buys twenty years' worth of everything money can buy—cars, homes, everything.

"Then the rich man says to you, 'Now, I've bought everything you could ever want for the next twenty years. If you need it, want it or desire it, just come and knock on the door. I have it in a big warehouse, and it's for you.'

"Now, if you went to the door and said, 'I could sure use such-and-such,' would you be pushing that person around or treating him like a 'butler'? No, you'd be taking him at his word."

You might say, "Well, if God spoke to me like that, I'd believe Him." But He gave you sixty-six books, and in every one of those books He spoke to you! He said, "By Jesus' stripes, you were healed," so healing is yours. He said, "God supplies all your needs," so all your needs are met.

We're not pushing God around. Don't be concerned about that. He's big enough to handle Himself. No one pushes or controls God.

So just take God at His Word and choose to believe that what He has said, He will do.

Confession:

I go to the Word, my spiritual "warehouse," and obtain the benefits God has given to me. I'm blessed with all spiritual blessings in Christ Jesus, who paid the price for everything I need. I take God at His Word and believe healing is mine!

Thou preparest a table before me in the presence
of mine enemies: thou anointest my head with
oil; my cup runneth over. —Psalm 23:5

The Table Set Before You

Some folks think the table in Psalm 23:5 refers to the marriage feast of the Lamb in heaven. But that can't be right. The marriage feast of the Lamb won't be held in the presence of our enemies; there won't *be* any enemies in heaven!

No, God has prepared a table before you right in the presence of your enemies down here on earth. Sickness may come running up, ready to attach itself to your body. But you have a table set before you with a big plate of bread right in the middle. When sickness presents itself, you can say, "God prepares a table before me in the presence of my enemies. Healing is the children's bread. Please pass me the children's bread!" (Mark 7:25-30.)

Everything you need is spread before you on that table. You have the fruit of the Spirit. You have the milk of the Word to help you grow in God. You have the meat of the Word to make your spirit strong.

So take advantage of the table set before you. No matter what enemy comes to harass you, just sit down at the table and feast on the Word and the children's bread. You'll be well taken care of, and there's not a thing in the world your enemies can do about it!

Confession:

A table is spread for me in the midst of my enemies.
I feast on God's Word, and it is life to me and medicine
to all my flesh. So please pass the children's bread!

DECEMBER 22

Watch Your Attitude Before God

And [Jesus] spake this parable unto certain which trusted in themselves that they were righteous, and despised others: Two men went up into the temple to pray; the one a Pharisee, and the other a publican. The Pharisee stood and prayed thus with himself, God, I thank thee, that I am not as other men are, extortioners, unjust, adulterers, or even as this publican. I fast twice in the week, I give tithes of all that I possess.

And the publican, standing afar off, would not lift up so much as his eyes unto heaven, but smote upon his breast, saying, God be merciful to me a sinner.

—Luke 18:9-13

I believe Jesus is trying to show us the difference between the two men's *attitudes* here. The Pharisee arrogantly boasted, "I do this and that and everything else, God; Your blessings belong to me now." The other man just humbly prayed, "Lord, I don't deserve anything on my own. Please just be merciful to me."

It's true we need to stand up in our righteousness. We are to come boldly before the throne of grace, believe and confess the Word and act in faith. Proverbs 28:1 says, "The righteous are bold as a lion."

But we shouldn't come with an arrogant attitude, saying, "God, I'm doing everything You said to do; You owe me."

We need to come and say, "Lord, I'm doing what You said in Your Word. Now I thank You for Your mercy."

God's mercy, compassion and grace provided everything we have in Jesus Christ, and we must treat His blessings as a gift. Because of God's grace poured out upon us, we can say, "If we believe and say what His Word says, it will come to pass." We are to be thankfully receptive, *not* arrogant, about it.

So be bold when you go before God, but always keep a watch on your attitude. Remember, it's only by God's grace that you stand!

Confession:

I go boldly before God's throne to receive my healing.
I don't deserve it on my own. But, praise God, Jesus gave me
His own right standing with the Father so I could receive it.

Blessed are the merciful: for they shall obtain
mercy.   *–Matthew 5:7*

Blessed Are the Merciful

The best thing you can do if you need healing in your body is to start praying for people to be healed. Believing God for others to be healed increases your capacity to receive healing for yourself.

Jesus said, "Blessed are the merciful." What are you doing when you're praying for the sick? You're showing God's mercy. "Blessed are the merciful." How are the merciful blessed? "For they shall *obtain mercy*" (Matt. 5:7).

People all through the Gospels cried out for mercy, and the blessing they received was *healing. You* will receive God's healing mercies as well, as you minister God's healing mercies to others. This is confirmed in Ephesians 6:8, where it says, "Knowing that whatsoever good thing any man doeth, the same shall he receive of the Lord, whether he be bond or free."

Paul states a spiritual principle here: If you're doing good things, the same good things will be given back to you. Therefore, the best thing you can do when you need healing is to thank God that healing belongs to you and then start finding people to minister to. Go pray for the sick.

Be out doing the work of the ministry, fulfilling the Great Commission, whether your body hurts or not. As you get busy seeking first the kingdom of God and His righteousness and ministering God's mercy to others, the healing mercies of God will be added to *you.* (Matt. 6:33.)

Confession:

Jesus is my healer. I show His mercy to people and help
them receive, and I obtain the healing mercy I need.

DECEMBER 24

A Treasure Hidden for Us

And he taught them many things by parables, and said unto them in his doctrine, Hearken; Behold, there went out a sower to sow.

—Mark 4:2,3

In this passage, Jesus began teaching a crowd in parables. Later, when He was alone with His disciples, they asked Him the meaning of the parable of the sower. In essence they said, "We don't understand what You're talking about."

Jesus said to them, "Unto you it is given to know the mystery of the kingdom of God: but unto them that are without, all these things are done in parables" (v. 11). Then He continued, "Know ye not this parable? and how then will ye know all parables?" (v. 13).

Jesus was saying, "This is the key. If you gain understanding of this parable, everything else will start to open up to you."

Some people read the Bible and say, "I don't understand the Bible. It's Greek to me."

Well, the Bible was written in code form. That's why God gave us the Holy Ghost—to translate, interpret and teach the Word to us. The reason many people have trouble understanding the Word is that they've never let the Holy Ghost be the teacher. They try to read the Bible with their own understanding.

But the Word is revelation truth. Verse 22 AMP says, "[Things are hidden temporarily only as a means to revelation.] For there is nothing hidden except to be revealed, nor is anything [temporarily] kept secret except in order that it may be made known." God's revelation truth was hidden not to keep it *from* us, but to keep it *for* us.

Every time you open your Bible, just ask the Holy Ghost to teach you. He is the teacher of the Church, and He will reveal to you what is written on the pages.

Confession:

The Holy Ghost is my teacher. He teaches me hidden truths and wonderful mysteries as I read and meditate on God's Word. I am planting the Word in my heart, and it is bearing rich fruit.

Behold, there went out a sower to sow.

And it came to pass, as he sowed, some fell by the way side, and the fowls of the air came and devoured it up.

And these are they by the way side, where the word is sown; but when they have heard, Satan cometh immediately, and taketh away the word that was sown in their hearts.

–Mark 4:3,4,15

DECEMBER 25

Don't Be a "Have-Hearder"

Jesus is teaching the foundation on which the entire kingdom of God operates: sowing and reaping. This spiritual principle applies to every part of life. If you sow the seed, you reap the harvest. If you don't sow the seed, you don't reap the harvest.

The seed here is the Word of God. Jesus begins to explain the parable to them: "The sower soweth the word." (v. 14.) The Word of God is the subject. "These are they by the way side, where the word is sown; but when they have heard, Satan cometh immediately, and taketh away the word that was sown in their hearts."

How was Satan able to do that? Why could he just come in and steal the Word away so easily? Look at the phrasing: "...but when they have heard...." Jesus says they are "have-hearders." He doesn't say, "They're hearing it"; He says, "They *have heard* it." The reason Satan could steal it away so easily is that they quit hearing God's Word and started hearing something else.

I remember when I thought I knew everything there was to know about Mark 11:24. I'd heard hundreds of different messages about that one verse. At one meeting, the minister said, "Open to Mark 11:24," and I just shut off my mind.

About six weeks later, I couldn't figure out why that verse wasn't working for me! The reason was that I'd turned into a "have-hearder," and the thief started stealing away what I'd already planted in my heart.

People often say, "I've already heard that. I don't need to hear that again." But we must hear every part of God's Word continually. What we're hearing *today* will bear fruit in our lives *tomorrow*.

───────── ✲ ─────────

Confession:

*I am a hearer, not a "have-hearder." I continually hear the Word.
I keep it before my eyes; I incline my ears to its truth. And as I
act on God's Word in faith, it bears much rich fruit in my life.*

DECEMBER 26

"Stony Ground" Hearers

And some [seed] fell on stony ground, where it had not much earth; and immediately it sprang up, because it had no depth of earth: but when the sun was up, it was scorched; and because it had no root, it withered away.

And these are they likewise which are sown on stony ground; who, when they have heard the word, immediately receive it with gladness; and have no root in themselves, and so endure but for a time: afterward, when affliction or persecution ariseth for the word's sake, immediately they are offended.

–Mark 4:5,6,16,17

We've all seen these "stony ground" people. They come to hear the Word of God, and they get really excited about it. They say, "Oh, man, this is so good! I've been looking for this for years!"

But these people are also "have-hearders." They don't settle down and continue to hear the Word. Therefore, the Word they've heard never really takes root in them.

The minute persecution and affliction come along for the Word's sake (and they will), these people stop hearing the Word and start hearing the persecution and affliction. In six months, we wonder where they are. They've just blown away with the wind.

When I first found out that by Jesus' stripes I was healed, I said, "Thank God, I'll never be sick a day in my life again!" Then I spent the next six weeks battling all kinds of symptoms!

As soon as you get a revelation in the Word, the thief will try to steal that away through persecution and affliction. If you're not careful, you'll end up saying, "Well, I tried that, and it didn't work."

Jesus said these people endure only for a short time because they have no root in themselves. (v. 17.) How does God's Word take root in us? By our hearing and hearing. What we hear on a regular basis is what bears fruit in our lives.

Confession:

I attend to God's Word, so it is rooted and grounded in my heart. When symptoms attack my body, His Word rises up in me to heal, strengthen and comfort me.

And some [seed] fell among thorns, and the thorns grew up, and choked it, and it yielded no fruit.

And these are they which are sown among thorns; such as hear the word, and the cares of this world, and the deceitfulness of riches, and the lusts of other things entering in, choke the word, and it becometh unfruitful.

—Mark 4:7,18,19

DECEMBER 27

Watch Out for Thorns!

How could anything gain enough strength or power to choke the Word and cause God's Word to become unfruitful? The cares of this world, the deceitfulness of riches and the lusts of other things don't have enough strength in themselves to do it. It's what we do with those "thorns" that causes them to choke the Word in our lives.

"These are they which are sown among thorns; such as hear the word." This person starts out right. He's hearing and feeding on the Word of God, and the Word is starting to grow and bear fruit.

"And the cares of this world, the deceitfulness of riches, and the lusts of other things *entering in....*" Then suddenly the cares of this world show up, and he starts listening to them. The deceitfulness of riches and lusts of other things follow right along, and soon he's feeding on them instead of God's Word. The "thorns" enter in and choke out the Word, making it unfruitful in his life.

Several years ago, I was trying to share the Word and pray for a man in a hospital but having little success. The man finally said, "I guess I was just born bad ground."

No, there's no such thing as anyone's being born bad ground. *You* decide what kind of ground you're going to be. You can be the kind of ground that never bears fruit, or you can decide to be good ground that bears a hundredfold return!

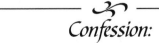

Confession:

I'm good ground for the Word. I cast my cares on the Lord. I seek the riches of my inheritance in Christ. The Word is planted in my heart and is bearing good fruit!

DECEMBER 28

How To Be "Good Ground"

And other [seed] fell on good ground, and did yield fruit that sprang up and increased; and brought forth, some thirty, and some sixty, and some an hundred.   *—Mark 4:8*

So what do you do to make sure you are good ground? Well, start out hearing God's Word. When the thief comes to steal it away, keep on hearing the Word of God. When persecutions and afflictions come because of the Word, (and they will come to everyone), keep hearing what God says.

First Peter 4:12 says, "Beloved, think it not strange concerning the fiery trial which is to try you, as though some strange thing happened unto you." What do you do when the fiery trials come? Do you feed on them? No, you keep on hearing the Word.

The cares of the world will try to distract you, but keep on hearing the Word. The deceitfulness of riches and the lusts of other things will try to get in your way, but just keep hearing the Word and plowing through. One day the fruit of that Word will start popping up on the other side of all the trials and distractions of life. You'll reap a harvest that is thirty-, sixty- or even a hundredfold!

The Bible says, "My son, attend to my words; incline thine ear unto my sayings" (Prov. 4:20). As long as we want abundant life, including healing in our bodies, we must incline our ears unto His sayings. We must hear God's Word coming from the pulpit, from tapes, from television and radio and, most importantly, from our own mouths.

Someone may ask, "How long do I have to hear the Word?" All through eternity! It's that good. It's not a chore—it's a pleasure!

Confession:

My ears are a gateway to my spirit. What I hear controls what fruit is produced in my life. I desire the fruit of divine health and abundant life, so I won't let anything distract me from hearing God's Word!

And he said unto them, Is a candle brought to be put under a bushel, or under a bed? and not to be set on a candlestick? For there is nothing hid, which shall not be manifested; neither was any thing kept secret, but that it should come abroad. If any man have ears to hear, let him hear. —Mark 4:21-23

DECEMBER 29

Shine Forth the Light of God

The margin in my Bible more accurately translates the word *candle* as lamp or light. Psalm 119:105 says, "Thy word is a lamp unto my feet, and a light unto my path." So this passage in Mark is talking about the Word of God. Is God's Word to be put under a bushel or a bed instead of set on a candlestick?

Jesus is saying that His Word isn't meant to be hidden or stuck on a shelf somewhere. It's meant to be placed on a stand, where it can shine forth and give life to everyone. In other words, God wants His Word to get on the inside of us so it can start producing life on the outside.

How do we get God's Word off the pages of the Bible and operating in our lives? How do we become living epistles, known and read of all men? (2 Cor. 3:2.) Mark 4:23 tells us: "If any man have ears to hear, *let him hear.*"

The Word shines forth when we take time to hear and feed on it. The more we hear the Word, letting the Holy Ghost teach us God's higher thoughts and ways, the more the Word gives us light, truth and understanding. Then we're able to pass its truth on to others.

You see, we're God's billboards on this earth. As the Word produces life in us, the love, health, peace and light of God then shine forth in every area of our lives to give life to those around us!

Confession:

I have ears to hear, so I choose to hear God's Word. The Holy Ghost opens the mysteries of the Scriptures to me, revealing the life and the ways of God to me. God's light and life are in me, shining forth so others can see.

DECEMBER 30

Live on the "More Besides" Side of Life!

If any man have ears to hear, let him hear. And he said unto them, Take heed what ye hear: with what measure ye mete, it shall be measured to you: and unto you that hear shall more be given. For he that hath, to him shall be given: and he that hath not, from him shall be taken even that which he hath. —Mark 4:23-25

Jesus explains in this passage that what we hear determines the kind of fruit we bear in our lives. In the parable of the sower, found earlier in this chapter, the "wayside" person quits hearing the Word, and the thief comes and steals it away. The "stony ground" person quits hearing the Word when persecutions and afflictions come. The third person begins by hearing the Word, but the thorns of this life—the cares of this world, the deceitfulness or riches and the lusts of other things—enter in and choke the Word, making it unfruitful.

Too often, people listen to the wrong things, meditate on the wrong things and feed on the wrong things. Jesus said, "Take heed what you hear." *The Amplified Bible* makes verse 24 even clearer:

And He said to them, Be careful what you are hearing. The measure [of thought and study] you give [to the truth you hear] will be the measure [of virtue and knowledge] that comes back to you—and more [besides] will be given to you who hear.

I don't know about you, but I want to live on the "more besides" side of life! We decide whether we live on the "barely-getting-along" side or on the "more besides" side.

But notice this: Jesus says, "More [besides] will be given to you who *hear.*" Will more be given to those who beg and plead or to those who pray all the time? No. Although it's important to pray, prayer will do no good unless we are doing what Jesus tells us to do. "More besides" will be given to us only when we set ourselves to *hear* the truth of God's Word.

Confession:

I continually hear God's Word, and the Holy Spirit constantly adds to my knowledge and understanding. "More besides" is given to me in every area of my life as I hear and obey God's Word!

Who hath believed our report? and to whom is
the arm of the Lord revealed? —Isaiah 53:1

DECEMBER 31

God Has Said!

Jesus said, "All things are possible to him that believeth" (Mark 9:23). The only qualification He gave us is that we must *believe.* So often that's the hard part for most of us. We say, "Lord, why did You make it so hard? Dear God, it's hard to believe."

Believing is the product, or the offspring, of God's Word planted in the human heart. Our problem hasn't been our lack of ability to believe; it has been not knowing *what* to believe. Believing has always seemed like an abstract, intangible mystery.

Someone says, "Man, I'm trying to believe God."

"What are you trying to believe?"

"I'm trying to believe *God!*"

But God gets a little more specific. He asks, "Who hath believed *our report?*" In any given situation, we need to find out what God is saying and believe His report.

In the Garden of Eden, God told Adam, "But of the tree of the knowledge of good and evil, thou shalt not eat of it: for in the day that thou eatest thereof thou shalt surely die" (Gen. 2:17). Later the serpent beguiled Eve, saying, "Ye shall not surely die" (Gen. 3:4). Now Eve had two reports. She'd never had this choice before—and she chose to believe the serpent's report!

When the Israelites were approaching the Promised Land, they sent in twelve spies. Joshua and Caleb returned and said, "Oh, yeah, it's just as God said, and we're well able to take it. Let's go do it!" But the other ten came back and said, "No way! We can't do it!"

In any situation in our lives, we have a choice. We can either believe what it looks like, seems like or feels like, or we can believe what God says. The serpent asked Eve, "Yea, hath God said?" (Gen. 3:1). Yes, He has. God has said something about every situation we'll ever run into. Let's look the problem straight in the face and say, "God *has* said!" If we want His power revealed in our lives, let's believe His report!

Confession:

God said that by Jesus' stripes, I was healed. I choose to believe God's
report. I fully expect His healing power to be revealed in my life!

ENDNOTES

March 22

[1]Leeser, p. 256.

March 26

[1]Leeser, p. 274.

April 6

[1]*Merriam-Webster's Collegiate Dictionary,* 10th Ed., s.v. "redeem."

May 3

[1]Vine, s.v. "life," Vol. 2, pp. 336-338.

July 6

[1]Strong, "Hebrew," entry #3068, p. 47; entry #7495, p. 110.

July 8

[1]Strong, "Hebrew," entry #5375, p. 80.
[2]Strong, "Hebrew," entry #5445, p. 81.

July 9

[1]Leeser, p. 724.

July 17

[1]Rotherham, p. 224.

July 22

[1]Rotherham, p. 176.

September 3

[1]Vine, s.v. "messenger," Vol. 3, p. 64.

September 27

[1]Strong, "Hebrew," entry #1897, p. 32.

October 16

[1]Vine, s.v. "profession," Vol. 3, p. 217.

October 22

[1]Vine, s.v. "confess," Vol. 1, p. 224.

October 30

[1]Strong, "Greek," entry #2476, p. 38.

November 22

[1]*The Companion Bible,* Appendix 101, part II, 14, pp. 146-147.

December 9

[1]Strong, "Greek," entry #2657, p. 40.

December 16

[1]Strong, "Hebrew," entry #4672, p. 70.

REFERENCES

Bosworth, F.F. *Christ the Healer.* New York: Fleming H. Revell Company, 1877.

Leeser, Isaac. *Twenty-Four Books of the Holy Scriptures.* New York: Hebrew Publishing Company, 1998.

Merriam-Webster's Collegiate Dictionary, 10th Ed., Springfield: Merriam-Webster, Inc., 1995.

Rotherham, Joseph Bryant. *The Emphasized Bible.* Grand Rapids: Kregel Publications, 1959.

Strong, James. *Strong's Exhaustive Concordance of the Bible.* "Hebrew and Chaldee Dictionary," "Greek Dictionary of the New Testament." Nashville: Abingdon, 1890.

The Companion Bible. Grand Rapids: Zondervan Bible Publishers, 1964, 1970, 1974.

Vine, *W.E. Vine's Expository Dictionary of Old and New Testament Words.* Old Tappan: Fleming H. Revell Company, 1981.

ABOUT THE AUTHOR

Since 1975, Mark Brazee has been teaching scriptural principles clearly and simply. With a vision to reach the nations with the Word and the Spirit of God, Mark and his wife, Janet, have traveled throughout the world spreading the Gospel.

Today Mark Brazee Ministries is reaching the world through DOMATA Minister's Training Schools, DOMATA School of Missions, DOMATA School of Missions for Children, DOMATA Team Missions, mission bases and a broad scope of media outreaches, including books, tapes, music, the Internet and television.

Additional copies of this book
are available from your local bookstore.

HARRISON HOUSE
Tulsa, Oklahoma 74153

THE HARRISON HOUSE VISION

Proclaiming the truth and the power
Of the Gospel of Jesus Christ
With excellence;
Challenging Christians to
Live victoriously,
Grow spiritually,
Know God intimately.